THE YOUNG LIONS

CONFEDERATE CADETS AT WAR

JAMES LEE CONRAD

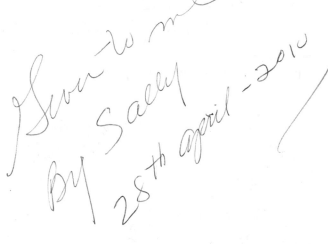

University of South Carolina Press

Cloth edition published by Stackpole Books, 1997

Paperback edition published in Columbia, South Carolina, by the
University of South Carolina Press, 2004

Manufactured in the United States of America

08 07 06 05 04   5 4 3 2 1

Library of Congress Cataloging-in-Publication Data

Conrad, James Lee.
   The young lions : Confederate cadets at war / James Lee Conrad.
      p. cm.
   Originally published: Mechanicsburg, Pa. : Stackpole Books, 1997.
   Includes bibliographical references and index.
   ISBN 1-57003-575-X (pbk. : alk. paper)
   1. Virginia Military Institute—History—19th century. 2. South Carolina Military
Academy—History—19th century. 3. Georgia Military Institute (Atlanta, Ga.)—History.
4. University of Alabama—History—19th century.
5. Military cadets—Confederate States of America. 6. United States—History
—Civil War, 1861–1865—Education and the war. 7. Military education—Confederate
States of America. I. Title.
   E586.V5C66 2004
   973.7'42'0835—dc22

                                                              2004018632

To All Cadets
Past, Present, and Future

CONTENTS

Introduction vii

CHAPTER 1 Schools of the Citizen-Soldier 1

CHAPTER 2 1861—Secession and Service 29

CHAPTER 3 1862—Transformations and Troubles 47

CHAPTER 4 1863—Coming of Age 63

CHAPTER 5 1864—"The Glory of . . . the Year 64" 85

CHAPTER 6 1865—"Come Retribution" 129

CHAPTER 7 "Entitled to All the Honor of . . . Soldiers" 151

CHAPTER 8 Reconstruction 161

Notes 169

Bibliography 186

Index 191

INTRODUCTION

DESPITE THEIR INHERENT DEMOCRATIC DISTRUST OF LARGE STANDING military forces, Americans have long been supportive of and fascinated by military schools. The nineteenth century was the heyday of these institutions, and today there are still numerous military high schools, preparatory schools, and colleges across the country. The states of the former Confederacy are home to most of them, including two of the country's premier military colleges and the nation's only state-supported military colleges—the Virginia Military Institute (VMI) and the Citadel. These two schools survived relatively unchanged for over 150 years until June 26, 1996, when the Supreme Court ordered both schools to admit women or forgo state support. The Citadel complied shortly thereafter, and VMI began admitting women in 1997.

Throughout the Civil War the graduates of the South's military academies commanded many of its regiments and trained many of its soldiers. Since they were trained as citizen-soldiers, these alumni were expected to respond to the calls of their states and, if need be, give their lives in their states' defense. That same sacrifice, however, was not initially expected of the wartime cadets of the Confederacy's military schools. Yet, because war does not respect expectations, many cadets found themselves committed to battle and, when called upon, these young men did their duty faithfully and with little complaint.

By 1860, eleven of the country's twelve private or state-supported military colleges were south of the Mason-Dixon line. Many were founded after the divisive Nullification Crisis of 1832 or in the decade leading up to the Civil War—for perhaps more than purely academic reasons. The South's distrust of the Federal government, arising from clashes over states' rights issues and attacks on its "peculiar institution," combined with its martial tradition, provided greater impetus for the establishment of military colleges, academies, and preparatory schools than existed in the more secure and less military-oriented North.

With the coming of civil war all but a handful of the South's military colleges closed their doors. Four of the remaining institutions—the Virginia Military Institute (VMI), the South Carolina Military Academy, the Georgia Military Institute (GMI), and the University of Alabama—operated throughout the war, and despite being state institutions, functioned as the Confederacy's de facto "West Points." In addition, cadets of each of these colleges engaged in operations against Federal forces. A fifth institution, the West Florida Seminary, or Florida Military Institute, also remained open on a much-reduced scale. Some of its cadets fought at the Battle of Natural Bridge, Florida, in March 1865.

Over the years the romance and tragedy inspired by the story of these supposed untrained boys thrown in front of the Yankee juggernaut have raised the cadets to superhuman proportions and their battles to near mythology. One of my goals is to scrape away some of the romantic varnish that has accumulated over the past 130 years, and to put these young soldiers into a more realistic context. I seek to give the reader a clear and comprehensive picture of a Confederate cadet's wartime world, as well as a meaningful, yet manageable, history of the military colleges themselves. To do this I found it necessary to paint with a broad brush; readers who desire more detail are encouraged to consult the bibliography for works on the individual schools. Also, given my focus, the contributions of the antebellum alumni of these schools are dealt with only tangentially. Finally, in order to give the reader a clear understanding of the motivations of the cadets and an appreciation of their day-to-day lives, it is necessary to discuss the academic and military systems of these four institutions.

I was once a cadet, and this book has been a labor of love for over ten years. During that period many people have assisted me in my effort and deserve thanks. William C. Davis, author of the definitive book, *The Battle of New Market* (required reading for every VMI cadet), encouraged me to continue this project at a time when I questioned whether anyone besides me would be interested in the story. Dr. Richard McMurry read an earlier version of the manuscript and gave invaluable advice and suggestions. Bruce Allardice shared some of his research results regarding antebellum Southern military schools. Mrs. Julia Yates Maloney shared with me her father's love of the Georgia cadets, as well as information and photographs from her collection. Mr. Jim Morris took time to show me around the former campus of GMI and the Marietta Confederate Cemetery, and to share his knowledge of Civil War Marietta. Mrs. Frank Owenby, the former owner of the GMI superintendent's quarters, graciously invited me into her home and answered many questions about the house. Mr. David J. Coles of the Florida State Archives supplied me with a copy of his yet unpublished article on the West Florida Seminary. Finally, Marvalyn "Bo" Johnson retyped the entire manuscript.

Special thanks are due to the librarians and archivists who answered questions and produced innumerable photocopies in response to my requests. Among them are Ms. Diane Jacob of the VMI Archives; Ms. Susan Jarvis and Ms. Diane Holland of the Cobb County Public Library; Dr. Jerry Oldshue and the staff of the William Stanley Hoole Special Collections Library, University of Alabama; the staff of the Citadel Archives; Ms. Charlotte Ray of the Georgia State Archives; and the staff of the South Caroliniana Library, University of South Carolina. If I have omitted anyone it is due to a poor memory and not ingratitude. One of the greatest rewards of this project was the opportunity I had to associate with all of these helpful, courteous, and professional people.

Thanks are also due to Cowles Enthusiast Media for allowing me to reprint my article, "The Katydid Cadets," which appeared in *Civil War Times Illustrated*, Volume XXI, May 1982. Portions of the article have been incorporated into sections of the book that deal with the University of Alabama Corps of Cadets.

Finally, I thank my late grandfather, Walter D. Wolf, a self-educated man who inspired in me the love of learning, and my parents, who divided my childhood vacations between the New Jersey beaches and the battlefields of northern Virginia. They instilled in me an abiding passion for the Civil War. Most of all, I thank my wife Susan, and my children, Katy and James, Jr., who have, for as long as they can remember, shared me with the ghosts of the young lions.

"Seed for the planting must not be ground."
—Goethe

CHAPTER ONE

Schools of the Citizen-Soldier

THE TOWN OF LEXINGTON, VIRGINIA, HAD A PROBLEM WITH SOLDIERS.
On a plateau north of town stood an arsenal established by the state in
1818. Here, sixteen militia guards watched over fifteen thousand to thirty
thousand stands of arms. The people of Lexington did not object to
having an arsenal in their town, but they did object to the way in which
the off-duty soldiers assaulted the serenity of their upper Shenandoah
Valley village. "The discipline was strict," wrote one prominent Lexington resident, "but could not prevent [the soldiers] from making use of
their leisure in ways that made them a very undesirable element in the
population of a small town."[1]

It was not long after the arsenal opened that there was talk about
converting the installation into an educational institution, with the students as its caretakers. No positive steps were taken in this direction,
however, and throughout the 1820s debate concerning the arsenal waxed
and waned among Lexington's more influential citizens.

In the early 1830s Hugh Barclay, a Lexington merchant, revived
interest in the project. During one of his semiannual business trips to the
North, Barclay accompanied the son of Mrs. Grigsby, a local widow,
to West Point to enroll him there. Barclay was mesmerized by the
well-disciplined cadets, technically oriented curriculum, and high moral
standards of Superintendent Sylvanus Thayer's military academy.
"The splendid drills and training of the academy were a revelation to
him," reported the *Rockbridge County News* almost a century later. "He
was so fascinated with them that he remained longer than his duty of

1

matriculating young Grigsby required, and watched the drills and looked over the handsome buildings. He returned to Lexington very full of what he saw."[2]

Barclay enthusiastically told his customers and anyone else who would listen what he had seen. His glowing reports of West Point revived the old idea of an arsenal/college, and in December 1834, the Franklin Society, a prestigious literary and debating society, discussed the question: "Would it be politic for the State to establish a military school, at the Arsenal, near Lexington, in connection with Washington College, on the plan of the West Point Academy?"[3] The members voted unanimously in favor of the proposition and resolved to assist in establishing such a school.

The following year, a series of newspaper articles regarding the establishment of a military academy appeared in the *Lexington Gazette*. On August 28, the first of three articles with the byline of "Cives" appeared. Cives was the pen name of John Thomas Lewis Preston, a member of the Franklin Society and a prominent young attorney.

In his first article Preston proposed the replacement of the present arsenal guard "by another, composed of young men, from seventeen to twenty-four years of age, to perform the necessary duties of a guard, who would receive no pay, but, in lieu, have afforded to them the opportunities of a liberal education."[4] Preston proposed to "have the whole Guard or School under military discipline, not only to secure the object of the state in establishing this military post, but likewise that industry, regularity, and health might be promoted."[5] He further explained the course of study contemplated and anticipated that students from across the country might be drawn to such a school. In his final article Preston shared his vision:

> Who would not wish to see those really handsome buildings which, upon their commanding site, adorn the approach to our village, no longer the receptacle of drones, obliged to be restrained by coercion of military rule, a discordant element in our social system —but the healthful and pleasant abode of a crowd of honorable youths pressing up the hill of science, with noble emulation, a gratifying spectacle, an honor to our country and our state, objects of honest pride to their instructors, and fair specimens of citizen-soldiers, attached to their native state, proud of her fame, and ready in every time of deepest peril to vindicate her honor or defend her rights?[6]

On December 11, 1835, the *Lexington Gazette* solicited support for a petition to the legislature requesting that the arsenal be converted into a military college. But there was opposition to the idea. One counterpetition proposed fireproofing the arsenal and hiring two nightwatchmen at the cost of one dollar to each man, per night. Another proposal suggested creating a "Deaf and Dumb Asylum" at the arsenal. The newspaper in nearby Buchanan, Virginia, printed a scathing indictment of the plan:

> It would not be safe to trust frolicsome, inconsiderate boys with the duty of guarding instruments of death. . . . Who would rest secure if his own life and that of his wife and children were perpetually dependent upon the vigilance and prudence of a boy . . . especially a Virginia boy . . . proverbially indiscreet as our youths are?[7]

The security of the arsenal aside, the author did not believe a military school would prosper in that part of the Old Dominion. As proof he reminded his readers:

> [O]ut of the ten cadets appointed from this Congressional District to West Point, not one remained to graduate, not from want of talent, but from the restive spirit of insubordination which so shamefully characterizes our youth. This may be considered a fair example of what the cadets at Lexington would do under the proposed system. Would our high Southern blood delight in scrubbing muskets and sewing up cartridge boxes, when they could obtain an education at Yale by blacking boots and doing odd jobs?[8]

But because of Preston's effective lobbying in Richmond, proponents of the school had their way. On March 22, 1836, the Virginia legislature passed an act to reorganize the arsenal as a military school of Washington College. Exactly one year later a board of visitors was appointed for the school. Claudius Crozet—a graduate of the renowned Ecole Polytechnique Military Academy of France, an engineer in Napoleon's Grand Armee, an instructor at West Point, and chief engineer of Virginia—was named its president. Crozet's legacy would be a school with academic and military systems based on both the Ecole academy and West Point. Despite the intent of the law, the trustees of Washington College declared the legislature to be without authority in ordering the linking of the two schools, and the infant military academy never became a part of the college.

Among the problems facing the board of visitors was the result of an August 1837 survey of the arsenal buildings, which revealed that the buildings were not sufficient to house the twenty-five cadets required to evenly distribute the arsenal guard duties so that time for study would not be severely diminished. The report to the governor of Virginia estimated that $2,500 would be required for the necessary alterations. But a bill amending the reorganization of the Lexington arsenal with an appropriation for the necessary funds was defeated in the state senate in April 1838, which delayed the opening of the school for at least another year.

The one positive event of that April was the appointment of Preston to the board of visitors. Soon after he took his seat, Preston made another contribution to his brainchild, and at the request of Governor David Campbell named it: "VIRGINIA—as a State institution, neither sectional nor denominational. MILITARY—indicating its characteristic feature. INSTITUTE—as something different from either college or university."[9]

By 1839 the board of visitors had new members—Hugh Barclay and three members of the Virginia General Assembly. With the assistance of these allies, the necessary legislation passed on March 29, 1839, and the board of visitors convened in Lexington two months later to begin organizing the school. The board drafted regulations, adopted uniforms, designated a course of study, and awarded a contract to erect additional buildings. The institute was not to be a carbon copy of West Point, since the objective of the school "was not to fit its graduates for a single profession . . . but to prepare young men for the varied work of civil life. . . . The military feature, though essential to its discipline, is not primary in its scheme of education."[10]

The board considered several applicants for the position of superintendent, and finally narrowed its choices to Francis Henney Smith and Joseph Reid Anderson. Twenty-seven-year-old Smith, an 1833 graduate of West Point, was a former instructor there and a professor of mathematics at Hampden-Sydney College, Virginia. Anderson, a West Pointer who resigned from the army in 1837, was Crozet's first assistant engineer. The board eventually selected Smith, with the rank of major and a salary of $1,500 a year. He would hold the position for the next fifty years. (Anderson went on to become a Confederate brigadier general and the proprietor of Richmond's Tredegar Ironworks.) J. T. L. Preston was hired as assistant professor, at a salary of $700 a year, and Barclay was appointed to the non-paying position of institute treasurer.

On November 11, 1839, the Virginia Military Institute admitted twenty-three cadets, and Cadet John B. Strange relieved the arsenal guard as the first cadet sentinel. All of the new students were classified as either regular (state-supported) or irregular (pay) cadets; the latter paid tuition. Until 1860, all the cadets were Virginians.

Home for these citizen-soldiers-in-training was the arsenal and its grounds. The arsenal itself was a three-story brick building, with walls two feet thick, enclosed by a ten-foot-high brick wall. South of the wall and parallel to it were buildings formerly used as quarters for the arsenal's garrison. Contract problems delayed completion of the barracks expansion that was recommend by the board of visitors. The cadets now numbered twenty-eight and were crammed into four half-finished rooms in the old soldiers' barracks. Since some of the rooms lacked serviceable roofs, Smith later moved six cadets into a log cabin. The lower room of the arsenal building was used as a mess hall and classes were held in a log cabin. "So intense was the cold in these comfortless rooms," Smith later recalled, "that it was impossible to write with chalk on the blackboard."[11] No supply of military clothing or equipment was provided, so the cadets wore whatever uniforms they made with their own cloth, although Smith did purchase some rough blanket overcoats for the sentinels' use. Conditions were so bad that the cadets almost mutinied, and a vote on the proposition that they disband and go home was only narrowly defeated.

By the following spring the barracks addition was completed and the cadets now had seven rooms available. Each room had a fireplace on the north side and was furnished with beds, two tables, chairs, a washstand, and pegs for hanging uniforms, arms, and accoutrements. Books and caps were required to be on the shelves, with shoes along the wall opposite the fireplace and near the door. That summer the barracks was completely renovated and expanded to seventeen rooms. One of these rooms was used as an office, and four cadets generally occupied each of the remaining rooms. The "Mess House" was completed by Christmas 1840. Its three stories provided the cadets with a kitchen, a mess hall, steward's quarters, recitation rooms, and a library.

Things steadily got better at VMI, which added three new barracks rooms in 1844, and by 1845 had six more rooms ready for occupancy.[12] In 1849 a hospital was constructed and throughout the 1840s and 50s, faculty housing was erected. But despite all the additions to the old arsenal barracks, by 1848 it became apparent that extensive renovation would be necessary. Cadets lived four to each 15-by-16 foot room. In the winter numerous wood-fueled fires burned continuously, which irritated the occupants with a blanket of eye-watering smoke. The small interior courtyard was sunless, and some rooms were often flooded. One member of the board of visitors complained that his "negroes were better quartered than the cadets."[13] A number of board members favored a new barracks; in 1848 they asked Alexander J. Davis, one of the country's foremost architects, to design such a building, not to exceed $46,000 in construction costs.

Davis designed a rectangular, four-story, castellated building in the Gothic style, with rooms opening onto a walkway (or in cadet vernacular, a "stoop") that ran around the inside of the building on each story. The new barracks was to be constructed around the existing arsenal building, but the legislature was slow to appropriate the necessary funds, and it was not until March 19, 1850, that ground was broken. Once built, the massive brick structure was finally occupied by the cadets on September 24, 1851. Davis's original plans, however, had to be scaled back to save money, so the barracks was constructed in a U-shape rather than rectangular. The rectangle was not closed until eighty-three years later. A new mess hall opened in 1854, which essentially completed the building program.

The physical plant expanded to meet the ever-growing number of cadets. Five years after the institute's opening, seventy-three cadets were enrolled. By 1846 eighty-three studied there. And by 1859 enrollment had risen to 131. As of July 4 of that year, a total of 1,084 cadets had been admitted since 1839 and 354 had graduated. The idea of a state-supported military college based on the West Point system had worked and the rest of the South had a guide to follow.

Governor John P. Richardson of South Carolina also had problems with arsenals. Richardson was concerned with the future of the Citadel in Charleston and the Arsenal in the state capital at Columbia. The former was established in 1783 and expanded in 1822 as a consequence of Denmark Vessey's abortive slave rebellion around Charleston, while the latter was erected in 1833 to consolidate the arms and ammunition of three other arsenals. By 1841 the two facilities were costing the state $24,000 a year just to maintain guards. This was too much to spend for support of men whom the governor described as:

the most profligate, licentious and abandoned of society—
men without local attachments—the indolent, intemperate and
depraved—outcasts from society, and sometimes fugitives from justice, whose crimes impel to this last resource for employment;
whose passions prompt to the first occasion of treachery or insubor-

dination, and whose character, however temporarily subdued by the restraints of discipline, can never be reclaimed, or fitted for the duties and obligations of useful citizens.[14]

Aware of what the people of Lexington, Virginia, had done in similar circumstances, Governor Richardson proposed to the General Assembly that the money currently appropriated for the arsenal guards be used to educate some of the state's indigent youths, and that the students constitute the arsenal guard at both locations. The bill failed to pass.

Richardson was undaunted and the next year he sent a small number of poor young men to the Arsenal and placed them under the instruction of two state guard officers. That same summer he mentioned his plan for the arsenals to General James Jones, a former adjutant general of South Carolina. But Jones disapproved of the plan when he discovered that Richardson wanted to establish little more than grammar schools for the teaching of reading, writing, and arithmetic. Jones argued that the proposed system was deficient in its standards of education and would produce neither soldiers nor scholars. Since Richardson would not be swayed, Jones used his political contacts to ensure defeat of the legislation should it be proposed in its present restricted form.

When the legislature convened later that year, Richardson formally proposed that the Arsenal and the Citadel be converted into military academies. The governor's message to the legislature outlined a much broader scheme than that discussed with General Jones. During this same legislative session, General David F. Jamison, chairman of the Military Affairs Committee of the House of Representatives, introduced a bill "to convert the Arsenal at Columbia, and the Citadel and Magazine in or near Charleston, into Military Schools."[15] The bill passed both houses on December 20, 1842, with little opposition. The law authorized the governor to appoint a four-member board of visitors with the power to establish by-laws for the management of the schools and the authority to appoint one or more professors. Otherwise, the law was purposely vague so the governor and board of visitors could design the curriculum as they thought best.

Governor Richardson retired soon after the legislation was passed, so the task of carrying out the mandate fell to his successor, James H. Hammond. The new governor quickly went to work. On December 21, he appointed Generals James Jones and David F. Jamison, W. J. Hanna, and J. H. Means to the board of visitors; they convened at the Arsenal that same day.[16] At its first meeting the board resolved to hire a superintendent for the Arsenal Academy and to establish rules and regulations for both schools. On January 13, 1843, the board elected Captain Alfred Herbert as superintendent and principal professor of the Arsenal Academy. First Lieutenant Joseph Matthews, a former private in the arsenal guard, was elected second professor. Then the first students were admitted—fifteen at the Arsenal and twenty at the Citadel. By March both schools were in operation.

The new cadets reported to fairly substantial facilities. Charleston's Citadel was located on Marion Square between King and Meeting streets on the east and west, and Hutson and Calhoun streets on the north and south. The building itself was a plain, two-story brick structure enclosing a quadrangle. As the school's enrollment grew so did the Citadel. In 1849 a third story was added, and five years later east and west wings were built. The Arsenal underwent similar expansion. Originally there were two unconnected two-story brick buildings on Arsenal Hill, fronting Laurel Street adjacent to Columbia's Sidney Park. They became a single unit with the 1852 construction of a three-story structure between, and connecting with, the original buildings. In 1855 a brick apartment building was erected to house the school's officers.

The first regulations for the two academies were promulgated by the board of visitors in 1843 and appeared in a thirteen-page pamphlet. In addition to admission requirements and a prescribed matriculation oath, the regulations established a military system based on the West Point and VMI models. Although independent institutions, the two schools operated under the same regulations and were so interrelated that in 1845, the Arsenal was made auxiliary to the Citadel and became responsible for training and instructing new cadets. After spending a year at the Arsenal, cadets would transfer to the Citadel.

The final change in this relationship occurred on January 28, 1861, when the legislature passed a bill providing that "the Arsenal Academy and Citadel Academy shall retain the same distinctive titles, but they shall together constitute and be entitled 'The South Carolina Military Academy.'"[17] The second section of this law required that the cadets and officers of each school be organized into companies constituting "the Battalion of State Cadets."

As at VMI, two types of students were authorized by law: state or beneficiary cadets and pay cadets. A total of fifty-four state cadets were appointed from South Carolina's thirty judicial districts. Starting in 1849 each state cadet was obligated to teach in the state public schools for two years after graduation. The number of both types of cadets rose steadily and by 1848, 91 pay and 218 state cadets had entered the academies since 1843. Of these, 231 were dismissed or had resigned and 21 graduated, leaving 57 enrolled. After 1850, enrollment was limited to South Carolina residents, but this restriction did not decrease the number of applicants. In 1857 the number of pay cadet applicants exceeded the number the academy could accommodate so 28 were denied admission. By November 1861 a total of 1,669 cadets (1,073 pay and 596 state) had entered the South Carolina Military Academy, and 202 had graduated. By then, 125 cadets were in residence at both academies, and both the Citadel and Arsenal had more than fulfilled the board of visitors' prediction in its first report to the governor:

The Board assures your Excellency, that this first year's experiment has succeeded beyond their hope; and they confidently predict that its future success will not disappoint the expectations of the Legislature in changing the nature of these institutions.[18]

Marietta, Georgia, had, by 1850, become a bustling community. Fine homes and well-stocked stores lined the streets, and the Western and Atlantic Railroad brought summer vacationers from other parts of the state. All in all, Marietta was "a desirable place to live."[19] Only one feature was missing—Marietta lacked a college.

Education was a serious business in Marietta and in surrounding Cobb County, where no less than six schools and three academies were in operation. However, if a young scholar wanted to continue his education, he had to travel to the University of Georgia in Athens, Milledgeville's Oglethorpe College, or out of the state. There was no question that north Georgia could support a college and, with the Mexican War just recently concluded, many advocated a military college. The proposal of one gained widespread support and soon eleven prosperous Mariettans contributed money to a joint-stock venture for establishing such a school.

The project moved ahead quickly. The organizers purchased 110 acres southwest of Marietta, along the Powder Springs Road, and began construction of the college buildings. A board of trustees was appointed, who hired as superintendent, with the rank of colonel, Arnoldus V. Brumby, an 1835 West Point graduate. James W. Robertson, an officer on a leave of absence from the U.S. Army, was named commandant of cadets. In July 1851, the Georgia Military Institute opened its doors with three faculty members and six cadets.

GMI grew rapidly and by 1856 six faculty taught 140 cadets. Unlike some of the other state military colleges, GMI did not restrict out-of-state applications, and by 1858 over one-third of the students were from other states. Alabama, Arkansas, Florida, Louisiana, Mississippi, North Carolina, and Texas were all represented in the cadet corps.

Although expansion of the college meant more income, it was never sufficient to cover expenses. Fortunately, the Georgia legislature, recognizing the value of a state military college, appropriated funds to support the school. In exchange for this support, the institute was allowed to award scholarships to needy applicants from each congressional district and to two others from the state-at-large. The recipients of these scholarships were then required to teach in Georgia public schools for two years after graduation. The state also provided the arms and accoutrements necessary for military training, including four six-pounder brass howitzers with Georgia's state seal and the inscription "Georgia Military Institute" on the barrels. With state aid came some state oversight in the form of a board of visitors. It met with the trustees "to formulate rules and inspect the public arms and other property."[20]

The lack of sufficient operating funds, however, still raised fears about the school's future. Colonel Brumby in his 1857 report to the board of visitors pointed out that "under its present organization, [the school] is liable at any time to be disbanded. As a state institution, it would be permanent. . . . If such institutions are of but little value as guards to liberty . . . why have Virginia and South Carolina organized such institutions?"[21] Popular opinion supported state purchase of the school and the institute's stockholders offered to donate the campus, buildings, and all other school assets to the state, which accepted the offer in early 1858.

For the redemption of $5,000 of stock, Georgia acquired a physical plant valued at $12,000. Included on the College Hill campus were a two-story classroom building with eight recitation rooms; fourteen single-story barracks, each with two rooms; a steward's building with attached kitchen and mess hall; an 18-by-30 foot gunhouse; and the superintendent's residence.

New ownership, however, had no effect on the day-to-day life of the cadets. Like the other military academies operated on the West Point model, the routine of a GMI cadet was rigidly prescribed. He was required to wear a uniform at all times and the mere possession of civilian clothes was forbidden. The contents of his four- or five-man room, to be purchased at his own expense, were set forth in the regulations: one iron bedstead, a pine table, mirror, wash basin, foot tub, water bucket and dipper, washstand, and candlestick. Cadets were forbidden to play cards, checkers, chess, or backgammon. Reading material not directly related to studies was prohibited. The high point of cadet social life was the Friday night "hops," which the young ladies of the town confessed to be the "most delightful of all dances given in Marietta."[22]

By the turn of the decade, as the 1860s opened, the future looked bright for the GMI.

The University of Alabama, unlike its counterparts, was not founded as a military institution. When it opened its doors in 1831 it was purely a civilian school, but as in the cases of southern schools elsewhere, the military college system was seen as a solution to a problem.

By 1855, when Dr. Landon Cabell Garland assumed the presidency of the university, the typical university student was the son of a plantation aristocrat—a young man supplied by his family with "costly and extravagant wardrobes, liberal supplies from the best jewelry establishments, and . . . the indispensable appendages of dirks, pistols, bowie knives &c."[23] These young men—who had grown up pampered and unrestrained, and had been waited on by slaves who catered to their every need—resented authority, particularly when wielded by someone they considered to be of inferior social status. Disciplining these unruly students became Garland's biggest challenge.

As the decade drew to a close Garland also observed the growing division between the North and South. Although it was later stated that "the introduction of drill and discipline at the State University had no connection whatever with any secession movement in Alabama," this widening schism undoubtedly influenced his promotion of the military system.[24]

While Garland could not be sure that adoption of a military system would solve the university's problems, he was convinced that the traditional college system had failed. He was well qualified to make this judgment; before coming to Tuscaloosa in 1847, he had been on the faculties of his alma mater, Hampden-Sydney College, and two other Virginia institutions, Randolph Macon College and Washington College. Garland was no soldier, however, and his unfamiliarity with the military college system prompted him to ask an old acquaintance, Superintendent Smith of VMI, some basic questions:

1. Does the system require a walled enclosure? 2. Does it require regular guard mounting, and what influence has this on feeble constitutions? 3. Does it curtail the hours of study? and as a consequence diminish the hours of study? 4. Does it prevent vice and immorality . . .? 5. Does it prevent disorders . . .? 6. Does it

require more than one superior officer . . .? 7. Are cadet officers, squad marchers, etc, reliable and faithful? 8. Does it require cadets to board in commons? 9. Are students often disposed to retire on account of the rigor of the system? 10. Is music essential to all parades? to what extent, and at what probable cost? 11. What does the wardrobe of one of your cadets cost per annum?[25]

After persuading the reluctant trustees of the university to finance the trip, Garland toured West Point, VMI, the Citadel, and Nashville University's Western Military Institute in search of more information. He returned more convinced than ever that the traditional college system was a general failure and did little to instill proper manners and decorum:

Beyond a few regulations, prohibiting the entering of a public room with the hat on or attending chapel or recitation in deshabille —or spitting on public floors—or some infraction of propriety, but little is done in our colleges for the improvement of a student in manners, and in the neatness of his room and person.[26]

Although they agreed with Garland's observations, the trustees were reluctant to support the transformation of the college into a military institution. The university was financially troubled and the cost of implementing Garland's proposal could be expensive.

Construction of suitable facilities, however, would not be part of this cost, for several buildings were already available. Thirteen buildings covered the campus site near the Black Warrior River, west of Tuscaloosa. The Rotunda, an impressive edifice "which perhaps had no equal in the south," dominated the center of the campus.[27] Directly behind it was the Lyceum, where most classes were held, and on both sides of the Lyceum was housing for the faculty. To the front and on each side of the Rotunda stood four three-story brick dormitories: Madison and Jefferson halls to the west, Washington and Franklin halls to the east. Also included on the campus was an observatory boasting some of the South's most modern equipment. Across the Huntsville Road from the main campus stood the college president's house.

In order to convert the university into a military college, the Alabama General Assembly would have to pass Garland's previously rejected proposal. In 1860, with the prospect of secession of the slaveholding states growing daily, both houses of the General Assembly finally authorized Garland to make the change. He wasted little time, and by September,

137 students found themselves metamorphosed into cadets. The newly commissioned State Colonel Garland was now their superintendent.

Garland adopted the West Point system and established the office of Commandant of Cadets to oversee military training. He chose First Lieutenant Caleb Huse, an 1851 graduate of the United States Military Academy and former West Point faculty member under Superintendent Robert E. Lee, for the position. Huse, a native of Newburyport, Massachusetts, took a leave of absence from the army to accept his new post. To assist the new commandant, Garland obtained the services of three VMI graduates: State Major James T. Murfee, who came with Francis Smith's recommendation, as assistant commandant, and State Captains Charles L. Lumsden and James H. Morrison as instructors in tactics.

The new cadets were issued uniforms and weapons and began four weeks of training in an encampment set up on the campus. The change must have been shocking to these young men, but miraculously, most seemed to thrive on it. One cadet did note, however, that it was "quite hard for the students who had lived under the old regime to bow to the yoke of military government."[28] The new cadets quickly became "brass-button conscious" and even those who formerly amused themselves by fighting or tormenting slaves found that "the quietude and order resulting from strict military discipline was an aid to those who wanted to study, and that the exercise required was conducive to health and physical development for all."[29] After just two months at the "new" University of Alabama, Cadet E. B. Thompson concluded, "It will be a fine college—from this time forward."[30]

Unlike West Point's mission to educate soldiers, these state-supported military colleges existed to teach citizens within a framework of soldierly discipline. Each aimed to produce a productive citizen who, when necessary, could take up arms in defense of his state or country. Consequently, there was less emphasis on the military subjects in favor of a more broad-based curriculum. But like West Point, and unlike many of their civilian counterparts, these schools tended to concentrate on technical rather than classical subjects.

In one of his articles, Preston set forth his suggested plan of study for Lexington's proposed military school:

> For the first year, let the higher branches of English be attended to, and the Latin language (or whatever might be substituted for it),

be commenced. In the second, Latin continued, and mathematics begun, and also modern languages; and in the fourth year, natural Philosophy, Chemistry, and the Military Art. This does not comprise the drill of a complete education, but it is sufficiently liberal to enable a young man to prosecute it further unassisted, or creditably to enter upon the study of any of the learned professions.[31]

Preston's "liberal" course of instruction was adopted and expanded upon by VMI's first board of visitors. The initial regulations for the institute established a course of study that included infantry tactics and military police, algebra, geometry, trigonometry, mensuration, descriptive and analytical geometry, differential equations, the English language and literature, French, German, topographical and architectural drawing, natural and experimental philosophy, astronomy, chemistry, mineralogy, geology, artillery science and practice, and civil and military engineering —all to be completed within three years. In 1845 the course of study was extended to four years, and for a brief period in the late 1850s and early 1860s, freshmen who failed examinations could repeat the first year's course of study.

The courses offered at other state military colleges in the South were similar. The course of study at GMI was almost identical to VMI's, with the exception of added courses in rhetoric and elocution, intellectual philosophy, and the law of nations. The same curriculum also existed at the Citadel, except that a class in vocal music was offered in 1858; it was a course unique among the military colleges and, in the words of one cadet, "something novel for this institution."[32] The Citadel's course of study also differed in that the normal completion time was four years and three months. The Arsenal's curriculum was not as extensive, and it concentrated on English, mathematics, and belle lettres to prepare cadets for further study at the Citadel.

The University of Alabama differed in its academic organization because of its civilian origins and its status as a university. Its curriculum was divided into nine major disciplines: ethics, logic, Latin, Greek, modern languages, pure mathematics, natural philosophy, chemistry, and military. Each discipline was further divided into three classes. Unlike cadets at the other military colleges, an Alabama cadet could choose his course of study. The university awarded three degrees: the diploma of graduation for cadets completing studies of the first and second classes of any department with a grade of not less than fifty percent; the degree of bachelor of arts for completion of the first and second classes of all nine departments with a grade of not less than fifty percent; and the degree of master of arts and sciences for cadets who completed all classes of all departments with a grade of not less than seventy-five percent. The time required for completing a course of study depended upon the chosen degree program. The University regulations opined, however, that "all of the studies of the University, with the exception of those of the Military Department, may be completed in the space of five years, by any student of average capacity and industry."[33]

Requirements for admission varied from school to school, but generally applicants were required to be males of good moral character, unmarried, and between the ages of fourteen and twenty-five.[34] The academic admission requirements of the schools varied. The University of Alabama required each applicant to have "a good knowledge of English Grammer, Geography, and Arithmetic."[35] In addition to these basic requirements, applicants were expected to meet other prerequisites for certain departments. For example, admission into the Latin department required completion of "Latin Grammer, including Prosody; Arnold's first Latin Book; Caesar's Commentaries, four books; Virgil's Bucolics and six Books of Aeneid; Cicero, six Orations."[36]

VMI at first required only the ability to read and write and a knowledge of simple arithmetic. The South Carolina Military Academy's entrance standards were similarly undemanding. This was intentional because the founders of both academies desired to offer a college education to those formerly deprived of one. "This liberal [admissions] policy," noted VMI Superintendent Francis H. Smith, "addressed itself to the poor boy at the plow handle, the apprentice at his work bench, and in general to all those whose circumstances in life had denied them the advantages of the usual preparatory training in the classical schools of the South."[37]

With the exception of the University of Alabama, cadets were divided into four classes: fourth (freshmen), third (sophomore), second (junior), and first (senior). Each class pursued one of four annual courses. Classroom instruction was by recitation. Each student was responsible for reading the day's lesson and being prepared to recite portions of it if called upon by the professor. The faculty was composed of professors of various standings, each having a military rank depending upon his professorial standing. Cadets who distinguished themselves in a particular course were sometimes appointed acting assistant professors for that course. Such an appointment was considered "an honorable distinction"

and brought with it privileges not enjoyed by the average cadet.[38] At the
Citadel, for example, cadet assistant professors wore a wreath insignia on
their uniforms and, at least until 1858, did not have to march to meals.

The full-time faculty was generally very good at all of the schools, but
not all faculty members excelled in all areas of the military college curriculum. For example, the best academician at the Citadel, Dr. William
Hume, professor of chemistry and physics, was a terrible soldier. When
drilling the cadets he would order, "Will you be kind enough, gentlemen,
to shoulder arms?"[39] He was also once run over by his own platoon during drill. He was later excused from all military duties. VMI's greatest
faculty soldier, Major Thomas J. Jackson, professor of natural history and
artillery tactics, was a poor teacher who "lacked the tact required in getting along with the classes."[40] In the classroom "his manner was grave,
earnest, full of military brevity, and destitute of all the graces of the
speaker" and his eccentricities led many to doubt his sanity.[41] The cadets
called him "Fool Tom Jackson" and "pointing significantly to their fore-
heads, said he was 'not quite right there.'"[42]

Examinations, usually a combination of oral and written tests, were
held twice during the school year in all courses. Cadets were orally examined on either a subject assigned by the professor or, as at the Citadel, a
topic drawn from a hat. Examinations were usually conducted in the
presence of the board of visitors or trustees, who were often accompanied
by distinguished guests or even the state governor. Governor Joseph E.
Brown attended the examinations at GMI in 1858 and declared that "the
young gentlemen acquitted themselves with much credit both to themselves and to the faculty."[43]

The military college course of study was difficult, and cadets who
failed to apply themselves or properly budget their time between
academic and military duties seldom graduated. Generally, the cadets
appreciated the efforts of their professors and perceived themselves to be
well prepared for life after graduation. Upon his graduation, one Citadel
cadet entered his observations in his journal:

> As to the Intellectual training which I have received; though for
> the profession which I have chosen [the ministry] it is deficient in
> the ancient languages, I think it as good, if not better, than I would
> have got elsewhere. My mind has been trained to study thoroughly
> and systematically, and the course is well suited to build on. The
> foundation is good.[44]

The academic philosophy of most state-supported military colleges in the South was accurately summarized by a former superintendent of the Citadel:

> Occupying the middle ground, they sought to reach the mean between the extremes of a purely classical curriculum on the one hand, and an essentially military and technical one, as at West Point, on the other hand. They sought to prepare the young for the practical duties of life; to fit them for scientific as well as liberal pursuits.[45]

Although the curricula of the military academies were a departure from the courses taught at most American colleges and universities, it was the military aspect which most set the academies apart from their contemporaries. And while the technical courses of study made these institutions valuable to their states during times of peace, it was the military system that made them invaluable to the Confederacy during the war.

From the start, the state schools saw the military system as only a means to an end: their goal was not the production of career military officers, but rather the molding of young personalities. "Military discipline," explained Preston, "was believed [to have] special advantages in promoting the health of its pupils, in training them in habits of subordination to lawful authority, to industry and punctuality, and to accustom them to prompt obedience to every call of duty, small or great, without regard to preference or self-indulgence."[46] Therefore, the philosophy of the schools made the military system secondary to academics; all the state colleges were careful to not let military training interfere with a cadet's studies. For example, a newspaper advertisement for GMI, informed parents of prospective applicants that each day cadets would be involved "about an hour and a half in military exercise; but at such times as not to interfere with their regular studies."[47] Nevertheless, the school superintendents would not tolerate interference with the military system from cadets or well-meaning outsiders. Alabama's Colonel Garland characteristically protested to the governor in response to parental complaints. "Take off guards from post after 10 o'clock at night, and wherein have you altered the old system?"[48]

The military college superintendents had complete confidence in the system. "Many bad subjects were sent here to be <u>reformed</u>," recalled VMI's Smith, "and, although it was by no means a desirable thing to be in any sense a Reformatory School, or 'House of Correction,' we started with the idea that we would admit such bad subjects, and try and see what could be done with them."[49] However, patience with those who failed to apply themselves was not unlimited. "Your son says he cannot stand our discipline and our fare," Superintendent Garland wrote to the parents of a dissatisfied cadet during the war. "The discipline is that of West Point, or the Virginia Military Institute or any other state Military Academy of high grade. The fare is better than my own or than three fourths of the families in the city of Tuscaloosa. . . . He has determined to desert his post and I have paid him $50 to bear his expense home."[50]

Cadets who stayed faced a highly regimented routine. At dawn, or soon thereafter, cadets were rudely awakened by reveille, played on fife and drum and sometimes accompanied by a blast from a six-pounder cannon. Mattresses and bed clothes were rolled up and strapped or neatly folded on top of the bed, and the cadets assembled for breakfast at seven o'clock. In the early-morning air they formed into as many squads as there were tables in the mess hall. Each squad was commanded by a carver, who marched in the cadets, hailed the waiters if necessary, and was generally responsible for the discipline of his squad's table. The mess hall itself was under the watchful eye of the superintendent of the mess, usually the ranking cadet captain. He prohibited walking about the mess hall and all unnecessary talking. Breakfast might consist of coffee or tea, hot corn cakes, fresh light bread, butter, and cold meat. Upon finishing the meal, all cadets rose in unison and were dismissed. After breakfast cadets had "free time" until formation for their first class, at eight o'clock. This free time, however, was often spent helping the room orderly put the room in regulation order for inspection.

Formation for classes was also heralded on the fife and drum. During assembly for class, the section marcher, the cadet whose name appeared first on the roll, formed his fellow students into two ranks, called the roll, and marched them to their classroom. At the end of the lesson, he marched his classmates back to their original assembly point and dismissed them.

At one o'clock the cadets formed into their squads for the day's big meal: two kinds of meat, two kinds of vegetables, and corn and wheat bread. Classes then continued until the daily drill at four o'clock. After the cadets completed drill, they marched to the mess hall for supper—a light meal of coffee or tea, bread and butter, and, once a week, plain dessert. Finally, the cadet retired to his room for an evening of quiet study until tatoo, the signal for lights-out, at nine-thirty, and taps ended the day at ten o'clock. This routine varied only on Fridays, with the addition of a full dress parade and on Saturdays, with a full dress inspection. Sundays were reserved for rest and religion.[51]

In addition to this busy and demanding schedule, each cadet stood his turn on guard. At VMI and the South Carolina Military Academy, the guard detail for the state arsenal was the primary reason for the school's existence. At GMI and the University of Alabama, guard detail was purely a means of instilling responsibility in cadets. Regardless of the reason, guard duty was an irksome, tiring detail from which there was almost no escape. As usual, the administration did not share the cadets' opinion of this duty. VMI's regulations proclaimed: "There being, perhaps, no better test of soldiership and the discipline of command than the manner in which the duties of the sentinels are performed, Cadets should understand the honor and responsibility of a soldier on post."[52] But after a twenty-four-hour stint on guard, cadets felt things other than honor and responsibility. "I was on guard today," wrote Citadel Cadet Tom Law in his journal, "and walking post in the sun almost blistered my face and neck . . . they were sore for several days."[53]

Throughout his busy day the cadet was governed by a myriad of regulations concerning his conduct. He could not have a waiter, horse, or dog. Possession or consumption of alcohol was forbidden, and smoking was either forbidden or allowed only in his room, and never during study hours. He could not play cards or any other game of chance. He could not leave the limits of the school without permission. His hair was required to be short, and mustaches and whiskers were prohibited. And, of course, he was not allowed to "beat or otherwise maltreat a citizen."[54] Every Sunday he was required to attend church, and on Tuesdays, Thursdays, and Saturdays he was required to bathe. Combinations under the pretext of redress of grievances were strictly forbidden as were combinations to "silence" a fellow cadet. Alabama regulations offered this advice for the proper conduct of a cadet: "The Cadets are not only required to abstain from all vicious, immoral, or irregular conduct, but they are enjoined, on every occasion, to conduct themselves with the propriety and decorum of gentlemen."[55]

For those who strayed from the "straight and narrow," the regulations provided for punishment. Minor offenses were dealt with by awarding demerits in accordance with a prescribed schedule. Cadets were given the opportunity to provide an excuse prior to punishment, but any cadet caught presenting a false excuse or giving evasive answers was dismissed.

If the maximum number of demerits (usually between 175 and 200) for the school year was exceeded, a cadet was subject to dismissal. If, however, a high number of demerits was received in any one quarter, a cadet officer could be demoted to private. Another punishment, one of the most onerous from a cadet's standpoint, was confinement to post or room, but the maximum punishment was dismissal. It was usually imposed by a garrison court-martial, but in cases of cadets "exceeding the limit of demerit, being willfully and culpably negligent of his duties or studies, or manifesting a disposition and determination to resist the authorities" of the institution, superintendents could dismiss without a court martial.[56] All dismissed cadets had the right to appeal to the governing board of the school.

The vehicle for tempering youthful exuberance, instilling respect for authority, and preparing the boy for the duties and responsibilities of being a man was the primary military organization of the school, the Corps of Cadets. The operational military unit of each corps was the battalion, and the number of companies in the battalion varied from school to school. On the eve of the Civil War, the VMI and Alabama cadet battalions had four companies while those of GMI and South Carolina Military Academy had two. In the latter's case, while on active service, one company came from the Citadel and the other from the Arsenal. Companies were identified by a letter from A to D. Cadet officers, assisted by tactical officers of the commandant's staff, led the battalions and companies. During the war, however, the tactical officers, many with previous combat experience, actually commanded the companies in the field.

The cadet staff at the corps level consisted of an adjutant, a quartermaster, and a sergeant-major. Company officers and noncommissioned officers (NCOs) were, respectively, the captain; three lieutenants; first, second, third, fourth, and fifth sergeant; and four corporals. A color sergeant and at least two color corporals made up the color guard. Cadet officers and NCOs were identified by a system of chevrons, which was fairly uniform among the schools. Generally, cadet officers were drawn from the first class, and NCOs from the second and third classes. Once appointed, they retained their grade unless it was reduced as punishment.

Cadet uniforms were patterned after those of the U.S. Military Academy. The dress jacket, or coatee, was the same gray wool garment adopted by West Point in honor of General Winfield Scott's similarly dressed victorious troops at the War of 1812 Battle of Chippewa, Canada. The buttons were the main difference. Those of West Point were spherical, brass "bullet buttons," while those of the state schools were often flat and usually had the state coat of arms stamped on them. The forty or more buttons on this uniform were its most distinguishing feature, leading South Carolina cadets to refer to the coatees as their "buttons." The tails were another unique feature of this waist length, tight-fitting jacket. Seeing University of Alabama cadets wearing them reminded one wag of winged insects. The name he used caught on, and the cadets were quickly dubbed "Katydids."

Fatigue jackets were worn by all cadets for day-to-day duties. The Alabama cadet wore an eight-button, gray wool fatigue jacket with a standing collar year round. In the winter he wore gray wool pants with a black stripe on the outer seam, and in the summer a white vest with white trousers. A "light cap of blue cloth" completed the Alabama Corps of Cadets fatigue uniform.[57] The VMI and GMI fatigue uniforms were similar to Alabama's except their cadets wore a nine-button fatigue jacket of brown, unbleached Russian drilling and a blue, visored fatigue cap while they drilled in the summer. South Carolina cadets were outfitted with gray wool uniforms for winter and, at least during the war, a cotton uniform of "white, with a dark stripe," made of "very flimsy material," for summer wear.[58] At some point prior to 1863, VMI authorized the wearing of a white fatigue jacket as part of the summer uniform. However, cadets were authorized to wear this fatigue uniform on post only. For trips outside of school limits the coatee was worn—with one exception: VMI first classmen were permitted to wear a more comfortable, eleven-button "furlough" jacket of dark blue cloth when they visited off-post. Between November and April cadets wore a gray *surtout,* a long overcoat with a cape extending to the coat's cuffs.

Until 1860, when it was replaced by the standard military-issue forage cap, the VMI fatigue cap was a visored, gray Mexican War-pattern dragoon cap, with "VMI" embroidered on the hatband. South Carolina cadets sported a blue fatigue cap with a patent leather visor. For dress parades, a tall black dress hat or shako (a "tarbucket" in West Point slang) was worn with the coatee. The front of the dress hat bore the school insignia: an engineer corps castle for VMI; a wreath embracing the letters ACC (Alabama Cadet Corps) for Alabama; the Georgia state seal, surmounted by a flying eagle, for the Marietta school; and a "brass tulip, shell and flame, with a brass Palmetto tree in front" for the South Carolina Military Academy.[59] The shako was topped with a black cloth "pom-pom" for privates and NCOs, and a black ostrich plume for officers. For dress parades and guard mountings the coatee and shako were worn, with white belts supporting a small cartridge box for enlisted, or a maroon or crimson sash and belt-carried saber for officers.

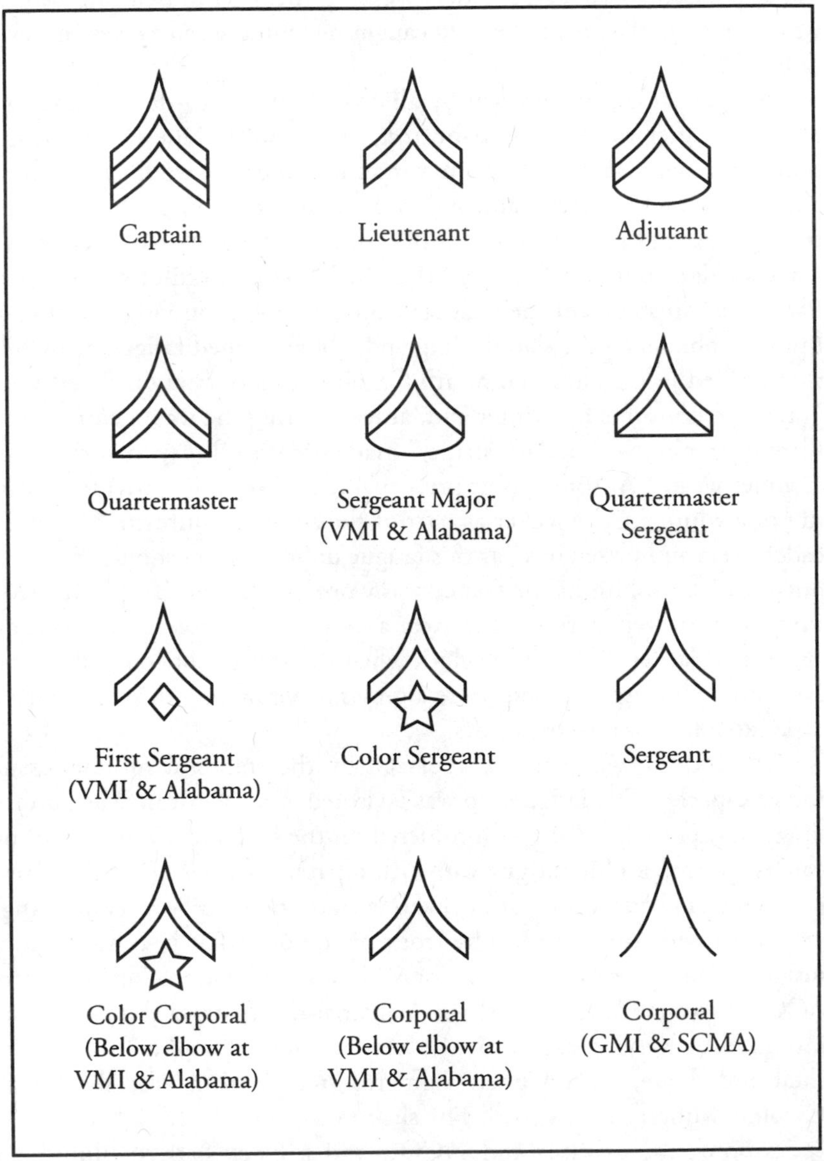

Captain

Lieutenant

Adjutant

Quartermaster

Sergeant Major
(VMI & Alabama)

Quartermaster
Sergeant

First Sergeant
(VMI & Alabama)

Color Sergeant

Sergeant

Color Corporal
(Below elbow at
VMI & Alabama)

Corporal
(Below elbow at
VMI & Alabama)

Corporal
(GMI & SCMA)

But these uniforms, though popular with the young ladies, did not necessarily make the cadets soldiers. The font of military knowledge and the man charged with the cadets' military training was the commandant of cadets. This officer was assisted by several lieutenants and captains known as tactical officers or "subs."[60] Then, as now, military training meant marching. But in the 1850s and 60s drills had a more practical purpose because the formations practiced at drill were also the formations used on the battlefield. Drill was performed according to *Scott's* or *Hardee's Tactics*. Military studies were taken seriously. In 1859 VMI created a Chair of Military Strategy—the first such chair of its kind offering advanced military instruction that was not even available at West Point.Each summer all of the cadet corps went into encampments for intense military training and to practice what they had learned. A Citadel cadet recalled the encampment of 1856:

> Having had the corps divided previously into two companies, and made preparations for the encampment, we shouldered our knapsacks and muskets about 4 o'clock, and set out for the ground, which is just south of Magnolia Cemetery and joining it. After arriving at the place, we pitched our tents, and entered upon soldier life. The novelty of the thing rendered it not very unpleasant at first, especially, if we could only have been relieved of the sand flies, which were a continual and sore plague during our sojourn there.[61]

As the specter of civil war grew more distinct, cadets were put to work on the more constructive aspects of the art of war. "A good portion of today was spent by my class, in . . . <u>ditching</u>," wrote a Citadel cadet in his journal on March 26, 1859. "We laid out a part of a Bastioned fort, and threw up a portion of the embankment. But finding it rather more tedious and laborious than we expected, we were very willing about three o'clock, to stop with what we had done, and give our blistered hands and tired backs a rest."[62]

Time was also spent in artillery theory and practice and cavalry theory. Training in the latter was hindered by the schools' lack of sufficient horses. The former was not affected as much, though, once it was discovered that fourth classmen made excellent substitutes for artillery horses.

Nineteenth-century military units were judged according to their proficiency on parade, and the superintendents of the schools were therefore eager to display their well-drilled units at every opportunity. While weekly dress parades showcased cadet corps to the local populations, state tours—especially trips to the state capital—were the best exposure the corps had to legislatures and taxpayers. Consequently, such trips were made by every one of the state cadet corps. West Point's Superintendent Thayer had taken his cadets on an exhibition tour in the 1820s and had excellent results. The trips of the VMI, South Carolina Military Academy, GMI, and Alabama Corps of Cadets were no less successful.

The VMI Corps made its first trip to Richmond in November 1841, where the cadets' semiannual examination was held before the General Assembly. The cadets drilled for the lawmakers on Richmond's Capitol Square and so impressed them that a pending bill to increase state aid to the institute was passed the following March.

By 1850, VMI cadets, under the guidance of Major William H. Gilham, who was commandant of cadets, "had attained a remarkable degree of military efficiency."[63] They were invited to Richmond, on February 22 of that year; there they escorted President Zachary Taylor to Capitol Square's equestrian statue of George Washington, where the cornerstone was being laid. Approximately 30,000 people were at the dedication ceremonies and saw the cadets in action. Taylor was so pleased with the young men that he ordered the Army Ordnance Department to cast a battery of four six-pounder cannon and two twelve-pounder howitzers for presentation to the VMI Corps.[64] The guns, each bearing the Commonwealth of Virginia's seal, were specially made and weighed two hundred pounds less than a standard piece. Taylor also presented the corps with bronze-barrel percussion muskets to replace its old flintlocks. From Richmond the corps traveled to Norfolk and Petersburg, and returned to Lexington on March 14. The legislature was again impressed and appropriated $46,000 for the construction of new barracks.

While in Richmond the alumni of the institute presented the cadets with new battalion colors, a handsome flag of white silk with the Virginia seal on the right field and the head of Washington on the reverse. Cadet Charles Denby, later a colonel in the Union Army during the Civil War, accepted the flag on behalf of the Corps of Cadets. These battalion colors were the only colors carried by the battalion until after the Civil War.

On February 22, 1858, the corps returned to Richmond to escort Governor Henry A. Wise to the dedication of the Washington statue. Years later the governor's young son John remembered the corps' appearance:

> The appearance of the Corps on this occasion the first on which I ever saw it, was sufficient to excite the wildest enthusiasm of a small boy, such as I was at the time. Never before had I seen

such trim alert figures; such clean saucy-looking uniforms; such machine-like precision and quickness of drills; such silence and obedience. From the first day my eye rested on the Cadet Corps, my ambition was to be a cadet.[65]

The Corps of Cadets of GMI made one of its first trips to the state capital at Milledgeville in November 1853. The citizens of the city were so impressed that they hosted a soiree in the boys' honor. A local newspaper reported, "The cadets . . . by their fine soldierly bearing and gentlemanly deportment excited universal admiration."[66] Even before this trip the cadets had already excited the admiration of their own board of visitors:

> The efficiency of the drill and the precision of movement was highly gratifying. The artillery instruction, but just commenced was also exhibited in the use of the six pounders . . . We think we may look forward to the time when the skill and ability of the graduates of the Georgia Military Institute to wield this tremendous arm of modern warfare may be measured without presumption with that of the best artillerists of the age.[67]

The corps became a common sight in Milledgeville, returning each summer for the state military encampment. During these encampments the cadets drilled with other militia regiments for the governor's Independence Day review and "did themselves great honor on the occasion and showed themselves every inch a soldier, as much so as their seniors."[68]

The first state tour for the cadets of the South Carolina Military Academy began on May 10, 1854, when the Charleston cadets boarded a train for Columbia to rendezvous with the Arsenal cadets. A two-day march from the capital brought them to Winnsborough where, with blistered feet, they paraded for the townspeople. The next stop was Yorkville, where its residents welcomed the cadets with a grand feast and a dance. Moving on to Limestone Springs the cadets were entertained by the young ladies of the local girls' school whose president "let down the bars" for the occasion.[69]

Leaving Limestone Springs as its band of black musicians played the "Girl I Left Behind Me," the corps passed through Spartanburg, Greenville, Laurens, and Newberry. At Newberry the battalion fired a volley over the grave of Captain William F. Graham, the Citadel's first superintendent. Upon returning to the capital city the boys had fond memories of the "picnics, dances and sumptuous dinners" they had enjoyed during their "grand tour."[70]

In 1861 the University of Alabama's financial condition was still perilous, so Colonel Garland, hoping that a favorable impression would gain
more funds for the University, decided to take his Katydids to Montgomery and show the legislature what a difference the military system had
made in the students' conduct. Both faculty and parents were skeptical of
his plan and pointed out that the capital city had many temptations to
offer boys who were, until recently, headstrong and undisciplined. They
predicted that Garland would be embarrassed by the cadets' conduct.
Garland left the decision to Commandant Huse who, despite having
recently weathered a rumored cadet mutiny to drive him back to "Yan-
keedom," trusted his cadets.

The cadets boarded a steamboat for Mobile, where they received a
warm welcome as it stopped to change boats for the trip up the Alabama
River to Montgomery, a city still in a state of excitement over Alabama's
secession from the Union only days before. On January 23, 1861, the
corps was reviewed by the legislature and Governor Andrew G. Moore.
One observer wrote that the cadets' "appearance on parade was much
admired."[71] The legislators must have also liked the cadets' look for they
increased the university's endowment from $250,000 to $300,000, and
the rate of interest on that endowment from 6 percent to 8 percent a year.

The cadets were also proud of themselves. Cadet Samuel Williamson
John wrote:

> During the entire trip of about ten days not a single infraction
> of discipline was reported; and when it is remembered that on every
> steamboat there was an open bar, it is a remarkable testimonial to
> the manly qualities of those young men who in less than five
> months had been trained into reliable soldiers.[72]

Another trip, which was a harbinger of things to come, occurred thirteen months before the Alabama cadets' triumphal trip to Montgomery.
The VMI Corps of Cadets was ordered to escort Governor Wise to and
provide security for the execution of the infamous John Brown, who had
seized the United States Armory at Harper's Ferry, Virginia, on October
16, 1859. It had taken Colonel Robert E. Lee and a detachment of U.S.
Marines to capture him and his twenty-two men. For his attempt to
incite and arm a slave rebellion, Brown was tried for treason and sen-
tenced to death. In late November, Majors William H. Gilham and
Thomas J. Jackson and sixty-four cadets, with two cadet howitzers, set
out for Harper's Ferry in response to the governor's call.

Brown's execution took place on December 2. Major Preston, who accompanied the cadets, vividly described the scene in a letter to his wife:

> The cadets were immediately in rear of the gallows, a howitzer on the right and left, a little behind, so as to sweep the field. The cadets were uniformed in red flannel shirts which gave them a gay, dashing, Zouave look, and were exceedingly becoming, especially the battery.[73]

VMI's Colonel Smith served as superintendent of the execution. When all was in order he said to the sheriff, "We are all ready, Mr. Campbell," and the sheriff sprang the trap beneath Brown's feet. Preston watched intently:

> There was profound stillness during the time his struggles continued, growing feebler and feebler at each abortive attempt to breathe. His knees were scarcely bent, his arms were drawn up to a right-angle at the elbow, with the hands clenched; but there was no writhing of the body, no violent heaving of the chest. At each feebler effort at respiration, his arms sank lower, and his legs hung more relaxed, until, at last, straight and lank he dangled, swayed to and fro by the wind.[74]

The "terrible partisan of Kansas" was dead, and the cadets had taken a part in it. In the ranks with them, during what some came to call the "first blow in the Civil War," was yet another connection to the forthcoming horrible struggle.[75] Standing with the color guard to get a good view of the execution, his long gray hair flowing from beneath his cadet cap, was sixty-six-year-old staunch secessionist Edmund Ruffin, who less than sixteen months later—while acting as a private in the Palmetto Guards, one of Charleston's twenty-two militia companies and one with strong ties to the Citadel—would pull the lanyard on one of the first cannon to fire on Fort Sumter.

CHAPTER TWO

1861: Secession and Service

THE STORM THAT HAD BEEN BUILDING THROUGHOUT THE 1850S FINALLY broke upon the nation on November 6, 1860, with the election of Abraham Lincoln as the sixteenth president of the United States. Unwilling to submit to the antislavery Republican administration, South Carolina's legislature, on November 13, called for an election of delegates to a convention that would decide the Palmetto State's future relationship with the Union. On December 17 the South Carolina convention convened in Columbia, but a smallpox epidemic in the capital city forced it to adjourn and reconvene in Charleston.

The port city enthusiastically received the convention and the Citadel cadets paraded in its honor. General David F. Jamison, author of the bill creating the Arsenal and Citadel Academies, was elected president of the convention. At 1:15 P.M. on December 20, the convention unanimously adopted an ordinance of secession and the Union was dissolved. One by one the remaining slave states of the Deep South followed South Carolina's lead: Mississippi, Florida, Alabama, Georgia, and Louisiana seceded in January 1861, and Texas joined them in February.

Once South Carolina reasserted her sovereignty, Federal forts and arsenals throughout the state were seen as an affront. Even before the ordinance of secession was signed, Charleston's Washington Light Infantry relieved the small guard at the United States arsenal. Castle Pinckney, located on a tiny island in the inner bay, was also "captured" from its lone caretaker sergeant. In Charleston only Fort Moultrie on

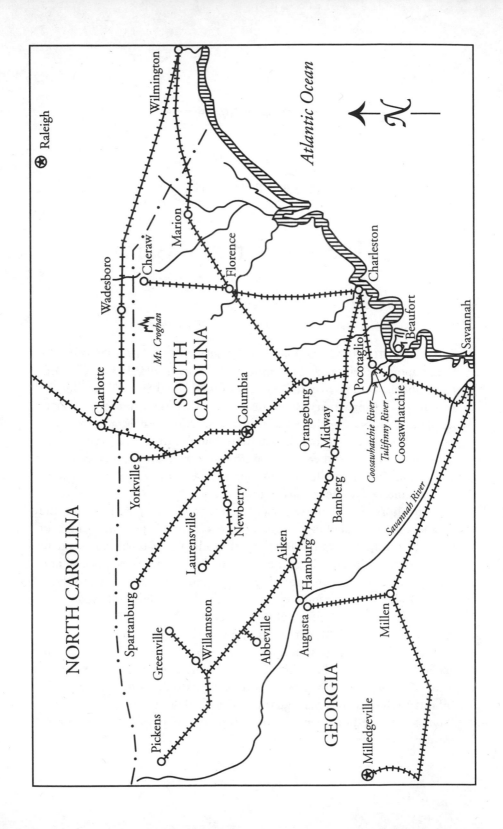

Sullivan's Island and Fort Sumter on its manmade island near the harbor's entrance remained to be dealt with.

Major Robert Anderson occupied Fort Moultrie with a battalion of regular artillery. Sumter was still under construction and had no garrison. Arrayed against Anderson were two regiments of South Carolina infantry, four batteries of light artillery, two cavalry troops, and the Citadel cadets, who were commanded by Superintendent Major Peter F. Stevens.

As long as they stayed at Fort Moultrie, keeping Anderson and his men bottled-up was an easy matter. But the day after Christmas, in 1860, Major Anderson spiked Moultrie's guns and secretly moved his troops to Fort Sumter. State authorities viewed this movement to a more defensible position as an act of aggression, and demanded that lame-duck President James Buchannan immediately order Anderson to evacuate the fort and return to Moultrie. Buchannan refused, which left Anderson in an untenable position since President Buchannan had earlier decided not to send supplies or reinforcements to Charleston, for fear of provoking a fight. Without logistical support Anderson would soon be left with no choice but to surrender. After consulting with his army chief, Lieutenant General Winfield S. Scott, Buchannan changed his mind and ordered the reinforcement and resupply of Sumter. On January 5, 1861, the chartered merchant steamer *Star of the West* sailed out of New York, loaded with supplies and two hundred additional men for Anderson.

While Buchannan agonized over what to do, the South Carolinians fortified their harbor. Fort Moultrie and Castle Pinckney were occupied, and on New Year's Day two militia companies and the Citadel cadets were sent to Cumming's Point on Morris Island to construct fortifications. Lieutenant N. W. Armstrong, professor of mathematics and military engineering, laid out a sand battery, and armed it with four smoothbore twenty-four-pounder cannon, manned by cadets who were more familiar with artillery than the militiamen. The finishing touch was the raising of a red palmetto flag that had been presented to the cadets by the ladies of a local family.

On January 7, Governor Francis W. Pickens received a telegram from friends in Washington informing him that a ship had set sail for Fort Sumter with reinforcements. The South Carolinian troops around the harbor were placed on alert with orders to prevent the ship from reaching the fort. The Citadel cadet gun crew was called out by the firing of three blank rounds from a fieldpiece run out in the barracks' sally port. Major Stevens formed up the forty-man gun crew and marched it to the Charleston-Morris Island ferry landing. After passing directly under

Sumter's guns, the ferry deposited the cadets at Cumming's Point, where they spent the rest of the day drilling and preparing their guns.

A guard boat in the harbor first spotted the *Star of the West* at daybreak on January 9 and signaled the defenders on shore. Cadet William S. Simkins saw the signal and sounded the alarm in the sand battery. The cadets rushed to their places, gunners poised with lanyards in hand. The *Star of the West,* "a beautiful ship decked from stem to stern; from water line to topmost mast as in holiday attire," passed into the channel and rapidly decreased the range between it and the cadet guns.[1] The officers in command of the sand battery garrison hesitated, undoubtedly deterred by the prospect of actually firing upon the Stars and Stripes. Stevens, true to his orders to stop the *Star of the West,* shouted, "Commence Firing!" Cadet Captain John M. Whilden passed the order: "Number One, Fire!" and Cadet George E. "Tuck" Haynsworth of Sumter, South Carolina, yanked his lanyard and sent a shell sailing over the *Star of the West.* Cadet Samuel B. Pickens fired the second gun. Then the firing continued at will. One of the militiamen remembered that "the vessel paid no attention to the first shots; then slowed down; turned and put out to sea."[2] The Federal ship did not escape totally unscathed; one shot struck abaft of the fore-rigging and stove in the planking.

On January 15 the *Charleston Mercury* gleefully reprinted a Yankee critique of the cadets' shooting that had appeared in the *New York Evening Post:*

> The military men on board highly complimented the South Carolinians on their shooting in this first attempt. They say it was well done; that all that was needed was a little better range, which they probably could have obtained in a few minutes. Their line was perfect; and the opinion is expressed that someone had charge of the guns who knew his business.... [The guns] were well manned. They were fired rapidly and with will.[3]

"The war has begun in earnest," wrote a correspondent from aboard the *Star of the West.* "The shots were fired by the Citadel Cadets under the command of Major Stephens [*sic*], who has thus had the honor, which he so much coveted, of opening the impending conflict."[4]

The cadets remained on Morris Island, and guarded against further Federal incursions into the harbor until February 4. They quartered themselves in the small rooms of an abandoned hospital. The straw, spread on the floors for bedding, also provided a convenient hiding place for a two-gallon jug of whiskey. When the order to return to Charleston was given, the jug was still half full. Rather than abandon it, Cadet C. Irvine Walker and his friends quickly disposed of the evidence. As a result, the marching of several cadets was "rather unsteady" on the way to the ferry.[5]

Upon their return to the Citadel, the cadets exhibited a restlessness that would soon infect most of their comrades at the other state military colleges. Cadet Joel D. Charles informed his sister on February 10, "I have got back to the city after six weeks hard service, and after all I am sorry we came back, for we are at our books and in the present state of affairs, it is hard to keep my mind on books."[6]

The war had begun, or so everyone thought, but there was still time for diplomacy, so as the cadets returned to the Citadel, statesmen labored to avoid further confrontation. However, in case diplomacy failed, the first classmen were busy drilling recruits on the Citadel Green and at other locations in and around Charleston. Cadet Amory Coffin was assigned as drill instructor for a company of coast guards. Each Friday afternoon he took the ferry to the unit's camp, drilled them that evening and all day Saturday, and took the ferry back to Charleston on Saturday night.

The South's military colleges expected and prepared for secession and war. In early 1860 VMI's Major Raleigh E. Colston anticipated that, in the future, the Corps of Cadets might be called out for service, and he worried about how ready they would be. Colston, holder of the Chair of Military Strategy, pointed out that while the cadets knew all there was to know about drilling squads, companies, or battalions, they did not know much about caring for men on the march or in camp. "Generation after generation of cadets," he reported with some exaggeration, "has gone through the Institute without having so much as seen a cartridge or heard of a knapsack."[7] More realism was needed in training, argued Colston. He recommended that Minie rifles be obtained and more small arm and artillery firing practices, as well as practice marches, be held. He also advised that the cadets be issued heavy shoes and socks for marching and that more practical field uniforms be obtained. That January the curriculum changed to stress military instruction, particularly artillery instruction, in anticipation of the corps being called into military service for the state.

Six months before Georgia's secession, Governor Joseph E. Brown, with similar foresight, recommended increasing the number of state cadets at GMI by admitting one from each county, noting:

It would . . . diffuse a knowledge of military science among the
people of every county in the state, which we must all admit, in
these perilous times, is a desideratum second in importance to no
other. We should not only arm our people, but we should educate
them in the use of arms and the science of war. We know not how
soon we may be driven to the necessity of defending our rights and
our honor by military force.[8]

On January 28, 1861, South Carolina readied its military academies
for conflict by incorporating South Carolina Military Academy's newly
created battalion of state cadets into the state's military forces, under the
direct control of the board of visitors.

Despite the preparations for war, not all of the military college superintendents immediately jumped on the secession bandwagon, nor did
their states. Virginia's secession was by no means a foregone conclusion
when VMI's Colonel Smith wrote his fellow Virginian, Lieutenant
General Scott, in October 1860. "I have no certain knowledge of the
course Virginia may take," he wrote. "She is now pressing forward with
earnestness her military defenses, until she will, I think, place herself in a
position of armed neutrality."[9] Smith also thought that Scott could do
much "to avoid the impending crisis."[10] Could the General but return to
Virginia and say to the country that either the Old Dominion's moderate
voice be heard and the Union preserved, or he would "count those as
common enemies of [his] state and country, who should persist in this
sectional strife." Smith somewhat naively believed the tensions between
North and South might be lessened.[11]

When South Carolina seceded, however, Smith considered Virginia
Governor John Letcher's criticism of the action unwarranted. Smith was
promptly accused of being pro-secession, and when Richmond news-
papers reported that the superintendent had made a secession speech at
a picnic, some legislators angrily declared that they would appropriate
no more money for VMI—an institution where "treason was taught."[12]
Smith denied that he was promoting disunion, but did state his opinion
that "the Union was valueless, if it had to be maintained at a sacrifice of
its constitutional guarantees. The Union was shattered when the spirit of
Union was gone."[13]

The cadets of VMI generally supported South Carolina, and on February 22, 1861, when Major Jackson supervised the customary thirteen-
gun salute to George Washington, a secession flag made of bed sheets and

shoe black proclaiming "Hurrah for South Carolina" floated from atop one of the barracks' towers. Jackson ordered the guard to haul it down.

"The spirit of Union" was definitely gone, and as April began it was clear that neither side was interested in talking further. The South still demanded the surrender of Federal installations within the seceded states, particularly Fort Sumter. President Lincoln viewed the surrender of any installation as a violation of his vow to preserve the Union, but he was loath to either provoke a war or to give upper states of the South a reason to secede by retaking Federal property by force. He therefore settled on a compromise that he would try out on Sumter. He notified Governor Pickens that the fort would be reprovisioned, but would not be reinforced nor its weapons resupplied. But the Confederates were unwilling to allow even this to happen.

Meanwhile, the Citadel cadets were preparing for graduation exercises, but on April 9 the board of visitors abruptly released the graduating class early by declaring "that in consequence of the imminent collision between the troops of the Confederate States and the forces of the United States in the immediate vicinity of the city of Charleston, the usual ceremonies of the Commencement be dispensed with."[14] The cadets were dispatched to their sand battery on Cumming's Point and to other Confederate positions around the harbor.

Shortly after 4:30 A.M. on April 12, 1861, Edmund Ruffin pulled the lanyard of his gun in Fort Moultrie and sent a shell arching toward Fort Sumter. Thirty-four hours later Anderson surrendered. On April 15, Lincoln called for seventy-five thousand volunteers to suppress the Southern insurrection. War had indeed begun.

The question of secession divided Virginians. Strong Union sentiment was present in the western portions of the state, and Rockbridge County, the home of VMI, was "thoroughly Union in feeling."[15] It was only a matter of time before the pro-secession cadets butted heads with some of the local Unionists. The inevitable collision came on April 13, 1861, as Lexington turned out to watch pro-Confederate forces raise a fifteen-star Confederate flag bearing the legend "Union of the South." That afternoon the Unionists attempted to raise their own flag, but the pole, weakened by holes drilled into it by some mischievous secessionists, broke and the flag crashed to the ground.

The Unionists suspected the cadets of the sabotage. Later that day several cadets were assaulted by a "violent man of the working class, probably excited by liquor . . . [who] drew a knife and revolver on them."[16] Cooler heads separated the combatants and a serious incident was avoided for the time being.

The Unionists, however, seemed to be spoiling for a fight, and one of them later attacked Cadet John K. "Put" Thompson on a Lexington street. One of Thompson's companions ran to the institute for reinforcements, and the word spread throughout the barracks that a cadet had been killed. Cadet First Captain Thomas S. Galloway commanded "Turn Out Under Arms" and soon the battalion, with loaded muskets, began marching on the town. Several members of the faculty, including "Old Spex" Smith* himself, tried to stop the cadets without success.

Meanwhile, the Rockbridge Rifles, a local militia company, was called from its customary Saturday afternoon drill and ordered to put itself between the cadets and the Unionists. Three hundred yards from the Rockbridge Rifles' line "drawn up across the street, supported by . . . citizens of the town and county, armed with shot guns, rifles and pistols," Major Raleigh H. "Old Polly" Colston reined his horse up in front of Galloway and ordered him to return the battalion to the barracks.[17] The order was obeyed. Smith decided not to discipline the young men since "the impulse which prompted them to rally to the call of an injured comrade was the spontaneous sentiment of generous, noble, young hearts that did not take time either to calculate the breach of order in their conduct or the results that might have followed it."[18]

On April 17, Virginia finally seceded from the Union. The following day the cadets turned out to salute the Rockbridge Rifles and a local cavalry company as they passed the institute on their way north to Staunton. All of Lexington was caught up in the excitement. As late as nine o'clock that evening, cavalry continued to clatter past the institute as Cadet Andrew C. L. Gatewood was writing to his parents. "That looks like war," observed Gatewood as he noted the passage of the horsemen in his letter, "it is bound to come."[19]

With war now a reality, the Confederacy's immediate problem was assembling an army. The thousands who flocked to the states' defense constituted little more than a poorly armed mob. To forge these men into an army would be the task of the cadets. This was not the kind of duty they had in mind, though, for the young men believed they knew a great deal about soldiering. "Tell Pa," Alabama Cadet Macon Abernathy wrote instructively to his sister, "when he is in ranks he must keep his eyes to

---

* The cadets dubbed Superintendent Smith "Old Spex" because of the gold-rimmed spectacles that seemed almost permanently attached to his face.

the Front Chin drawn in and hands down and he will make a good soldier."[20] This belief, coupled with youthful spirit and impetuosity, made the average cadet certain he was better suited to the battlefield than the drillfield. "I would rather die in defense of my country than any other way," one cadet declared with youthful bravado. "I will stand up and fight like a man for our rights with as light a heart as anybody else."[21]

It was not surprising, therefore, that soon after the firing on Fort Sumter, Colonel Garland received a petition from his Alabama cadets requesting that he suspend the operation of the university until October, at which time the petitioners would either return to their books or send for their discharges. Garland fully expected the cadets to be involved in training recruits or in supplying trained officers to the army and, while giving them "full credit for the purity of [their] motives," told them that he was "compelled to look upon the course you propose to pursue, as injurious to yourselves, to the University, and to the country which you wish to serve."[22] He explained that either the governor or the army would probably call upon the corps to supply them with officers or drill instructors. If they resigned now, Garland argued, "When the Governor, or companies make such demands on the Institution, I have to say that the University is disbanded and I can give you no aid. How reprehensible will the course of dissolution you wish to inaugurate appear."[23] Since he had no choice, he agreed to discharges for those who received their parents' permission. He hoped, however, that all of the cadets would "relinquish your purpose, and prove yourselves to be faithful to every interest for which you are here, whether civil or military. This is the path of duty, of interest and of honor."[24]

Cadets at all of the schools, nevertheless, resigned or deserted to join the army in the wake of Fort Sumter. This was the beginning of a problem that plagued the institutions throughout the war. For now, though, sufficient numbers still remained to allow the various corps to render their first, and perhaps most valuable, service to the Confederacy.

In the aftermath of Fort Sumter, camps of instruction rapidly sprang up throughout the South and the cadets were quickly called upon to train the recruits. They had quite a job on their hands—faced as they were with thousands of men who were not only totally ignorant of drill and discipline but who also did not relish the idea of taking orders from a boy. The volunteers would swagger in with their squirrel-guns, horse pistols, shotguns and Bowie knives, dressed in all manners of "uniforms," from red shirts to coonskin caps. Each was convinced that "the true soldier must present a dare-devil aspect with the unkempt hair and scraggly

beard of the border ruffian."[25] These new "soldiers" eyed the neatly uni-
formed, clean-shaven cadets with suspicion and contempt. To them they
were play-soldiers, dandies, and young whippersnappers. But the cadets
knew the mysteries of flanking movements and by-company-into-line,
and this knowledge earned the grudging respect of the thoroughly mysti-
fied recruits.

Although the volunteers obeyed and perhaps even respected their
young drill instructors, some recruits never came to like them. The
opinion of Virginian George Bagby concerning military life in general
and his youthful drill instructor in particular was probably shared by
many recruits:

> I was three and thirty years old, a born invalid whose habit had
> been to rise late, bathe leisurely and eat breakfast after everybody
> else was done. To get up at dawn to the sound of fife and drum, to
> wash my face in a hurry in a tin basin, wipe on a wet towel, and go
> forth with suffocated skin, and a sense of uncleanliness to be drilled
> by a fat little cadet, young enough to be my son . . . that indeed
> was misery. How I hated that little cadet! He was always so wide-
> awake, so clean, so interested in the drill; his coat-tails were so short
> and sharp, and his hands looked so big in white gloves. He made
> me sick.[26]

The Citadel cadets had been training recruits in and around
Charleston since January, and in late April the cadets of the Deep South's
other military schools began to do their part. The Arsenal cadets demonstrated the art of drill for the neophyte 4th South Carolina Volunteer
Infantry on April 26. In June Arsenal Superintendent James B. "Benny"
White took twelve cadets to nearby Camp Hampton to assist in the training of Colonel Wade Hampton's Legion.

The cadets of GMI were first detailed to Camp Brown, four miles
south of Marietta, on April 23, 1861. Here they trained the officers and
NCOs of the General William Phillips Brigade. These men gave up their
ranks and submitted to the command of Superintendent Major Francis
W. Capers, a former Citadel superintendent who replaced Brumby in
1859. The cadets honored the newly formed brigade with the loan of its
national flag, which had been presented to them by the ladies of Marietta
just a few weeks earlier. The first day of training was spent setting up
camp in regulation order and teaching the novices how to properly
assemble. The second day the men were organized into one company and

the next several days were spent learning the duties of the guard. During the second week the recruits were organized into a battalion of companies and were drilled in infantry, artillery, and cavalry tactics.

In mid-June the cadets were called upon to train the recruits gathered at Camp McDonald, a large instruction camp located in Big Shanty (today's Kennesaw), Georgia, six miles up the Western and Atlantic Railroad from Marietta. The corps under Superintendent Capers, Commandant Captain Joseph E. Eve, and Cadet Captain A. C. McKinley, were State Adjutant General William Phillips's staff of instruction. Governor Brown also kept a tent at Camp McDonald.

The training at Camp McDonald was on a much larger scale than at Camp Brown. A brigade of four regiments of infantry, a squadron of cavalry, and two batteries of artillery waited to be trained. The cadets tackled their new job with a will. A reporter for Milledgeville's *Southern Recorder* praised them, writing, "It is surprising to see with what accuracy these young men of the Georgia school drill. You would find in some squads old gray-headed men drilled by a boy of fifteen years old."[27] The cadets put the recruits through drill, dress parades, and mock battles—often before spectators from Marietta and other communities. When their work was finished, Capers wrote with justifiable pride, "The Governor's review of [the] brigade . . . repaid the cadets for their diligent instruction, for it furnished an object lesson in the evolution of troops in line of battle, which could not then be seen elsewhere."[28] Some of the cadets at Camp McDonald left for the war with the companies they had trained. Undoubtedly many others tried.

In the Old Dominion, 185 VMI cadets were also hard at work, training recruits at Camp Lee. This instruction camp was established on the state fairgrounds in Richmond under command of Colonel Gilham. The cadets arrived on April 22 and were billeted in the central exhibition hall of the fairgrounds, but they took their meals of beef, bread, and beans at long tables set in the open air.

Recruits from all over the South came to Camp Lee for training. The cadets here were able teachers because the drill of fourth classmen or "rats" was a pastime from which every upper classmen had "graduated with honors."[29] The rats themselves were very willing to dish out to recruits a little of what they had received from the senior cadets, and they relished drilling men who were every bit as clumsy and inept as they had once been. "Tell Mr. Stofer I want to get him down here in my squad and double quick him some," one of the rat drillmasters wrote home. "I know I can run him to death without getting tired myself."[30]

The cadets were determined to train their charges as thoroughly as possible, and their attitude toward their duties was even noticed by the women who often visited the camp. "We were often astonished at the patience and diligence displayed by the cadets in training recruits," one of these lady visitors wrote. "Never showing weariness, they took delight in teaching the prospective soldier."[31]

Every other hour of the recruits' twelve-hour day was devoted to drill, and the results of the cadets' efforts were soon apparent. "The dress parade at the Hermitage Fair Grounds, yesterday evening, was of a very imposing character," the *Richmond Daily Examiner* reported on April 27. "The cadets are progressing finely in their instructions to recruits and have vastly improved some of the previously organized companies of volunteers."[32] Approximately fifteen thousand recruits were trained at Camp Lee, and the demand for cadet drillmasters increased so much that Major General Robert E. Lee, commander of Virginia's land and naval forces, informed Colonel Smith, "They are wanted everywhere."[33]

Although "wanted everywhere," some cadets felt unappreciated. "I don't care so much for the money," Cadet Gatewood explained in a May 29 letter to his parents, "but everybody else are getting paid but the cadets and they are doing more good for the State than all the other officers put together. We drilled ten thousand men well, whilst we were in Richmond . . . we don't get any thanks for what we are doing."[34] On June 22, a grateful state belatedly awarded each cadet drillmaster $20 plus subsistence for his services.

While the corps was at Camp Lee, Superintendent Smith, who had served on the governor's "Committee of Three" to advise him on the state's military preparedness, decided to leave the institute for active service in the field. On June 20 he proposed to lead the Richmond cadets into battle as the cadet battalion. They "respectfully declined" his offer the following day, however, saying they could render more valuable service as officers. But if commissions were not forthcoming, "We will select from our own body such officers as we think qualified and attach ourselves to what regiment we deem proper and die, if necessary, in defense of our homes."[35]

Many of the cadets at Richmond were, in fact, elected officers of the regiments they drilled. One of them, Cadet Tignal Jones Morton, a rat, became colonel of the 53d Tennessee Infantry at age nineteen. Another, first classman Henry King Burgwyn, Jr., left Camp Lee and became known as the 26th North Carolina's "boy colonel."[36] By early July, the VMI Corps of Cadets had practically ceased to exist, with not more than thirty "old" cadets remaining. The usual Fourth of July graduation exercises were dispensed with and the cadets were dismissed with directions to report when further orders were issued.

After his cadets petitioned him to close the university, Landon Garland, hoping to still their restlessness, loaded them aboard the steamboat *Southern Republic* for a trip to Montgomery. The corps was reviewed by Governor Moore, who undoubtedly talked to Garland about his desire to use the cadets as drillmasters. Rather than being moved to a single camp of instruction, however, the cadets were detailed to various companies throughout the state. Cadet H. Austill recalled his experience as an instructor of recruits:

> It fell to the lot of the writer to go with Clarence Ellerby and Lucius Pincard to Sumpter country [*sic*], to drill Capt Winston's company. When we reached the camp of this gallant company, we found the Captain doing his best, with Hardee's tactics [*sic*] in his hand. In two weeks we had the company in pretty good shape and were then recalled to stand examination.[37]

Many of these drillmasters also became elected officers of their pupils' regiments. One of them, John Caldwell Calhoun Saunders, became a brigadier general at the age of twenty-three.

As cadets resigned, deserted, or joined the regiments they had trained, the university's enrollment rapidly declined. On May 20, Garland wrote Francis H. Smith, "I have succeeded in holding about 80 of our cadets together, whom we detail, as they are required to drill the volunteer companies in the neighboring counties. They are doing valuable service to the state, and acquiring much reputation for the University."[38] By June the Katydids had trained nine companies. That same month, although very few cadets remained, Garland published a message to the people of Alabama declaring that while many other colleges and universities were closing their doors, the University of Alabama would continue its normal curriculum.

In addition to stripping them of cadets, the first months of the war also deprived the military schools of key faculty. Commandant Huse resigned from the University of Alabama to act as one of the Confederacy's purchasing agents in Europe. Despite his Yankee background, Huse was respected by the cadets, and Cadet James A. Hall wrote to his father that he believed "the prospects of the university changed for the worst lately. Colonel Huse the commandant has left. . . . There is no doubt but that he was an excellent officer [and] in losing him the university has lost its best officer."[39] Major Murfee, the assistant commandant, also resigned to become lieutenant colonel of the 41st Alabama Infantry. Captain Lumsden served as commandant until Murfee's return in 1862. Then he too went to war as commander of Lumsden's Alabama Battery. At GMI, Superintendent Capers was appointed a brigadier general of militia by Governor Brown and took a leave of absence that autumn to organize and command the state troops along the Georgia coast. Major John M. Richardson served as superintendent until Capers' return in the spring of 1862. On August 8, 1861, Citadel Superintendent Stevens resigned to become commander of the Holcombe Legion; he was replaced by Major Benny White, a transfer from the Arsenal. Captain John P. Thomas replaced White at the Columbia school. VMI lost the services of Smith, Gilham, Major Scott Ship, Colston, and Jackson. The first three later returned, but Colston and Jackson, upon asking for and receiving leaves of absence for the war, did not. Consequently, at the time of his death the mighty Stonewall Jackson still held the title professor of natural and experimental philosophy, VMI.

By July 1861, the parade fields of the South's military colleges were quiet, but ominous rumblings were heard from the fields surrounding Bull Run, a northern Virginia creek. It would be on these fields that the first cadets would die.

When the VMI Corps of Cadets marched with Major Jackson to Camp Lee on April 21, forty-seven of its comrades, "in tears that they cannot share danger and glory," stayed behind to guard the arsenal.[40] The cadets who remained at the institute began training the Rockbridge Greys, which later became Company H, 4th Virginia Infantry.

Despite their important duties, the cadets of the arsenal guard felt disgraced and dishonored. But this "disgrace" lasted only one day. On April 22, Cadet Charles R. Norris and nine of his comrades, under the command of Lieutenant John D. Ross, assistant professor of French and tactics, were detailed to escort five wagonloads of gunpowder to Harper's Ferry. Upon their arrival the cadets found newly-promoted Colonel Jackson in command of the garrison. Jackson, not about to let nine trained cadets escape him, retained Lieutenant Ross and his detachment to train his raw troops. Norris and Cadet Charles C. Wight were assigned to instruct the 27th Virginia Infantry. Cadet Junius L. Hempstead was assigned to drill the 5th Virginia Infantry. He later remembered that once they reached Harper's Ferry, "drill, drill, drill was the order of the day."[41]

Some of the Camp Lee cadets also came to Harper's Ferry to help out; among them was John Stuart Moffett, who was assigned to train the 4th Virginia Infantry. On May 23, General Joseph E. Johnston relieved Jackson of the command of Harper's Ferry. Jackson was given command of the 2d, 4th, 5th, and 27th Virginia Infantries, as well as the Rockbridge Artillery, which had "borrowed" some of the cadets' cannon. These regiments, with the later addition of the 33d Virginia, were designated the First Brigade, Army of the Shenandoah and were later honored with the name Stonewall Brigade.

Brigadier General Irvin McDowell's Federal Army of North Eastern Virginia, later the Union Army of the Potomac, was on the move in July. Goaded by the popular cry of "On to Richmond," McDowell launched his own army of volunteers against the Confederates around Centerville, Virginia, about twenty miles southwest of Washington. On July 17, after McDowell's men shoved aside Confederate outposts near Fairfax Court House, Major General P. G. T. Beauregard, the hero of Sumter and commander of the Confederate Army of the Potomac, fell back upon Bull Run and telegraphed for reinforcements. Richmond ordered General Johnston, now bivouacked near Winchester, Virginia, to his aid.

The First Brigade of the Army of the Shenandoah arrived by train at Manassas Junction late in the afternoon on July 19. In its ranks as acting volunteer captains were Cadets Norris, Hempstead, Wight, and Moffett. In the ranks of the 18th Virginia of the Army of the Potomac, also serving as an acting volunteer captain, was their classmate Robert D. McCulloch.[42] Charlie Moore was also somewhere on the field in a volunteer officer capacity.

McDowell continued his advance down the Warrenton Turnpike until the morning of July 21, when he confronted the Confederates along the banks of Bull Run. Sometime near daylight, a massive thirty-pounder Parrott-rifled cannon, posted near the stone bridge over Bull Run, sent a shell whistling toward Rebel positions. The Federals began a noisy demonstration and the Southerners covered the stone bridge and the Bull Run fords closely. But McDowell had a trick up his sleeve—a strong flanking column that crossed Bull Run against the unprotected Confederate left flank. Major Nathan G. Evans rushed his small brigade to the threatened sector and, with the help of Brigadier General Bernard Bee's and Colonel Francis Bartow's brigades, fought a gallant delaying action. As Evans and company began to give ground, Jackson took up a position on the Henry House hill in their rear. As Bee reached the hill with his exhausted men, he spotted Jackson and his brigade, standing "like a stone wall," and rallied on the Virginians. Jackson was still dressed in the blue frock coat and forage cap of a VMI professor.

When McDowell launched his attack against the Henry House Hill, he sent the batteries of Captains Charles Griffin and James B. Ricketts up the hill to an advanced position. The men and horses of both batteries were decimated—one volley alone from the 33d Virginia killed or wounded 54 men and 104 horses. The Union guns were soon abandoned and captured by the Confederates. The Federals counterattacked and regained them only to be driven away in turn. Five times that hot afternoon the eleven cannon changed hands. Through the charges and countercharges the cadets, still dressed in their coatees, advanced and retreated with their regiments. Cadet Norris was leading his company during one of the Confederate assaults calling, "Come on boys, quick and we can whip them!" when a bullet tore through his chest and killed him.[43] About midafternoon Cadet McCulloch and the 18th Virginia joined in the fight. The fighting was furious until around 4:30 P.M. when Federal soldiers, first in small groups, then in whole companies, and later in entire regiments, stopped fighting and began to melt away. The Confederates streamed down Henry House Hill after them, and soon the retreat became a rout. Some of the panic-stricken soldiers ran until they reached Washington, twenty miles away.

"Those little soldiers, with buttons all over their coats," as the cadets were described, paid a high price for victory.[44] Moore, Moffett, and Norris were dead, Wight and McCulloch wounded. One Confederate, while walking the battlefield the next morning, passed by the positions of a Rhode Island battery on Henry House Hill and noticed that "the nearest one killed to the cannon was a fair-haired boy in V.M.I. cadet uniform, hardly fourteen, who was shot through the heart. . . . I shall never forget how brave and handsome he looked with his little dress sword clenched in his hand."[45] The dead cadet—so vividly remembered—was probably young Charlie Norris, whose body was later found by his older brother. When Bob McCulloch heard of Moore's death, he searched the battlefield for his friend's body. Finding him among the other human debris of the battle, he buried his classmate in a marked grave, from which the body was later retrieved by the dead boy's mother.

The first cadets to die were VMI's, but the South Carolina Military Academy received the honor of performing the first field service of the war as a unit, when they were ordered in November 1861 to guard Charleston against a feared Yankee gunboat attack from recently captured Port Royal, South Carolina. Stationed at Wappoo Cut, the cadets supported Charleston's Washington Light Artillery. Their service was uneventful and the forty-two Arsenal cadets were back in Columbia by November 22, while the Citadel cadets returned to their books early in 1862. Prior to its service in Charleston, the Arsenal cadets guarded Union prisoners on the long walk between the railroad station and the Columbia city jail.

The summer rush of cadets volunteering for war had emptied the military colleges, leaving the institutions' futures uncertain. Garland, who had already expressed his determination to keep the university open, lowered the admission age to fourteen in an attempt to attract students. He was optimistic that he would have a full-strength corps in August, despite the war, because "the wealthy want their sons prepared for the contest."[46] His optimism was not misplaced: Enrollment that fall was 158 cadets, although new cadets far outnumbered the old. The Citadel and Arsenal academies reopened and by January 1, 1862, had 133 and 139 cadets, respectively. The same phenomenon was also observed at GMI; few old cadets returned, but applications for admission were higher than ever. Garland's observation was accurate: Throughout the war the military schools found themselves almost besieged by applicants. But desertions and resignations to join the active forces continued to remain high, and had a profound impact on the upper classes.

In the months following the battle at Bull Run, VMI's fate remained the most uncertain. William H. Richardson, Virginia's adjutant general, championed the cause of continuing the work of VMI, realizing then what General Lee would later declare: "We never wanted the advantages of military instruction more than now and the Virginia Military Institute is the best and purest fountain from which we can be supplied."[47] Richardson enlisted the aid of both Governor Letcher and President Davis, and on September 11, 1861, the board of visitors ordered the institute to reopen on January 1. Colonel Smith was directed to "put into full operation the regular exercises of the school."[48] Interestingly, Smith was one of the chief advocates for closing the school for the duration of the war. He frankly stated his opinion regarding the reopening of the school:

[It w]as against, my wishes, judgement and protest. I presented
to the Board, in emphatic language, the many difficulties that
would attend the effort to continue the work of the school pending
the war, the restlessness of the cadets, the impossibilities of securing
supplies of provisions, clothing, fuel, books, etc. difficulties that
would increase as the war progressed.[49]

Smith's concerns were well-founded and the problems he foresaw
only worsened the longer the war lasted. Manassas had shown that it was
going to be a long war.

CHAPTER THREE

1862: Transformations and Troubles

THE DAWNING OF THE FIRST FULL YEAR OF WAR WITNESSED SOME FUNDA-
mental changes in the educational philosophies of the state military
schools. After the initial resignations of West Point-trained army officers
and military school cadets, the Confederacy had no reliable source of
supply for the trained officers needed to command its forces. Out of
necessity, the state military colleges altered their educational schemes
from producing citizen-soldiers, who may have to serve in the military, to
producing trained officers specifically for service in the military.

All of the superintendents endeavored to keep their respective
academic programs intact, but some subjects had to be neglected to
create the time necessary for more intensive military training. Infantry
drill and tactics sometimes replaced Latin, and chemistry often made way
for gunnery. From an educational standpoint this was unfortunate, but
even educator-soldiers such as Colonel Garland recognized the need for
the sacrifice: it was becoming apparent that the conflict would be "war to
the knife and the knife to the hilt." Therefore, it was crucial that "the
military state of the Corps . . . be considered as more important than its
scholastic, during the period of our struggle for independence."[1] Garland
lamented the possibility that the war-caused interruption of so many
colleges and universities would leave the South "destitute of cultivated
intellect." Nevertheless, he wrote to VMI's Smith, "We will fight as long
as there is a man to level a gun, and then we will bequeath our women
and children, to the Crown of England, or France, rather than [to] the
domination of Northern fanatics."[2]

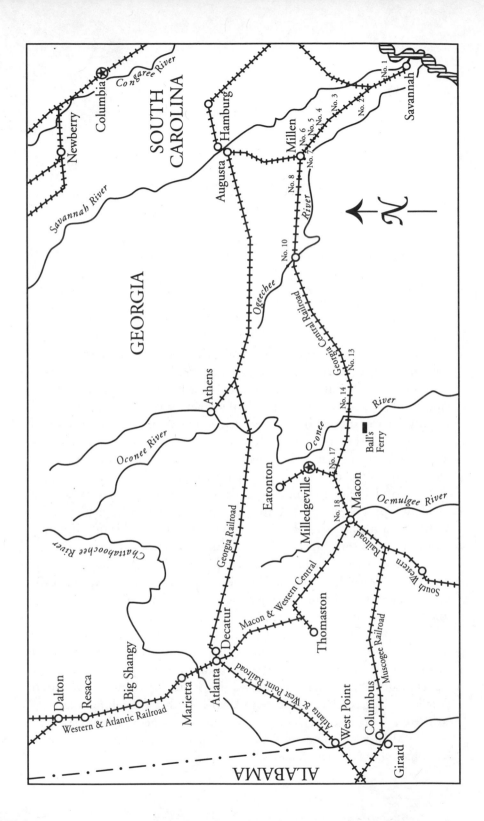

Such dedication to the cause and to their colleges was shared by offi-cers of all the military schools. These men struggled to keep their institu-tions open and to transform them into nurseries for the Confederate Army's future officer corps. In the spring of 1862, rumors continued to abound that one or the other school would close. When GMI's Superin-tendent Capers was appointed brigadier general in the militia and sent to the Georgia coast to command state troops there, speculation increased that the Georgia Military Institute would cease operation. In response to these rumors, Major John M. Richardson, the acting superintendent, proclaimed, "When Georgia is subjugated, her military school will be closed; as long as Georgia stands erect and maintains her sovereignty, the military school will be kept open."[3] Only dedication and determination such as this would counter the three major threats to the schools' contin-ued viability: the continued loss of "old cadets," the beginning of wartime shortages, and conscription.

The resignations and desertions that began after the bombardment of Fort Sumter continued unabated in 1862. "The cadets are resigning very fast . . . all think they ought to be in the army," wrote VMI Cadet John B. Snodgrass to his sister on March 29, 1862.[4] Sometimes a cadet's parents encouraged leaving the college, but those cadets who could not obtain the required parental permission to resign often deserted. The typical deserter was an upperclassman who had reached the legal enlistment age of eighteen, although some were younger. Some cadets who joined the corps at the beginning of the 1861–62 session planned to desert from the start, and stayed only long enough to learn how to drill a company.

None of the superintendents countenanced desertion for any reason, but Colonel Garland was particularly severe with those who deserted the Alabama Corps of Cadets. When a cadet deserted, an order was published dismissing the offender from the corps for violating the oath he took at his matriculation to "discharge all my duties as a Cadet with regularity and fidelity."[5] The order also pronounced him to be a disgrace as a soldier. Garland declared that "these are not the materials we want," and he never allowed a deserter to return to the corps.[6]

Still another category of cadets plagued the officers of the schools. Unable to secure their parents' permission to resign, but wanting to avoid the label of deserter, these cadets sought to force their dismissals by "rais-ing hell" or neglecting their studies. VMI's new commandant of cadets, Major Scott Ship, was confronted with so many of these cadets when he returned from active service in January 1862 that he was forced to grant their wishes to maintain good order and discipline among the remaining cadets. Ship promptly dismissed any cadet neglectful of his military duty or deficient in academics. After one examination alone, seventy cadets were dismissed. At the Arsenal, twenty-one cadets were suspended after attempting to force "their parents' consent to leave, and failing in that 'to leave any-how.'"[7]

Due to desertions, resignations, and dismissals, by July only 143 of the 268 cadets enrolled in January remained at VMI. There was no first class to graduate. The same situation prevailed at all of the other military colleges.

The schools made efforts to stem the loss of cadets by appeals to patience and patriotism. Each cadet who did not complete his course of study was considered a loss of a fully trained officer for the Confederacy. Sometimes these appeals had an effect. One VMI cadet lamented that he and some of his comrades would have to wait to leave the institute for the army and: "As General Smith says, be soldiers in the next army, after the present one has been killed off."[8] Garland was more subtle, but his appeals also occasionally deterred those who were not dead set on leaving their studies. Major White of the Citadel employed the oratorical skills of future governor Judge Andrew G. Magrath to stem a summertime exodus of cadets. Magrath eloquently and forcefully reminded the cadets of their duty to their state. After the address, as Captain Hugh S. Thompson remembered, they "returned to their duties with fresh energy and spirit."[9]

Garland was particularly distressed by the hero's welcome deserters were given by the local community, but in reality, these young men were deserting a relatively safe duty for one far more dangerous. The number of cadets leaving for the war was such that whole units were formed almost exclusively of cadet deserters. In June, after being recalled from the field by the board of visitors, thirty-six dissatisfied Citadel cadets deserted and formed a cavalry company dubbed the Cadet Rangers. Former Cadet Miles B. Humphrey acted as captain. The Cadet Rangers joined the 6th South Carolina Cavalry and were officially designated as the regiment's Company F in September. These "deserters" soldiered throughout the war, and refused to surrender with the rest of General Joseph E. Johnston's army on April 26, 1865. Instead, they disbanded the following day. Deserter units formed from the University of Alabama were Captain Charles P. Stoor's Cadet Troop and Captain Bascom T. Shockley's cavalry company, the escort of Brigadier General Daniel W. Adams. Both units were active until the end of the war.

While desertions adversely affected the stability and continuity of the cadet corps, these losses were replaced from the ever-growing number of new applicants. No relief was in sight, however, for the shortages that begin in 1862, in everything from food to textbooks. War-related shortages affected VMI earlier than the other colleges, perhaps because Virginia had been the most active battleground since the war's beginning. Major General Smith dealt with the shortages by using the broad procurement powers given to him by the board of visitors when the Institute reopened in January.

With admirable foresight, Smith purchased three hundred head of cattle that produced a supply of beef throughout the war. "Old Spex" never missed an opportunity to add to VMI's larder, as demonstrated when he returned from a business trip to Vicksburg, Mississippi, with fifty barrels of molasses, which he had somehow convinced the Confederate Quartermaster to transport to Lexington. Foreign sources of supply were also tapped. He procured textbooks in Europe with a £2000 loan-of-grace from the London firm John K. Gilliat & Company, and obtained uniforms, buttons, and shoes from other British sources. Supplies purchased overseas were loaded aboard blockade runners, often through the assistance of Major Benjamin F. Ficklin, one of the Confederacy's European purchasing agents and a VMI graduate.

Smith knew that the supply situation could not greatly improve; therefore, he preached conservation to his cadets. General Order Number 23, published on February 5, 1862, sought to change the cadets' wasteful ways by appealing to their patriotism: "The Superintendent deems it his duty to impress upon all cadets the importance and necessity of the most rigid economy in all their expenditures. At such a time as this it is the duty of every patriot to husband the resources of the country that they may be not extravagantly or wastefully used."[10] In keeping with this policy, cadets were asked to turn in their old cotton and linen underwear for recycling into bandages. And a supreme sacrifice was made in the interest of conservation on Founder's Day, November 11, when the traditional cannon salute was cancelled because, "we have not more powder than we may be allowed upon at any day to use from shotted guns against the invaders of our soil."[11] But despite the best efforts of all involved, the supply situation continued to worsen.

The difficulties caused by the loss of experienced cadets and supply shortages would last throughout the war. They were not, however, as much of an immediate threat as the problems caused by an act of the Confederate Congress. In an effort to stimulate volunteers for the army, the Congress passed on April 16 the first Conscription Act. It removed men between the ages of eighteen and thirty-five from the control of their

states and placed them at the disposal of President Davis. Several classes
of exemptions were provided for, which included the academies' faculty,
but the Congress refused to exempt students at military colleges for fear
that the institutions would become havens for draft dodgers. The advent
of conscription did, in fact, stimulate enrollment at the colleges as parents
sought to protect their sons from the draft. Undoubtedly, bona fide draft
dodgers did enroll, and applications from young men of conscription age,
especially those without prior military service, were carefully scrutinized
to prevent this as much as possible. Without a congressional exemption,
however, the superintendents were understandably alarmed at the
prospect of overzealous enrolling officers swooping down on their cadets
as soon as they turned eighteen.

Each of the governors shared this concern and attempted to protect
his cadets from conscription. Governor Brown of Georgia wrote President
Davis on April 22: "I would . . . invite your attention to the fact that the
State owns and controls the Georgia Military Institute, at Marietta, and
now has in the institute over 125 cadets, a large proportion of whom are
within the age of conscripts. If they are not exempt this most important
institution is broken up."[12] Governor Shorter of Alabama assured Colonel
Garland that he would not permit the conscription of cadets and later
authorized the superintendent to use force if necessary to prevent it. In
Richmond, Governor Letcher sought to induce President Davis to
exempt VMI cadets from the Conscription Act, but Davis informed him
that it was not within his power to grant exemptions not specifically provided for by the Congress. He suggested that Letcher allow a cadet to be
drafted and then test the law by applying for a writ of habeas corpus for
the draftee. Letcher chose not to take such a gamble, and instead, he
ordered Smith not to surrender any conscripted cadet until the constitu-
tionality of the Conscription Act was decided. The executive council of
South Carolina dispatched a plea to Secretary of War George W. Randolph on behalf of its two military academies:

> The students of the academy are always ready, being well offi-
> cered, organized, armed, and equipped. We have always held them
> as a most efficient reserve, and if occasion should require they will
> be far more effective organized as they are than they could be if
> thrown out separately and absorbed in the various corps of the
> army. I earnestly hope that it may be consistent with your views of
> policy to issue very soon an order giving effect to the request of the
> Governor and Council in this particular.[13]

Randolph's reply was the same as the president's response to Letcher: The Confederate Congress had provided no exemption for cadets and he was powerless to create one.

Although the Congress refused to exempt cadets, it had no desire to break up these valuable institutions, and trusted President Davis to exercise discretion and not draft cadets unless absolutely necessary. Consequently, cadets enjoyed a practical exemption from the draft, although the actions of eager enrolling officers caused the battle over conscription to be joined anew periodically throughout the war.

In the spring, studies at most of the military colleges were again interrupted by field service. In March, Governor Shorter of Alabama called out the Katydids to train twelve thousand recruits assembled at twelve state camps. The soldiers were organized into over thirty regiments of infantry and cavalry and a number of artillery batteries. The cadets performed well, and the university was besieged by applicants who had seen them in action and now wanted to be cadets. Another consequence of their success was that when the university reopened in September, no seniors and only three juniors returned. As in 1861, most of the missing cadets had been elected to officer the regiments they trained. To help replace these men, Garland began admitting fourteen-year-old boys for preparatory instruction.

The cadets of GMI may have also returned to Camp McDonald. And after the April theft of the locomotive "The General," from nearby Big Shanty, they may have also guarded railroad bridges throughout north Georgia.

That spring, Professor Stonewall Jackson spent his sabbatical in Virginia's Shenandoah Valley playing hide and seek with overwhelming Federal forces. His former boss, General Smith, watched the events to the north with mounting concern. If Jackson was defeated, the way would be open to the institute itself, and the protection of the school was Smith's primary duty. On April 22, Old Spex offered the services of his corps to Jackson and suspended recitation in Latin, French, geography, and natural philosophy in order to concentrate on military training. In making this offer, Smith liberally interpreted the governor's instructions to keep the cadets ready to defend the institute. He reasoned that the school's best defense was a successful offense by Jackson.

A new spirit of efficiency and discipline came to each cadet at the prospect of active service. "Last Sunday," wrote Cadet Private John B. Snodgrass on April 29, "the news came that the Yankees were about entering Staunton. Academic duties were suspended and our time was devoted to three drills a day—preparing to meet the invader, should he attempt to drive us away from the V.M.I. General Smith told us he would lead us out to meet them if they came a thousand strong."[14] On April 30, Jackson sent for the cadets, and early the next morning, Cadet Snodgrass hastily reported to his sister, "The Corps of Cadets leave the Institute this morning to go to Staunton to reinforce General Jackson. All of us are in fine spirits—anxious to get a shot at the enemy."[15]

The corps, less eleven left behind as a guard, formed up before Washington's statue in front of barracks with their blankets, haversacks containing two days rations, and a tin cup and plate, "not equipped as soldiers at all," according to one cadet.[16] The column of about two hundred set out on the Valley Pike for Staunton with two wagons and two smoothbore six-pounder cannon.[17] In the afternoon a cold rain began that plagued the march almost all the way to Staunton and created bogs through which the cadets marched knee-deep in mud. The soggy battalion reached Staunton, a supply and transportation center about thirty miles north of Lexington, on Sunday, May 4.

The board of visitors had operational control of the VMI Corps of Cadets, and Smith had neither requested permission to offer Jackson the corps' services nor to respond to his later call. Smith did, however, inform the board of his actions. The first indication that the board did not share Smith's rationale for cooperating with Jackson came in the form of a letter from Adjutant General Richardson, an ex officio member of the board, written the day the cadets departed Lexington. "The members present today," Richardson wrote, "were unanimous in their disapprobation of the cadets being in any wise subjected to the risk of battle unless in the immediate defense of the Institution at Lexington and if we can get a board a resolution will be passed positively forbidding any portion of the corps being sent to join Jackson. There is no authority for it and the board thinks it would be a breach of good faith on the part of the Institution towards parents and guardians."[18]

At Staunton, Smith found two telegrams waiting for him. The first contained the board's resolution that it had no authority to grant leave or to order the cadets to enter military service. The second informed Smith that the board refused to give instructions concerning what to do with the cadets. Smith chose to force the issue and telegraphed that if he received nothing to the contrary by the next morning, he would treat the board's resolution as an order not to cooperate with Jackson. A reply from Richardson came that afternoon: "Your dispatch . . . was sent to the governor who endorsed it 'I do not see now how the cadets can be sent back. I think it best to let them go on. The mischief is done and we shall have to let it alone.'"[19]

Smith was not satisfied with this grudging permission to continue assisting Jackson. So when Stonewall returned to Staunton with his army from Brown's Gap in the Blue Ridge Mountains on May 6, Smith sought his guidance. After detailing the interchange between Richardson and himself, Smith confessed that he was "unexpectedly and painfully embarrassed, by the action of the Board, and the opinion of the Governor." He addressed Jackson directly: "In what way, and to what extent, I may take the responsibility of acting in opposition to the express wishes and order of my immediate superiors."[20]

Jackson, a stickler for the proper regard of military authority and the chain of command, refrained from counseling the superintendent. Instead, he only said, "The safety of this section of the Valley, in my opinion, renders your continued cooperation of great importance."[21] This was enough for Smith, who replied that it was his duty to have all of the cadets—with the exception of those under eighteen who did not have their parents' permission to be in the field—assist Jackson. Well aware that parents sent their sons to VMI to get an education and not to fight in the war, Smith rationalized his decision to Jackson as "a means, under Providence, by which you may be enabled, with your gallant army, to ensure to the cadets, at the end of the contemplated service, a safe return to their accustomed duties, with the satisfaction that they have at least endeavored to render a patriotic service."[22]

The cadets camped on the grounds of the Deaf and Dumb Asylum in Staunton, and on May 6, Jackson reviewed the sharp-looking, well-drilled young soldiers. Conscious of the cadets' high standards, the usually shabby Jackson arrived at the review freshly barbered and in a new Confederate general's uniform. That evening an order was read at Dress Parade that attached the cadets to Brigadier General Charles S. Winder's Stonewall Brigade.

Despite his calm appearance at the cadets' review, Jackson was anxiously awaiting intelligence on his two main opponents: Major General Nathaniel Banks, who was coming down from the north, and Brigadier General Robert H. Milroy, who was descending on Staunton from the west. But that evening Jackson learned that Banks had pulled back and that Milroy had retreated into the Allegheny Mountains with Brigadier General Edward "Allegheny" Johnson in pursuit. The next morning Jackson sent his troops, which now included the cadets, trudging west out of Staunton to assist Johnson.

Among the VMI cadets was Sergeant Benjamin A. "Duck" Colonna, who had been this way before when he had briefly served in Gilham's 21st Virginia Infantry the previous summer. On his last trip into the mountains Colonna had halted at Buffalo Gap, but now with Jackson's "foot cavalry," the gap was quickly reached and passed. The men continued to march, and soon passed the second campsite of Colonna's previous expedition. Here, thought Colonna, they would surely halt. "It was getting monotonous, and though I did not like to own it, I was getting a little tired of carrying that musket and other toggery," Colonna recalled. "But no; we were called to attention and soon found ourselves climbing the Shenandoah Mountain."[23]

The cadets, though worn, kept pace with the veterans. Nearing the mountain hamlet of McDowell, Jackson's soldiers heard the rumble of cannon fire and the rattle of musketry. Johnson was engaging Milroy's bluecoats, who were now reinforced by Brigadier General Robert C. Schenck's troops. The noise of battle gave the cadets their second wind, and they quickened their pace toward the direction of the firing. But the sound of combat gradually died and the corps halted and bivouacked.

The cadets were sorely disappointed at not being able to "see the elephant," as soldiers described the first battle experience, but Jackson never intended to use them in battle. When he had requested the cadets' services, Jackson had told Smith that he could arrange for them to perform duties behind the lines and free others for battle. "The duty I know would not be congenial to the feelings of our brave Corps," wrote Jackson, "which I am well satisfied would desire to advance; but the patriot (and I regard each one of them as such) is willing to take any position where he can best serve his country."[24]

The Battle of McDowell was a Confederate victory and Schenck burned his camps and retreated up the road toward Franklin around nine o'clock that night.

The battle was small in comparison to others yet to come, with only a total of about eight thousand troops engaged on both sides. Jackson outnumbered his opponent by almost two-to-one, yet suffered 75 dead and 428 wounded, while Federal losses were half that. On May 9, in order to harden them against war's horrors, Jackson assigned the cadets the grisly task of burying the dead and collecting the wounded. Many paled at their first sight of the torn bodies but soon overcame their disgust and began clearing away the dead. Searching for wounded, Colonna and some cadets entered the parlor of a fine brick home and found:

> [A] dead man laid on top of the piano, and in the dining-room
> on the table there was a litter with a man on it. This man had a
> triangular hole knocked in the top of his head, and his brains had

run out on the floor, leaving the front half of his skull entirely empty; yet he breathed, and when we gave him water from a sponge, that we found in his mouth, he sucked it vigorously and opened his eyes.[25]

Dr. Robert L. Madison, the corps surgeon, examined the man and told the cadets to stop giving him water—it would only prolong his agony. He died half an hour later. Colonna and a cadet detail buried the two Federals along the banks of the Cow Pasture River.

Dragging the shattered bodies of their comrades and enemies to their graves was unpleasant, but it was not as arduous as the twenty-two-hour, forty-four-mile march of the day before, and the cadets welcomed the respite. "The Corps of Cadets were nearly all broken down," remembered one of them. "All were lame with sore feet."[26] The rest and recuperation was needed because Jackson intended to pursue Schenck and Milroy and push them as far from the Valley as possible.

On May 10, the Valley Army set out after the defeated but still dangerous enemy. The Federals, in order to conceal their whereabouts and to generally harass their pursuers, set smoking forest fires and ambushed the Confederates as they followed the retreat. Jackson caught up with the enemy the next day at the village of Franklin, thirty miles northwest of McDowell. Fighting was light and inconclusive, but was not rejoined because Stonewall had decided to turn loose of Schenck and Milroy to pursue General Banks, who was hunkered down in the Shenandoah at New Market. He hoped that attacking Banks would cause Lincoln to transfer troops from Major General George B. McClellan's army in front of Richmond to the Valley to ensure that Jackson would not move on Washington. Luring Federals away from Confederate General Joseph E. Johnston's army, which was fighting for Richmond's life, was Jackson's primary mission.

The return march was even harder than the march out. It began raining on May 12, and continued for five days. With their heads bent against the rain and sodden uniforms clinging uncomfortably to their bodies, the troops trudged on, accompanied by the constant sound of marching feet breaking free from the mud's suction. Their soggy shoes began to dissolve and many men marched fifteen miles a day barefooted. Others straggled or fell out of the line of march altogether. The cadets tied their shoes together with strips of cloth and pieces of string and continued the march. But despite their discomfort and Jackson's blistering pace, they were full of enthusiasm and felt stronger than when they had left Lexington, for the campaign had hardened them.

On the evening of May 14, the soldiers reached McDowell, and here the decision was made to return the cadets to the institute. The following day Jackson published an order thanking "Major General Smith and the officers and cadets under him, for the promptitude and efficiency with which they have assisted in the recent expedition."[27]

The cadets parted with Jackson's army at Lebanon Springs on May 16, and marched twenty miles to Staunton, losing about half their number along the way because of lack of shoes. But when the remnant of the corps reached Staunton, cadet pride and training outweighed physical exhaustion and pain. Colonna looked on with admiration as the cadets halted in front of their quarters "faced to the front and ordered arms. It was simply perfect; every gun came down at once on the brick pavement."[28] For them the Valley Campaign was over.

Not only were the cadets impressed with their performance, but so were Jackson's veterans, despite the merciless harrassment they inflicted upon the cadets. Cadet Snodgrass proudly wrote home on May 18, the day after his return to Lexington, that the Corps had survived "one of the most toilsome marches of 10 days ever endured by an army."[29] His pride was still evident a month later when he wrote his sister: "The New York Herald says General Jackson has been reinforced by 2000 well drilled cadets. They are sightly mistaken in their numbers—we were not 200 strong."[30]

Even General Smith himself was proud. In his annual report that July he reminded the board of visitors of the positive aspects regarding the cadets' time with their old professor "Fool Tom":

> It showed them that war was not a pastime, but was an irksome and laborious duty; and most of the restlessness among them . . . has been quieted. Besides, this military expedition has, in a measure, vindicated the manhood of those, many of who, although below the legal age for military service, were restless under the reputation of a peace establishment.[31]

War, so it seemed, could also be part of the educational experience, although the experience cost Cadet Private John T. D. Gisiner his life, who died from an illness he developed during the campaign.

In South Carolina that spring, the Citadel cadets of Company A, Battalion of State Cadets, served as provost guards in Charleston after their return from Wappoo Cut. In May they were then called to James Island by Confederate General John C. Pemberton, commander of the District of Georgia, Florida, and South Carolina. Here the cadets mounted eight heavy guns, requisitioned from the Citadel, in the fortifications west of Newton's Cut. Once the guns were mounted, however, Pemberton decided to retain the cadets because of the increased Federal activity on the island. But the Citadel cadets were also under the control of their board of visitors, and Superintendent Major "Benny" White would be embarrassingly reminded of this fact.

Having responded to Pemberton's initial call without consulting the board, White now sent Captain Hugh S. Thompson, professor of belle lettres and ethics, to Columbia to request General Jones' permission to keep the cadets in the field. In his meeting with Jones, Thompson detailed White's reasons for taking the corps to James Island. Jones listened without interrupting and then wrote a note ordering White to return the cadets to the school and to report to him in person.

When Thompson returned to White with Jones's order, the agitated superintendent hurried to Pemberton's headquarters in Charleston and requested that Pemberton relieve the corps from further duty so White could obey the order. Pemberton refused. White, caught between the two men, was luckily rescued by the intervention of Pemberton's chief of ordnance, who had asked that the cadets be called out in the first place. The young soldiers were totally demoralized by Jones's order and, upon their return to the Citadel around June 8, began the mass desertion that gave birth to the Cadet Rangers.

Despite the disputes regarding the role of the cadets in the war, Federal armies were not the only dangers they might have to face. There existed within the Confederacy a circumstance that could become more terrifying than any Yankee legion—the potential for a slave uprising. Alabama's Colonel Garland became especially concerned about this after Lincoln's preliminary Emancipation Proclamation on September 22, 1862. Garland believed a slave rebellion was part of the overall Yankee war strategy.

"Lincoln knows," wrote Garland to Governor Shorter on October 31, "that any general insurrectionary movement in the slave states would dissolve our armies. Our soldiers would fly to defend their firesides from a domestic foe, and our regiments on the border would melt away like snow before a summer's sun."[32] Garland wrote that abolitionists would corrupt slaves scattered among the plantations, arm them, form them into "bands of midnight assassins," and send them forth for the purposes of destroying property and "butchering our wives and children."[33] To "protect" the slaves from these abolitionists, the superintendent proposed creating internment camps for male slaves between the ages of fifteen and sixty.

Garland maintained that should his dire predictions come true, the cadets would have a role in defending the populace. "While the Cadets should not be needlessly exposed to destruction in an assault against superior numbers of the enemy," explained Garland, "yet in the event of insurrectionary movement anywhere in the dense slave population of the middle counties, I shall not hesitate to fly as rapidly as possible to the defense of women and children."[34]

Of course, Garland's slave rebellion never materialized, so his cadets were spared the further interruption of their studies. And despite the wartime revision of the colleges' educational philosophies and the interruptions caused by field service, academics were still considered important in the training of military officers. Professors labored hard to teach the cadets, though they sometimes thought they were "casting pearls before swine." Lieutenant John B. Patrick concluded that at the Arsenal, "we have a set of boys here this year who do not love to study. They find great difficulty with the Binomial Theorem, more I think than any class I have taught."[35]

Nevertheless, the teachers kept on trying and some students profited. VMI Cadet Fourth Class Private J. Henry Reid was a beneficiary of Smith's efforts to maintain a viable academic program. "General Smith seems determined to pick Math into our heads," Reid reported to his father. "He gives us 20 or 30 pages of Algebra every day."[36] Smith's perseverance paid off and at the conclusion of VMI's abbreviated 1861–62 school year, Smith was able to report progress in all sections of all classes, save the lower sections of the third and fourth classes who were less able to catch up after their studies were interrupted by the corps' two week sojourn with General Jackson. So Smith decided to cancel VMI's normal summer military encampment in favor of a summer of study to make up for the missed fall 1861 semester.

The beginning of the 1862–63 academic year produced the largest number of applicants for admission to the colleges so far. The Citadel received over three hundred applications, VMI more than five hundred, and Alabama approximately four hundred. So overwhelming was the number of students seeking to enter the South Carolina Military

Academy that discussions were held in November regarding the expansion of the Arsenal or the establishment of a branch campus at Yorkville, South Carolina. Alabama's Colonel Garland accepted more cadets than could be boarded in the barracks, so the overflow was housed in tents. GMI was forced to turn away numerous applicants for lack of barracks facilities; by November of the following year Governor Brown urged the legislature to expand the institute.

Such success increased the Confederate government's faith in the state military academies and was demonstrated early in 1862 when a group of Confederate States cadets enrolled at VMI, the oldest of the colleges and the closest to the seat of government. Thereafter, the government periodically sent cadets to VMI throughout the war, and its generals detailed or recommended deserving enlisted men to attend the institute, as well as the other military colleges.[37]

The end of the first full year of war found the state military colleges plagued with external problems beyond their control. Balancing their duty to their state against the demands of a central government, which pushed for total mobilization, and balancing their mission of educating officers against the increasing calls for field service, would become a progressively more difficult trick for the superintendents.

CHAPTER FOUR

1863: Coming of Age

THE YEAR OF 1863 WOULD PROVE TO BE A TURNING POINT IN THE fortunes of the Confederate nation. Although the previous year had seen some setbacks for Confederate arms—the captures of New Orleans and Roanoke Island; the surrenders of Forts Henry and Donelson; the bloody defeat at Shiloh; and Robert E. Lee's repulse at Sharpsburg—the overall prospects for Confederate independence remained bright. Large Confederate armies were still in the field, the war had been carried to the enemy by Lee in Maryland and Braxton Bragg and Edmund Kirby Smith in Kentucky, and George McClellan's Army of the Potomac had been turned away from Richmond. Although Lincoln's transformation of the war with the Emancipation Proclamation into a moral struggle troubled some of the South's admirers in Europe, there was still a realistic hope that England or France would recognize the Confederacy. It was possible that 1863 could be the year of triumph, and the faculty and cadets of the military colleges shared in this guarded hope.

However, also by 1863, problems that had started as mere annoyances to the superintendents of the South's military colleges began to have a telling effect on the operation of the schools, as well as their cadets. As the Federal blockade of Southern ports became more efficient and the Confederacy's transportation system began to deteriorate, shortages of food and other supplies became more alarming. Textbooks were in such short supply that cadets at the military schools were asked to turn in their used books for issue to the next class. Later, because the blockade raised the cost of books even higher, cadets had to rent them for their classes.

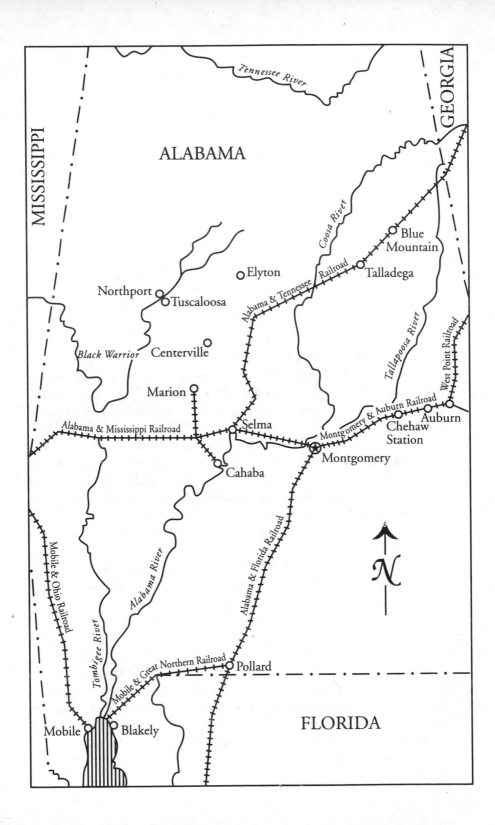

Some young entrepreneurs sought to supply the academic needs of their classmates. VMI cadet Jacob Kent Langhorne gratefully acknowledged the receipt of some texts sent by his brother, but wished "he had sent a dozen coppies [*sic*] of French Grammar as . . . I could sell every coppy [*sic*] for two $ apiece."[1] More commonplace items such as window glass were nearly impossible to obtain and General Smith felt it necessary to remind VMI cadets to lock their casement windows so the wind would not catch them and break the precious panes.

Cloth was also at a premium, and cadets at VMI were required to furnish their own, much of it homespun, to be made into uniforms. Smith tried to obtain cloth from the army, but with little success. When some was finally acquired, it was issued only to those who never had a "regulation" uniform. The Citadel was so starved for cloth that when a Charleston merchant helped locate a supply, he promptly received the official thanks of the board of visitors. Colonel Garland also had problems clothing his cadets. He was forced to use curtains and sheets to line their jackets and trousers, which had been made with the limited supply of cloth available. To ensure an ample supply of uniform cloth for the university, Garland urged the governor to seize a nearby woolen mill, which was rumored to be the target of Confederate impressment for the state.

Obtaining shoes for cadets was also a challenge. "General Smith says he cannot and will not furnish us shoes," wrote Cadet Langhorne plaintively to his parents, "and I am nearly barefooted."[2] The colleges procured some footwear by local purchase and through the blockade, or made the shoes themselves. Garland established a cobbler shop at the university, and managed to have an experienced shoemaker detailed from the army to run it. He also bought beef on the hoof so there would be a supply of leather for the shoemaker.

As the year wore on, shortages caused necessary changes to be made in the colleges' heretofore strict uniform regulations. The use of homespun cloth, with its uneven quality and color, changed the uniform cadet gray of the battalions to a hodgepodge of varying shades. When regulation black collar-stocks became hard to obtain, bow ties were substituted. The situation became so bad that Smith was forced to restrict the wear of the practically irreplaceable cadet coatee to only "drill or dress duty."[3]

The shortage of food, however, was a more alarming problem. "We have very poor fare here," wrote VMI Cadet Edmund Berkeley:

> Today for breakfast we had only two pieces of bread and about
> half a gill of milk with what we call growly—which is made of

mutton, beef, beef feet or anything else they can make. For dinner
we have beef or cabage [*sic*] or turnips one day and beef-steak and
soup the next. We have nothing that I would have eaten at home,
but I am so hungry when I go to meals that I think even turnips
delicious.[4]

Citadel Cadet Joseph Barnwell had similar comments regarding the mess
at Charleston:

The material was inferior and the cooking worse. Hominy with
the husks left in and rice badly boiled, coffee with brown sugar and
no milk, tough beef for dinner and hash for breakfast made up the
usual course, but on Sunday we were given poultry for dinner. At
supper we had cornbread mostly.[5]

Some cadets were convinced that the poor quality and insufficient
quantity of the food was a plot by the administration to ruin their health.
"I understand Dr Madison said this morning that the fare here was calcu-
lated to give anybody the Typhoid fever," wrote VMI Cadet J. Henry
Reid to his father.[6] Another complained about the ersatz rye coffee; he
proclaimed it to be poison and swore to his mother, "they are starving
us now."[7]

The school superintendents did all they could to supply sufficient
rations of good quality, and usually investigated cadet complaints about
the food. Garland sent the university's steward throughout the South in
search of food. He had some success, and it appears that food was more
abundant at the University of Alabama than at some of the other colleges.
Nevertheless, the quality, quantity, and variety of the meals did not meet
cadet standards and complaints were frequent. But when Garland looked
into some of these complaints, he found them to be "misrepresented and
greatly exaggerated."[8]

As the war dragged on there was less patience with cadet complaints.
In May 1864, Adjutant General Richardson, on behalf of the board of visitors, investigated cadet complaints about the food at VMI. He reported
with some disgust: "The Corps of Cadets is far better subsisted than any
private family I know. Gen. Lee himself lives almost entirely upon vegetables, leaving what meat there is for the soldiers—and to descend from the
sublime to the ridiculous, I am very near the point of having no meat on
my own table."[9]

Complaining about food was, and still is, a main source of enjoyment
for cadets. Garland was undoubtedly correct in his finding that many of

the mess's deficiencies were exaggerated. Yet, as elsewhere in the South, there were very real inadequacies regarding the supply of food at the military colleges. In September Colonel Garland resorted to a novel way to obtain needed rations: each cadet had to pay part of his tuition with bacon. This often amounted to a tidy sum of money. For instance, when the Stephens brothers matriculated each "paid" 111 1/2 pounds of bacon with a value of $669 as part of his tuition. Since money was often easier to obtain than bacon, some parents balked at the new requirement. But Garland was firm with those who claimed an inability to pay and told one recalcitrant parent, "Bacon is an indispensable condition to the reception of your son."[10]

Many complaints were sent·along with the bacon, and to the complainers Garland patiently explained that he could not accept students if he had not the means to feed them. "What can I do," he asked these parents, "in a market which is not offering a single pound for sale, except in the way of barter for salt, or thread, or something else which I cannot command?"[11] In 1864 VMI adopted a similar payment-in-kind requirement.

The fact that General Lee had no meat and that it was difficult everywhere did little to quiet the cadets. Their letters home continued to be filled with complaints about their poor fare, as well as with descriptions of their resourcefulness in filling their stomachs. "I know the fare we get is not sufficient," wrote a cadet to his father. "I have therefore made an arrangement with a servant to supply me with some chicken, some butter and some good bread, every five days in a week at $1.25," and since the regulations prohibited bringing food into the mess hall, "he brings it to me in my room."[12]

Those cadets with little money but large appetites resorted to less honest ways of satisfying their hunger. VMI Cadet Private Samuel F. Atwill explained to his father how he and his roommates acted as their own commissariat: "Yesterday one of my roommates 'as it was his time' went out in the country foraging and about 12 o'clock he came in with two very nice chickens with their heads looking like someone had hit them with a rock. . . . We had a very nice breakfast this morning in old [room number] 45."[13] Local farmers soon complained to Smith about foraging cadets, and the superintendent was not amused. He warned the corps that, "Every facility will be afforded for the detection and conviction" of foragers.[14]

Citadel cadets supplemented their rations by raiding orchards and fruit trees in various bombed-out Charleston neighborhoods. As Federal shelling of the city increased, so did the danger of these fruit raids, but the "grapes, figs, and peaches" hanging "temptingly from vine and tree" were too good to pass up merely because one might be blown to bits by a Yankee shell.[15] Cadet John Kershaw, son of Confederate Major General Joseph B. Kershaw, made frequent raids with his hungry comrades, "dodging the shells when necessary and timing ourselves so as to pass . . . in the intervals of firing."[16]

Cadets who wished to avoid the practice of foraging and its accompanying risks hunted game in their free time or bartered for food. Uniform items seemed to be a popular medium of exchange with local civilians, and despite the cloth shortage, a VMI cadet reported, "I have seen many a cadet jacket traded off for half a peck of apples; and if a cadet were really hungry, I think he would trade the coat on his back for one apple-pie."[17]

The cheapest way of eating well, and with a clear conscience and a coat on your back, was to dig into a box of goodies sent from some cadet's home. The opening of such a box was a time for rejoicing and almost Bacchanalian behavior:

> The best simile description of cadets around a box from home is that of feeding a kennel of hounds. With undisguised impatience they watch the display of food. With frank gluttony they fall upon it. With pop-eyed satiety they turn away only when all is consumed. And then they lie about in a semi-comatose condition refusing to attend meals until nature relieves itself of overloading.[18]

Though it was not of immediate importance to the cadets, a shortage of serviceable, efficient military equipment and ammunition was a pressing problem for their leaders. Most of the modern muskets that had been in the hands of the colleges had been turned over to arm the volunteer regiments at the start of the war, and were replaced by smoothbore Austrian and Belgian muskets or some other antiquated, outmoded weaponry. Obtaining or retaining artillery also proved troublesome. GMI managed to hang on to its artillery; VMI lost four guns; the Citadel "donated" several to Charleston's defenses; and Alabama pestered the governor for cannon. Garland finally obtained two guns, but a request for horses to pull them was denied, so he contracted with citizens of Tuscaloosa for the use of their horses.

After much begging, Garland also received some better muskets for his cadets. However, he was unable to make bullets because the local supply of lead was exhausted. He searched in desperation for any available lead and reported a somewhat ghoulish find to Governor Shorter. "There are about 1,000 pounds on a vault in this vicinity in which I have had an eye in case of necessity," Garland confided, "but it is the vault of the late Capt. Wm. T. King, whose wife's grief at his loss is such as to preclude the propriety of speaking to her on the subject of dismantling her husband's tomb."[19]

VMI's weapons problems were not solved until November, when Adjutant General Richardson obtained two captured, three-inch rifled cannon and two hundred Austrian rifles from the Confederate Ordnance Department. At the same time Smith received sixteen thousand rounds of musket ammunition and four hundred rounds of ammunition for the new cannon, as well as canteens, haversacks, and knapsacks.

Compounding the problem of shortages was the inflation ravaging the Confederate economy. Even when goods could be located the purchase price was often outrageous. By late 1863, a copy of Levizac's *French Grammar* obtained through the blockade cost $30. In December VMI's milk contractor almost quadrupled his price from 20 cents per gallon to 75 cents. In Richmond that month, poor-quality bacon was selling for $3.25 a pound, butter for $4.50 a pound, brown sugar for $3.25 a pound, and molasses for $14 a gallon. In January 1863 these items had sold for $1, $1.75, $1, and $8 respectively. Uniform items also increased in price. Cadet pants which had cost $8 five years before cost $30 in September 1863.

In an effort to keep up with rising costs, the schools had to raise tuition. The increases at the Citadel were typical: In 1861 a cadet's tuition was $200 per year; by 1862 it was $400, and each cadet was required to furnish his own underclothing, shoes, combs, and brushes; a year later tuition was up to $800; and in 1864 every matriculate paid $1,200 and supplied his own shoes, underclothing, combs, brushes, towels, sheets, and pillowcases.

Support from the Confederate government would have done much to ease the colleges' supply problems, but little was forthcoming. The government vacillated between policies of indifference and niggardliness, and soon became an active competitor with the military colleges for scarce supplies. In 1863, Garland, at least, still had faith that the government would recognize that the war would be a long one, and would also realize that the Alabama Corps of Cadets was an integral part of the Confederate military establishment. Garland hoped this realization would bring more government support, including the ability to purchase surplus army supplies from the quartermaster. Unfortunately, he was disappointed.

Despite adversity, the wartime cadets did not lose their youthful impishness or zest for life as they sought to maintain their individuality and sense of humor in a military system that stressed uniformity during one of the most humorless times in American history. The camaraderie of the cadets did much to make a bad situation bearable. It was further enhanced by the fact that inside of barracks, family and fortune meant little because the military system was a great leveler. Although some cadets were members of prominent families—GMI's Julius Brown was the governor's son, VMI's John S. Wise was the son of former governor Henry A. Wise, and the Citadel's Henry T. Beauregard was the son of General P. G. T. Beauregard—all were brothers in adversity.

The average wartime cadet was between seventeen and eighteen years of age, although some were as young as fourteen and others were "old men" of twenty-four. Not surprisingly, the opposite sex figured prominently in their thoughts and desires, and they were always on the lookout for young women. "Today . . . we were compelled to attend church," one cadet wrote in his diary. "The day being very muddy and sloppy there was an unusual display of legs by the young ladies of the Seminary."[20] Even during hot and dusty marches a sharp eye was kept out for women. "As we marched past a female school," recalled a cadet, "every window of which was filled with pretty girls, the fifers were laboring away at 'The Girl I Left Behind Me'. . . . Not one of us were thinking of the girls we left behind us. The girls we saw before us were altogether to our liking."[21] Girls were on the mind of VMI Cadet Charles T. Haigh so much that in his diary he created a mythical accusation against himself for talking in ranks on the way to church and answered it with a young man's Victorian fantasy:

> Excuse . . . there was a young lady—yes? a most lovely one! who was so unfortunate as to be in the center of the whirlwind—immediately her dress and all her under clothing was over her head and then—good gracious? what a sight for mans eye to behold—I could not restrain my feelings—it was an impossibility—but all I did was exclaim? "look Selden what a beautiful 'gambe.'"[22]

The young ladies had as much interest in the cadets as the cadets had in them. Many veterans found their sweethearts "snaked" by cadets whenever the impressive young men were about. One cadet noted that the veterans, especially the officers, "could not and would not understand why the girls preferred these little, untitled whippersnappers to officers of distinction."[23] "Veterans," he concluded, "forgot that youths love youth."[24] But interest in women sometimes had its price, as one cadet discovered. "I had nearly the limit of demerits," he recalled, "for besides other weaknesses, I had developed a love affair uptown with a pretty little Presbyterian, and, being caught out of limits, had been confined to barracks, and assigned several extra tours of guard duty."[25] But while boldness in romance was seen by cadets as a virtue, the same quality was not admired in young women. "I got . . . a lovesick note from Miss Falk," Arsenal Cadet Carey Thomas confided in his diary concerning a girl he'd met only four days before. "I am disgusted with fast girls."[26]

A good sense of humor and a love of pranks were almost universal among cadets. In response to being placed on report for missing reveille, a joking cadet wrote, "Excuse—I dreamed I was O. D. [Officer of the Day]—and I did not have to go."[27] The officers of the schools were also a source of merriment. Cadet Sam Atwill told his father about seeing Superintendent Smith seated at the table of examiners during his most recent exam: "'Old Spex' as big as life, resembling an old owl with a standing collar, and a pair of spex on; but I will not say anything about the looks of this venerable gentleman for he certainly is as good looking as any monkey you ever saw; with a mouth sharp enough to pick peas out of a porter bottle."[28]

Practical jokes were popular sport, and many victims found that their accoutrements had been hidden before dress parade or that shoe polish had been put on their musket minutes before a white glove inspection. While the usual targets for practical jokers were fellow cadets, it was not uncommon for pranksters to loosen the axle nuts on the artillery and stifle their laughter as the wheels separated from the gun carriage during drill. The officers tried to control pranks aimed at school property or facilities and sometimes, as when Arsenal Lieutenant John B. Patrick confidently proclaimed that his remarks to the corps after someone doused the garrison's lights would "stop that kind of amusement," they were foolish enough to believe they had succeeded.[29]

As amusing as these practical jokes were, the cadets thirsted for more proper entertainment, which was hard to find within the confines of a military college. One inmate described his school as "one of the dullest and meanest places in Christendom," but the cadets always seemed to come up with something.[30] Animal fights were one diversion. VMI Cadet Haigh and his comrades caught a ground hog on one occasion and fought him against a rat and two dogs. Haigh later reported, "[T]he first round—they fought nearly three-quarters of an hour—neither seemed hurt much—but the second round did not last quite so long—but the principal reason was because we had two dog's [*sic*] on him—but he still fought until the last."[31]

Fights between cadets also supplied an exciting diversion from barracks routine. Some fights were in the nature of duels that were organized and well publicized in the barracks beforehand. Most, however, were spontaneous affairs brought on by a "transgression" that someone felt deserved an immediate thrashing. Whatever the cause, the opponents gave it their all. "My adversary walked away," remembered a former contestant years later:

> He was no beauty . . . But I? My! oh my! but I was a physical wreck. My jacket, where I had held his head so long, was fairly soaked with gore. Two or three buttons were torn off, and my collar was under one ear. The toe of his shoe had raked off about an inch of skin from the ridge of my nose. A knot as large as a pigeon's egg was on my forehead, and the last I saw of him he was picking my hair off his fingers.[32]

Like most other sources of cadet entertainment, fighting, of course, was against school regulations. So too was the favorite sport of upperclassmen—hazing new cadets. Regardless, it was prevalent and became a tradition at most of the military schools. Several forms of hazing were practiced. Initially, the new cadet suffered through a one-time initiation, which was known at VMI, for example, as "bucking." A cadet described his bucking as follows:

> A bed-strap was buckled about my wrists; I was ordered up on the table and compelled to draw up my knees, over which my bound arms were slipped; a ramrod was run under my knees and over my arms, and then I was rolled over on my side, and Louis and Colonna, with a bayonet scabbard, spelled CONSTANTINOPLE. The taps given me by these laughing friends were light, but sufficiently stinging to make me appreciate what it might have been.[33]

A typical initiation at the Citadel was to confine new cadets in a room full of cigar-smoking upperclassmen. As the room filled with noxious blue smoke, the old cadets guffawed at the choking newcomers. Cadet John Kershaw brought his session to a quick conclusion, however, when he pulled out his own pipe and belched forth clouds every bit as blue, thick, and nasty as his tormentors'.

Another form of hazing, less painful but more embarrassing, was known—at least at VMI—as "greening." Greening took the form of practical jokes such as sending a new cadet to the quartermaster sergeant for a left-handed ramrod, convincing him he was on guard when in fact he was not, or telling him the superintendent wanted to see him when there was no such summons. Cadet Joseph Barnwell's experience was typical. Upon his first entry into the Citadel mess hall, an upperclassman growled that he was to be tested on his knowledge of the school's regulations by several upperclassmen. Only after he began earnestly committing various trivia to memory was he informed by another grinning upperclassman that it was all a joke.

Sometimes physical hazing was meted out as punishment for new cadet "impudence." "Hold up" was a painful punishment that consisted of ordering the cadet to hold up his hand, whereupon his arm was twisted behind his back. Other forms of punishment were much more severe. After a fight with an upperclassman, VMI rat J. Henry Reid was jumped by his opponent. He later recalled: "As I was coming off guard with my gun lying carelessly across my shoulder [they] tied me & hung me over the door until I had no life in me & they had to throw water in my face & bathe my head to bring me too [sic]."[34] This episode changed Reid's opinion of VMI. "In regard to my maltreatment," he wrote his father, "if I had known . . . how I was to be treated I never would have consented to come."[35] Reid later left the institute and joined the army.

The practice of hazing at VMI became the subject of legislative investigation in 1863 after a former cadet, William A. Daniel, filed a complaint. The General Assembly took a dim view of the practice and held debates during which some legislators voiced unflattering opinions about the institute and its cadets. "The legislature is still cutting up about our maltreating the new Cadets . . . ," explained Cadet Thomas B. Davis to his sister. "I enclose you a part of the proceedings of the Legislature. . . . You will see from it what a reputation we have. The Legislature says that we are a set (the most of us) of precocious youths who came here to avoid Conscription."[36] Superintendent Smith defended his opposition to hazing by pointing out to the lawmakers that since 1846 he had issued twenty orders prohibiting the practice. He also shared his opinion that "the evil cannot be entirely removed . . . until the spirit of mischief, natively alive in every child's heart, and prominently developed in many a rude boy's growth, is entirely removed—then, and not till then, will this universal evil, common to all schools, be fully and completely eradicated."[37] As a result of the Daniel complaint, Smith again prohibited physical hazing and ordered the cadets to cease bucking, and substitute greening in its place.

Neither Smith nor any other superintendent could eliminate "the spirit of mischief" in his cadets, but the war tempered it with other qualities. The impetuosity of youth, so disconcerting to college officers, gave rise to an ability to disdain fear. The cadets' sense of humor enabled them to withstand the rigors of the march and the field with little complaint. When tempered with the determination to contribute to their states' and their new country's defense , these traits produced an élan akin to a young lion—an almost fearless spirit that which would recognize no power greater than itself. Smith commented upon this trait when he noted his cadets' "cheerful alacrity in the discharge of every duty, the patient endurance under great hardships, such as only veterans are accustomed to, and the buoyant spirit, not daunted by . . . disaster."[38] The great tests of the "young lions" were still in the future, but 1863 brought service that developed this spirit and further honed the weapon of the cadet battalions.

The first four months of the year passed relatively uneventfully for the various corps of cadets. Citadel cadets were called out for a time in January to man the battery protecting the New Bridge, which linked James Island and Charleston.

In early May the Katydids were called out to meet a force of fifteen hundred "abolitionists" marching on Tuscaloosa from Elyton (present day Birmingham). It was Garland's nightmare come true—a force of anti-slavery fanatics bent on corrupting slaves and inciting an orgy of death and destruction. Within six hours of the first alarm, the Alabama cadets were on the march. "It was gratifying," Garland reported to Governor Shorter, "to witness the ardor and enthusiasm with which they marched to the anticipated conflict."[39]

It was a false alarm. There was no abolitionist column, but the incident gave Garland some valuable insights. First, when fewer than a dozen of Tuscaloosa's citizens responded to his call for assistance in repulsing the rumored raid, he became convinced that his cadets were the only reliable force in the area. Second, he realized how uncomfortably vulnerable his college was to enemy raiders. Garland had no illusions concerning the results of a Federal raid of Tuscaloosa:

If the enemy should ever reach this place, they would not leave at this University one brick standing upon another. At Oxford, Miss., they totally destroyed buildings, Library, and Apparatus and the private residences of the Officers. Yet that was not a Military Institution. If they did that in the green tree what will they not do in the dry?[40]

To help make the university a rallying point during Federal raids and to protect the campus, Garland convinced Governor Shorter to impress 150 slaves from the local area to construct fortifications. They dug trenches and prepared thousands of pickets. However, on December 28 the newly elected governor Thomas Hill Watts received a petition from 101 Tuscaloosians urging that the slaves and tools be released for work in the fields. The fortifications, they alleged, were of little use and the impressment of laborers was both "unnecessary and unavailing."[41] Watts ordered that hired laborers be substituted for the slaves. Garland protested that hired laborers could not be found at any price and, except for occasional labor performed by the cadets, the work on the fortifications essentially ceased.

A solemn duty resulted for the VMI Corps of Cadets that May, as Robert E. Lee's Army of Northern Virginia faced Joseph Hooker's Army of the Potomac in the tangled Virginia wilderness around a cluster of buildings known as Chancellorsville. After withstanding Federal attacks on May 1, Lee decided to take the offensive, and Stonewall Jackson, now commander of Lee's Second Corps, proposed stealing a march on Fighting Joe Hooker and attacking his right flank. Lee agreed, and at 8 A.M. on May 2, Stonewall set his corps in motion. After an eight-hour march, his troops arrived on the Federal's unprotected flank.

Standing with Colonel Thomas T. Munford of the 2d Virginia Cavalry and watching his corps form for the assault, Jackson noticed many of his former students and faculty colleagues in the ranks and remarked to Munford, who was a VMI graduate, "The Institute will be heard from today."[42] At 5:00 P.M. Jackson turned to former VMI professor Robert E. Rodes and asked, "Are you ready?" Rodes replied that he was, and the Second Corps rushed forward, striking Hooker's flank, and rolling it up like a blanket. It was to be hailed as Stonewall Jackson's greatest day.

That night about nine o'clock, Jackson rode out beyond his lines on a reconnaissance in preparation for a night attack. During his return to his own lines, the general and his staff were mistaken for Yankee cavalry by the 18th North Carolina's pickets. Shots rang out and several of Jackson's staffers fell from their saddles. Jackson's aide and brother-in-law, Lieutenant Joseph Morrison, and Major General A. P. Hill both tried to stop the firing, but a second volley sent a bullet tearing through Jackson's right hand and two more into his left arm. Jackson, in great pain, was taken to a field hospital at Wilderness Tavern, where his left arm had to be amputated.

Adjutant General Richardson, who was in Richmond, kept Superintendent Smith informed of Jackson's condition. "The Governor tells me today that he has rec'd intelligence that Gen. Jackson will lose his right hand and his left arm," Richardson telegraphed on May 5.[43] Five days later Smith received an update: "Rumored that Gen. Jackson's condition is critical."[44] Richardson's information was correct: the mighty Stonewall Jackson died of pneumonia on May 10. Two days later a dispatch from the quartermaster in Staunton communicated this information on to Lexington.

Arrangements were made for Jackson to be buried in Lexington, and VMI cadets, who felt the loss "irreparable," were to take their old professor to his grave.[45] On May 13, in preparation for the arrival of Jackson's body, Smith ordered that the cadet battery fire a volley every half hour the following day, that Jackson's old lecture room be draped in mourning for six months, and that all officers and cadets wear black mourning bands for the next thirty days.

On May 14 the body arrived from Richmond aboard a canal boat. The corps was waiting at the canal terminal and "with reversed arms and muffled drums bore him back to the Institute."[46] All along their route "the lilacs and early spring flowers were just blooming."[47] Upon arrival at the institute, the cadets placed Jackson's body in his former lecture room, where "it lay in state throughout the night, banked high with flowers and guarded by cadets."[48]

The following day his body was placed aboard a cadet battery caisson, and the escort regiment, under the command of Commandant Scott Ship, formed up around it. Eight of the escort's companies consisted of the Corps of Cadets. Slowly, solemnly, the procession marched down the institute's plateau and up the hill on Main Street. It passed within sight of Jackson's home and in front of the Presbyterian church where he taught

Sunday school for the slaves. Then, upon entering the gates of the church cemetery, the procession laid General Thomas Jonathan Jackson to rest. The entire South paused to mourn its fallen hero, but the war continued.

On July 10 the South Carolina cadets were called out when the Federals occupied the lower end of Morris Island. Brigadier General Roswell S. Ripley, commander of the First Military District, dispatched the Citadel cadets to the island. However, while the cadets waited at the wharf Ripley sent word to Superintendent White that events had made their services unnecessary. Cursing their bad luck, the cadets reluctantly marched back to Marion Square. Had the young soldiers made the trip, there would have been plenty of work for them. On July 11 and again on July 18, the Federals attacked Morris Island's Fort Wagner. Each assault was bloodily repulsed.

Soon after the disappointment, Captain John P. Thomas and the Arsenal cadets arrived in Charleston, where they were detailed to guard government supplies stored at different points around the city. An Arsenal professor was troubled by the city's apparent lack of concern about the military situation and declared there was "no more excitement than if the enemy was not in a thousand miles of the city. I should prefer to see a little more interest manifested for the safety of the city."[49] Perhaps the professor mistook calm for indifference, for there was sufficient concern on the part of the city's defenders who wanted to keep the battalion of cadets in service throughout the summer in and around Charleston, as part of Colonel Wilmot G. De Saussure's Fifth Subdivision of the First Military District.

The battalion was finally released from duty on September 28, whereupon it assembled to hear the reading of an order from General P. G. T. Beauregard:

> The battalion of South Carolina Cadets, under Maj. J. B. White, are hereby relieved from duty in this city. In relieving this battalion, the commanding general tenders his thanks to the cadets and their officers for the promptness with which they responded to his call, and their zeal and discipline while under his orders. Should the enemy threaten a land attack on this city, they will be again called upon to assist in its defense. Meanwhile, they will return to their appropriate duties, daily more and more qualifying themselves

for the important positions to which they may ere long be called, in the defense of their country.[50]

Fine words though these were, the cadets' summer of duty had done little to satisfy their thirst for glory and adventure. Most cadets felt ill-used and cheated of opportunities to strike a blow for the Confederacy. Spirits were also low because that summer's service claimed the life of Arsenal Cadet William Ravenel, who died from typhoid fever.

The long period of field service also brought a realization to some that such service might ultimately have an unwanted effect on the school. As the Arsenal's Lieutenant Patrick observed:

[P]arents will not consent for their sons to serve the Confederacy for an indefinite period while they are paying the State to educate them. If they have to remain in service, their parents will withdraw them from the Academy and let them serve in an organization that will not require pay of them.[51]

Besides bringing disappointment to the eager South Carolina cadets, July brought bad news from the Confederate armies in the field. After a bloody three-day battle at Gettysburg, Pennsylvania, Lee's Army of Northern Virginia was repulsed in its second invasion of the North. On July 4 the battered army abandoned the field and returned to Virginia. As Lee retired, Lieutenant General John C. Pemberton, since transferred from the Charleston area to the West, surrendered the key Mississippi River bastion of Vicksburg, along with almost twenty thousand men to Major General Ulysses S. Grant. With this loss, the Confederacy was cut in two by the barrier of the Mississippi.

The Fourth of July was a happy day, however, for the cadets of VMI, who were yet unaware of these twin disasters. Although many of the first class cadets had left the institute to join the army upon Jackson's death, the remaining fourteen received their diplomas and Bibles from Superintendent Smith and with the singing of "Auld Lang Syne," the rats became "yearlings." The day also marked the beginning of the first summer training encampment since the beginning of the war. The cadets were to remain at Camp Jackson, as it was named to honor the fallen general, until the start of the fall semester. But on August 13 fifty mounted cadets, under the command of Lieutenant Henry A. "Old Chinook" Wise, were sent out to capture army deserters who had supposedly encamped southwest of Lexington. Whether the mission was successful is not recorded, but it would not be the last time cadets engaged in this potentially hazardous duty.

Deserter hunting would not be the only interruption of Camp Jackson's routine. On August 25 Colonel William L. "Mudwall" Jackson, a second cousin of Stonewall and a former lieutenant governor of Virginia, called for help in dealing with Yankee cavalry raiders. Under orders from Union Major General John C. Fremont, Brigadier General William Woods Averell set out from Winchester, Virginia, in early August with thirty-five hundred men, eight guns, and the objective of destroying the vital saltpeter works and gunpowder factories of western Virginia. Mudwall and his force of about nine hundred men constantly skirmished with Averell, but by August 19 the Federals reached Franklin and destroyed its saltpeter works.

A week later Averell was approaching Bath Alum Springs, twenty-seven miles northwest of Lexington, and Jackson called for help. Smith responded by arming two companies of home guard with weapons from the arsenal and ordering Acting Commandant William E. Cutshaw to march to Jackson's aid with four cannon and two companies of cadets. Smith informed Adjutant General Richardson of the movement, and explained that it was imperative that Jackson be supported. "Otherwise, we should be exposed to the depredations of a successful march upon our frontier."[52] Since another Confederate force under Major General Samuel Jones was approaching the area, Smith did not expect the cadets to be absent "more than two or three days."[53]

Smith was correct; by August 27 Averell was in retreat after a two-day fight near White Sulphur Springs. The cadets returned to VMI that evening after marching more than fifty miles. They were "broken down sorefooted, and quite mad that they were not permitted to go on and engage the enemy."[54]

While the cadets saw nothing good come out of their jaunt up the mountains, Smith used the incident to settle a matter that had rankled him ever since the McDowell campaign of the previous year. In his report to Richardson, Smith mentioned that Mudwall had asked him to join in the diversion planned against Averell, but Smith had refused since he did not feel authorized to "take the cadets upon any military operations except in protection of the state property, which they were appointed to guard."[55] Smith then formally requested specific guidance from the governor regarding what he should do during emergencies when

Confederate authorities requested the assistance of the cadets. "I want to do my whole duty," Smith explained, "but before doing it, I must know what my duty is."[56]

Smith received a response on September 4. The corps' sole military duty, wrote Richardson on behalf of the governor, was to defend the institute. However, the decision of whether that defense be made in the streets of Lexington or at some distant point was Smith's. The only restriction on his discretion was that "needless exposure of the corps of cadets shall be carefully avoided."[57] This was what Smith wanted to hear. There would be no embarrassing repeat of the McDowell campaign.

By November Averell had assembled a force of five thousand men at Beverly, West Virginia. Supported by Brigadier General Alfred N. Duffie, who was to join him at Lewisburg after pushing east from the Kanawha Valley, Averell this time aimed for the bridge at Dublin, Virginia, which carried the strategic East Tennessee and Virginia Railroad over the New River. Averell marched out of Beverly on November 1 with two regiments of infantry, four regiments of mounted infantry, part of a cavalry battalion, and two batteries of light artillery. Four days later he collided with Jackson near Mill Point. Jackson retreated to the crest of Droop Mountain where he was joined by Brigadier General John Echols and an infantry brigade from Lewisburg at nine o'clock the next morning. Averell attacked, and by three o'clock that afternoon, the Confederate line had collapsed.

Echols and Jackson fell back toward Dublin, and Averell continued his march southwest toward Lewisburg. Smith received the first report of Averell's new threat while Echols, Jackson, and Averell fought it out on the slopes of Droop Mountain. In a dispatch from Colonel J. Q. A. Nadenbousch, commander of Staunton's military post, Smith learned that Brigadier General John D. Imboden's cavalry was riding to Jackson's support, and that, while Staunton was felt to be safe, Averell might enter Rockbridge County. Smith issued arms to the home guard again and dispatched Captain Marshall McDonald to find Imboden and arrange for the cadets' cooperation.

On November 7, Smith ordered Lieutenant Colonel Ship, now returned from his "sabbatical" as a private in the 4th Virginia Cavalry, to prepare four pieces of artillery and issue two days cooked rations to each cadet. Soon, 225 cadets, as well as a number of county home guardsmen, were on the road northwest toward California Furnace. The column reached the furnace that afternoon, but were informed that their services would not be needed since they could never keep up with the pace Imboden's horsemen must set if they were to catch Averell. But before the cadets marched back to Lexington, Imboden changed his mind and ordered them and the home guard to march for Covington. The next day, they arrived at Clifton Forge, a little over half way to Covington, and were joined by their superintendent. Imboden made his headquarters at Covington that night and asked Smith to have the cadets and home guard march at dawn to join him.

While Imboden tried to assemble his available forces, Averell and Duffie joined up at Lewisburg. Here Averell determined that his tired horses and Duffie's footsore infantry could never make it to Dublin, so he decided to turn back. Duffie was ordered back to his camps while Averell sent his two infantry regiments to Beverly with the wounded and prisoners, as well as captured property. Averell and his mounted troops took a more easterly route and discovered Imboden in a position one and one half miles west of Covington, near his line of march. Two squadrons of the 8th West Virginia Mounted Infantry were dispatched to push Imboden away, but they hastily retreated when the Confederates opened up on them with cannon. Imboden then pulled back to a more defensible position east of Covington. At 2:30 P.M. he sent a dispatch to Smith, who had been on the march since dawn, telling him it was not necessary to advance further. Averell's second raid was over.

The cadets returned to the institute on Founder's Day, November 11. Their performance in the field brought Imboden's thanks and admiration and Superintendent Smith praised their soldierly conduct "in the midst of privation and discomforts which a veteran might even shrink from."[58] Although the cadets never saw a Yankee, Union scouts may have seen them. One of Averell's reasons for abandoning the raid was a report he had received claiming that strong reinforcements from Lee's army were on the march. The cadets, though, were disappointed that they still had not "seen the elephant."

But William Woods Averell was persistent, and in December his target was the East Tennessee and Virginia Railroad, southwest of Lexington at Salem. To screen the actual objective, feints were planned against Staunton and Dublin.

Averell set out on December 8 and picked up supporting units along the way. He faced only light Confederate resistance, and by December 16 had reached Salem, where he proceeded to destroy three supply depots, the water station, turntable, three railroad cars, five bridges, and fifteen miles of track. That night, in a heavy rain, Averell left Salem for New Castle, to the northwest, after telling some inquisitive citizens that he was headed for

Buchanan, to the northeast. Two days later Averell reached New Castle, where the Federal commander then heard that Major General Fitzhugh Lee's cavalry was on his right flank and Brigadier General Sam Jones's infantry was to his front. A trap had been set for the Federal raiders.

The cadets received the call from Imboden on December 14, while he was skirmishing with Averell near McDowell. Fearing that the Federals were attempting to gain access to the Valley in order to join Yankee forces reportedly advancing on Staunton, Imboden requested that the passes at Panther Gap and Goshen be occupied. The cadet battalion, about 180 strong, set out the next morning, followed by the Lexington Home Guard, and camped that night just short of Rockbridge Baths.

Two days later they reached Bratton's Run, which, because of the incessant rains, was now a raging torrent that stymied their attempts at a quick crossing. The cadets spent the night at a campsite on the stream's bank dubbed "Camp Starvation." The next day the cadets waded waist deep into the swollen stream to construct bridges over which the artillery could cross. They then pressed on to Cold Sulphur Springs, wading "through mud & water a foot deep near ten miles," but in high spirits "hallowing & singing the whole time."[59]

The home guard had been recalled to Lexington before they crossed Bratton's Run, and the cadets bivouacked alone at Cold Sulphur Springs on the evening of December 17. "There was a still house at this place," recalled Cadet Private Jacqueline B. "Jack" Stanard, "and every boy got enough to drink to make him sleep and to keep him from taking cold. In fact the majority of the boys were quite merry."[60]

The home guard had been recalled because Averell's misinformation about moving to Buchanan in southern Rockbridge County had been duly reported to Confederate authorities. At noon on December 18, Ship received similar orders. The march back to Lexington was painful. Rain came down in sheets, freezing as it fell, adding to the agony of the many shoeless, hungover cadets marching along the frozen roads. The cadets reached Lexington the next afternoon, but by then Averell was slipping between Lee and Jones and heading for Covington. Eight miles from Covington he dispersed a Confederate force of three hundred and crossed the Jackson River before the bridges could be destroyed. Mudwall Jackson struck the four-mile-long Federal column soon after it crossed the river, but Averell managed to slip away with minimal losses.

The cadets started for Buchanan on a very cold December 20, but they soon received word of Averell's crossing at Covington. Fitz Lee then ordered them to join Jackson somewhere in that vicinity. That night the cadets reached a point eight miles from Clifton Forge, where they were informed by Jackson that Averell was escaping and the cadets could return to barracks, "as Infantry cannot pursue Cavalry."[61] They were back home on December 21, again not having been engaged. A veteran of the march summed up the campaign to his mother: "Well dear Mother we reached our journeys end Monday evening and nar'e yankee did we kill or see after marching us all over this plagued mountainous country, and ruining our feet, we being badly shod at the time . . . . Although we were so near drowned, yet there was no grumbling."[62]

So ended 1863. The military colleges were still thriving; all had larger enrollments in the fall than they had in the spring. All of the corps, with the exception of GMI's, had seen field service of one sort or another. This service had hardened them both physically and mentally to the outrage of war, but it had also forged an esprit de corps that most regular army units had not seen since the war's early days. The young lions were coming of age.

CHAPTER FIVE

1864: "The Glory of . . . the Year 64"

THE LONGER THE WAR DRAGGED ON, THE MORE THE CONFEDERACY'S cadets itched to be part of it. Many were ashamed that they stayed in school while others fought. "You ought to hear," wrote VMI Cadet John H. Shields, "the galling taunts they hissed at the 'Conscripts Exempts' as they called the, Full-grown, over eighteen cadets. No less than 100 have resigned since I have been here, as fast as they reach the age of eighteen, they resign, and more is thought of them, than if they did not."[1] And many were impatient. When Smith was advised in March to fortify the mountain passes because of the threat of yet another Averell raid, nineteen-year-old Jack Stanard complained to his mother, "Is this what I was sent here for, to shovel with the spade & dig with the hoe for the protection of the Rockbridge Negroes? . . . I think you had just as well give your consent at once to my resigning and entering the Army. I want to have some of the glory of . . . the year 64 attached to my name."[2] But Stanard needn't have worried; there was going to be enough glory, as well as death and destruction, to go around.

Enemies closer to home, not conflict with the Yanks, were the immediate concern of the military colleges' administrators. Despite the ever-increasing shortages caused by the general decline of the Confederacy's fortunes, a bare minimum of supplies continued to trickle into the military colleges from various sources. Food was obtained domestically, but much of the necessary military and academic material was obtained from foreign sources and run through the blockade. Much got through, but losses were becoming more common. In January the blockade runner

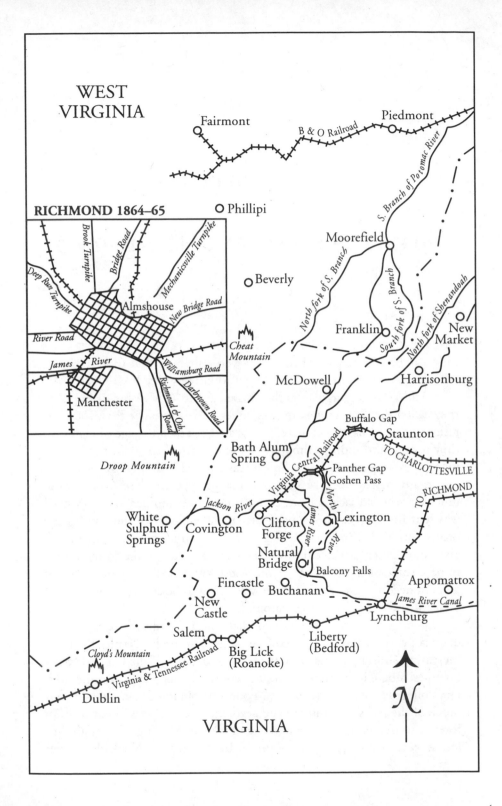

WEST VIRGINIA

Fairmont

B & O Railroad

Piedmont

RICHMOND 1864–65

Phillipi

Brook Turnpike

Bridge Road

Mechanicsville Turnpike

Deep Run Turnpike

Almshouse

New Bridge Road

River Road

James River

Manchester

Williamsburg Road

Darbytown Road

Richmond & Osb. Road

Beverly

Cheat Mountain

North fork of S. Branch

Moorefield

S. Branch of Potomac River

South fork of S. Branch

North fork of Shenandoah

Franklin

New Market

McDowell

Harrisonburg

Buffalo Gap

Staunton

Droop Mountain

Bath Alum Spring

Virginia Central Railroad

TO CHARLOTTESVILLE

Panther Gap
Goshen Pass

TO RICHMOND

Jackson River

White Sulphur Springs

Covington

Clifton Forge

James River

North River

Lexington

Natural Bridge

Balcony Falls

Appomattox

Fincastle

Buchanan

James River Canal

New Castle

Lynchburg

Salem

Big Lick (Roanoke)

Liberty (Bedford)

Cloyd's Mountain

Virginia & Tennessee Railroad

Dublin

VIRGINIA

N

Dare was run aground by Federal warships near Georgetown, South Carolina. On board were books, buttons, one thousand pairs of badly needed shoes, and other supplies for VMI. On January 18, Adjutant General Richardson informed Smith that "Most of the cargo was safely landed, and the goods for the Institute, especially shoes and cloth, were plundered and appropriated on the spot by the Confederate cavalry—and so lost."[3]

This was not the only instance of Confederate interference with efforts to keep the South's military schools adequately equipped and supplied. In the spring, Confederate authorities attempted to impress the contract horses of the Alabama Cadet Corps' artillery. This prompted a frank letter from Colonel Garland to the commander responsible, Lieutenant General Leonidas K. Polk. "I hope, Sir," wrote Garland, "that you will furnish me with an order, to any officer on such service, to leave the horses of this Battery unmolested, and not drive me to the disagreeable necessity of protecting them by force."[4] The letter had the desired results and Polk ordered his impressment officers to keep their hands off of the cadet battery's horses.[5]

Often the clash between the needs of the colleges and the requirements of the Confederate army did not end so favorably. In March, Confederate supply officers seized from a local farmer 210 bushels of corn intended for VMI. Acting Superintendent Preston immediately ordered the school's assistant chief of subsistence, Captain A. C. Whitwell, to "follow after said train until he overtake it, and . . . demand of [the officer in charge] in the name of the Commonwealth of Virginia, that the corn impressed . . . be released and returned to the possession of the Va. Mil. Institute."[6] After this incident, General Richardson spoke to Confederate Secretary of War James A. Seddon regarding protection for cadet supplies from army quartermasters. Seddon told the general that the impressment officers were acting under military necessity; therefore, he had "no authority over the case."[7]

In addition to the impressment of college supplies, the government tried to throw a wide net when it came to conscription. It again tested the resolve of the superintendents and the states to protect their cadets from the draft. The stands taken by Garland and Smith in this latest round of the conscription fight left no doubt as to where the primary allegiance of the superintendents lay.

Garland's conscription problems began in January, after Congress drew into the ranks those who had previously furnished substitutes and obtained an exemption from conscription. Four Alabama cadets who had furnished substitutes prior to entering the university were threatened with

conscription under the new law. Garland saw this as an affront not only
to the university but also to the state. He wrote to Governor Watts:

> It is probable that the Action of Congress may render it neces-
> sary to procure from the proper Authority, the exemption again of
> Cadets over 18 years of age. Be that as it may, the highest authority I
> recognize is the Executive of the State of Alabama. Our present dif-
> ficulties have come upon us, by the doctrine [that] the Federal
> Govt. is superior to that of the State. We are fighting for the sover-
> eignty of Alabama, and there is no power on earth that I acknowl-
> edge to be above that of my State. The allegiance that I owe to the
> Confederate Govt. is under that I owe first to Alabama—and where
> the two collide, my obedience shall be rendered to that of the State.
> Therefore, it is my desire to have your instructions in the matter,
> and they shall be my law.[8]

Watts, undoubtedly moved by this expression of allegiance, wrote
Secretary of War Seddon. If the law were applied to the cadets, as each
turned eighteen, Watts explained, they would be snatched up by an
enrolling officer and the corps would cease to exist. Seddon accepted this
logic and the four cadets were not conscripted.

Smith's problems arose in September when Seddon, desperate for
men to defend the capital, requested the board of visitors to order the furloughed VMI Corps to assemble in Richmond. When the board refused,
Seddon threatened to call all cadets of suitable age into the army as
reserves and not release them. True to his word, Seddon issued Special
Order No. 102 on October 3, and ordered all cadets seventeen and over—
the new draft age as of February 17—to report to Richmond. However, he
promised to release them in time for the upcoming school session. Smith
complained that the call-up violated the governor's 1862 order against
cadet conscription and wrote to Adjutant General Richardson:

> The authorities of the Virginia Military Institute have no dis-
> position to withhold the cadets from the service of the country in
> this hour of its peril and need. . . . But the State, through its Mili-
> tary Institute, stands as guardian, in her sovereign capacity, to
> these young soldiers, and it seems to be just and proper that when
> their services are required on the field of battle they should be sent
> forth under the authority of the State whose servants they are, that
> the care and protection which has been assumed and promised to

them may be rendered. . . . If Special Orders No. 102 be persisted in, the organization of the Virginia Military Institute will be destroyed."[9]

The cadets were released from duty in mid-December and the government never attempted to use such heavy-handed methods again. Colonel Garland found the whole attitude of the Confederate government toward the military colleges annoying and perplexing. With only a few military academies of any sort remaining in the country, "It seems to be as much to the interest of the Military affairs of the Gov't. as of the Civil that these institutions be allowed to receive all they can accommodate" and, he might have added, receive the full support of Confederate authorities.[10]

The actions of the central government were of no immediate concern to the cadets of GMI. They had been able to pay attention to their studies thus far, although they suffered from the same impatience to fight as did their counterparts. As Capers explained to the state adjutant general, "The Cadets of Georgia Military Institute, have sought active field service from the beginning of the war. This desire had become almost a passion. Under its influence we had lost our higher classes and might have lost the existence of the Institute."[11] But as long as Georgia remained unthreatened by the enemy, the cadets' only struggles would be against boredom, shortages, and sagging morale.

By the spring of 1864, however, the war, in the form of Federal Major General William T. Sherman's army from Chattanooga, was creeping closer and closer to Marietta and GMI.[12] By the first of May academic work was abandoned in favor of intensive drill, and the cadets were placed on provost duty in Marietta. On the night of May 13, "the 'long roll' was sounded on the drum . . . [and] the brave boys sprang from their beds . . . and assembled in front of the building for roll call. . . . Orders were given to march to the depot, in Marietta, and take a train to 'go to the front,' which was then about Resaca."[13] With their musicians, Cornelius and Charley, to provide marching music on the fife and drum, the cadets marched down College Hill to the Marietta station.

Confederate General Joseph E. Johnston's Army of Tennessee had occupied positions around the railroad settlement of Resaca on May 12, after having been flanked out of a strong position at Dalton by Union Major General James B. McPherson's Army of the Tennessee, part of Sherman's command. McPherson, however, missed the opportunity to sever Johnston's railroad lifeline before Resaca was occupied. Now a major battle was brewing between Johnston and the bulk of Sherman's army. The cadets were called upon to bolster the lines.

The cadet battalion of two companies, under the command of Major Capers (he was rarely referred to by his militia rank of brigadier general), arrived at Resaca on May 14, as the battle began. Capers was intimately familiar with the earthworks near the town, having laid them out himself earlier in the year. The cadet companies accompanying Capers were commanded by faculty members: Commandant of Cadets Captain James S. Austin commanded A Company, and Captain Victor E. Manget, a South Carolina Military Academy graduate and professor of French and history, commanded B Company. Still dressed in their multi-buttoned coatees, the cadets were attached to Major General William H. T. Walker's Division of Lieutenant General William Hardee's corps.

Lieutenant James Oates of the 9th Illinois Mounted Infantry was part of the Federal force attacking Resaca. He later recalled, "It was during the advance that . . . we came in contact with the Georgia Cadets from the Military Institute at Marietta, who had come out from the woods at Resaca and formed their line behind a rail fence."[14] As Oates and his comrades advanced, the cadets let go with a volley that killed several of the attackers; they then withdrew into the works around the town. On May 15, after heavy fighting, Johnston found himself in danger of being flanked again and evacuated Resaca that night. The cadets were back on their College Hill campus by the next day with vivid memories of their first combat and grateful prayers that none of them had been hurt.

As the Georgia cadets watched Sherman's advance with a paradoxical mixture of joy and dread, the VMI cadets engaged in a solemn duty. On May 10, the Corps gathered in the Lexington cemetery to raise a silk Confederate flag, the gift of a European admirer, over the grave of Stonewall Jackson. Academic duties were suspended for the day, but the evening dress parade went on as scheduled, and despite sad memories of the fallen professor, it was a beautiful day. From his place in the ranks at parade, John Wise savored the moment:

> Groups of girls in filmy garments set off with bits of color, came tripping across the sod and children and nurses sat about the benches at the Guard-Tree. The battalion was put through the manual. The first sergeants reported. The adjutant read his orders. The fifes and drums played down the line in slow time, and came back with a jolly, rattling air. The officers advanced to music, and saluted. The sun sank beyond the House Mountain. The evening

gun boomed forth. The garrison-flag fell lazily from its peak in the barrack's tower. The four companies went springing homeward to the gayest tune the fifes knew how to play. Never in all its history, looked Lexington more beautiful.[15]

But an ominous cloud was boiling in the North and heading straight for Lexington. The storm it carried broke upon them that night.

Around nine o'clock a mounted courier clattered along the brick roadway in front of the barracks, dismounted, and hurried through the Washington Arch. Soon the drums beat out the "long roll." As the cadets fell-in, they saw several officers clustered around the statue of George Washington, reading something by the light of a lantern. The grumbling cadets, expecting to be dismissed to their barracks soon, were surprised when the adjutant stepped forward and ordered the corps and a two gun section of artillery to march at dawn. Major General John C. Breckinridge, commander of the Department of Western Virginia, needed them. Cadet Corporal John Wise remembered how he and his comrades greeted the news:

> Still silence reigned. Then, as company after company broke ranks, the air was rent with wild cheering at the thought that our hour was come at last. Elsewhere in the Confederacy, death, disaster, disappointment may have by this time chilled the ardor of our people, but here, in this little band of fledglings, the hope of battle flamed as brightly as on the morning of Manassas.[16]

Breckinridge, a prominent Kentuckian and former vice president in the Buchannan administration, had no choice but to call out the cadets, for he was facing formidable odds. As part of the plan for Lee's army, Lieutenant General Grant had sent a column of nine thousand men and twenty-eight cannon up the Shenandoah Valley, under the command of the politically popular German-American Major General Franz Sigel. Grant's purpose in doing this was to divert Lee's attention from his own offensive against him. Sigel was to destroy anything of value to the enemy and keep Rebel forces pinned down in the Valley.

Breckinridge had only three brigades, totalling four thousand infantry and twenty-six hundred cavalry, to defend the Valley. After sending Brigadier General Albert Jenkins's one brigade to confront Major General George Crook's simultaneous advance into southwestern Virginia, Breckinridge dispatched the remaining two, under Brigadier Generals Gabriel

C. Wharton and John Echols, to Staunton. Needing every man he could get to confront Sigel, Breckinridge summoned the cadets and the local Augusta-Rockingham County Reserves to the Staunton rendezvous. John Imboden's cavalry and partisan rangers under Captains Harry Gilmor and John S. "Hanse" McNeill did their best to slow Sigel's advance. By May 10, after twelve days on the march, Sigel had only reached Woodstock, a disappointing fifty-six miles from his starting point at Martinsburg, West Virginia.

While Sigel camped at Woodstock, Colonel Ship and 247 cadets marched out of Lexington on the morning of May 11 and covered eighteen miles before bivouacking at Midway. Lacking tents, the young soldiers were forced to find other shelter from the rain that had been with them all day. Some climbed through the windows of the Midway Presbyterian Church, lay down on the pews, and "slept where many a good follower of Calvin had slept before us."[17]

Early the next morning the cadets formed up on the Valley Pike and continued the march to Staunton. As they entered the outskirts of the town they passed some of Breckinridge's veterans along the road. When the old soldiers got a good look at their youthful companions-in-arms, their band struck up "Rock-a-bye-Baby" and the veterans cradled their muskets in their arms, rocking them back and forth. The angry cadets went into camp north of Staunton where soon many of the town's young ladies came to visit. Later that night many cadets slipped into Staunton to visit friends or relatives, attend various dances, or perhaps steal some young girl's heart. As the cadets left the town on May 13, the revelry of the previous evening was driven from their minds when they passed a slaughterhouse on Staunton's outskirts. Leaning on his gate, the Irish butcher puffed his pipe as he watched the column pass and exclaimed, "Begorra, an' it's no purtier drove av pigs hev passed this gate since this hog-killing began."[19]

Sigel continued his advance. As the cadets marched out of Staunton, he sent ahead his First Brigade commander, Colonel August Moor, with three regiments of infantry, one thousand cavalry, and six cannon, to probe Imboden's delaying position at Rude's Hill. Moor did well and by 9:00 A.M. the following day, he and his men had pushed Imboden back to the town of New Market. Sigel ordered a general advance at 5:00 the next morning to link-up with Moor. Breckinridge, after ordering Imboden to establish a defensive position south of New Market, started his march at 1:00 A.M.; he was determined to quickly cover the remaining ten miles to New Market and confront Sigel there.

Breckinridge's troops arrived at New Market on the damp, misty morning of May 15, well ahead of Sigel's main body. Near the reverse slope of Shirley's Hill, on the summit of which Imboden's line had been established, the cadets passed the men of Wharton's Brigade, strung out along the road and cooking breakfast. The veterans quickly began hurling the usual taunts at the cadets. Some of them ambled out to the road to ask the "seed corn" battalion what kind of coffins they desired, and one went through the ranks with shears, offering to collect "love-locks" to send to their mothers when they were dead. Ahead of the main body of cadets, Cadet Lieutenant Collier H. Minge's thirty-two-man, two-gun artillery section thundered down the road, turned left, and strained up Shirley's Hill. With drill-field precision the cadets unlimbered and began shelling Moor's position in New Market. For the moment the cadets forgot their tormentors and watched their comrades. "We counted it a good omen," noted one of the observers, "when, at the first discharge of our little guns, a beautiful blue-white wreath of smoke shot upward and hovered over them."[18]

Breckinridge spent most of the morning trying to lure Moor into attacking his positions on Shirley's Hill. By eleven o'clock it was apparent that Moor would not oblige, so the Confederate commander decided to advance. In a light rain, Breckinridge's men moved toward Moor's positions south of New Market with the objective of driving his troops out of the valley, which ran perpendicular to the foot of Shirley's Hill. With the valley to shield them, the Rebels would be safe from Federal artillery atop Manor's Hill to the north. The Confederate battle line rapidly followed its skirmishers. The men of Wharton's brigade ran down the hill and gained the safety of the valley without a single casualty. Echols' brigade followed suit and fell into line. Only the cadets remained on the hill.

The cadets stripped for action, discarding all items except muskets, cartridge boxes and canteens. It was a sober moment. "Every lip was tightly drawn, every cheek was pale, but not with fear. With a peculiar, nervous jerk, we pulled our cartridge-boxes round to the front, laid back the flaps and tightened belts."[20] General Breckinridge rode up and addressed the corps. "Young gentlemen," the imposing Kentuckian announced, "I hope there will be no occasion to use you, but if there is, I trust you will do your duty."[21]

"Atten-tion! Battalion forward! Guide center," ordered Lieutenant Colonel Ship. Cadet Color Sergeant Oliver "Big" Evans unfurled the white battle flag, the fifes and drums struck up a lively tune, and the cadets stepped off. Sergeant Major Jonathan Woodbridge "ran out and posted himself four paces in advance of the colors, as direction guide, as if we had been upon the drill-ground."[22] Ship ordered him back for this was no parade.

All eyes were on the cadets as they advanced down the hill, since they showed a uniformity and organization that had not been seen in the Confederate army since its early years. "The cadets acted splendidly," wrote Wharton later, "closing up ranks and moving forward in beautiful, military procession and order."[23] Colonel George H. Smith of the 62d Virginia commented that "nothing could have been handsomer than the perfect order in which they moved."[24] Both the enemy and the townspeople were puzzled by the natty cadets with their short, sleek shell jackets and white battle flag. Some civilians thought they were foreign mercenaries, and at least one small girl, upon seeing their advance, ran home shouting, "The French have come!"[25]

The cadets paid for their orderly yet slow march down Shirley's Hill. As he watched, Wharton, a VMI graduate himself, regretted not having formally briefed Colonel Ship to rush down the hill as his and Echols' troops had done. A Federal shell suddenly exploded in the midst of Companies C and D. The C Company commander, Captain A. Govan Hill, went down "bathed in blood, with a frightful gash over the temple . . . gasping like a dying fish."[26] Cadet Private Charles E. Read was hit over the right eye by a shell fragment that bent the barrel of his Austrian musket.[27] In B Company Cadet Private Pierre Woodlief was painfully wounded and Cadet Private James L. Merritt was hit in the abdomen by a piece of shrapnel that knocked him down but did not penetrate. Seventeen-year-old Cadet Corporal John S. Wise was also hit: "It burst directly in my face: lightings leaped, fire flashed, the earth rocked, the sky whirled round . . . and I fell upon my knees. Cadet Sergeant Cabell looked back at me pityingly and called out, 'close up, men!' as he passed. I knew no more."[28]

"Great gaps were made through the ranks," Ship remembered, "but the cadet true to his discipline, would close in to the center to fill the interval, and push steadily forward."[29] Soon the Corps reached the protection of the New Market valley.

The Confederates remained in the relative safety of the valley until mid-day, when Sigel arrived with most of his force. He forgot to tell Brigadier General Jeremiah Sullivan's 28th and 116th Ohio Infantries and Captain Henry DuPont's Battery B, 5th U.S. Artillery about the advance. Moor's 123d Ohio Infantry gave way without resistance as the Confederates advanced out of the valley, but the 18th Connecticut and 1st West Virginia stood their ground. Before the opposing lines made heavy contact, Sigel ordered the two regiments to fall back. By 1:00 P.M. Moor had been driven from New Market. In the wake of Moor's withdrawal, Cadet Charlie Faulkner brought in twenty-three of Moor's Germans, "each large enough to swallow him."[30] Faulkner claimed that he and Cadet Winder Garrett had captured the Germans all by themselves.

Sigel, meanwhile, established his main defensive line on Bushong's Hill, north of the tidy white buildings of the Bushong farm. The line was anchored on the high bluffs of the Shenandoah River's North Fork on the right and in a thick cedar grove straddling the Valley Pike on the left. Near the bluffs stood two six-gun batteries. To their left were posted the 34th Massachusetts, the 1st West Virginia, and the 54th Pennsylvania. To slow the Rebel advance, Sigel placed the 123d Ohio, the 18th Connecticut, and Captain Albert Von Kleiser's 30th New York Artillery behind a stone wall on Manor's Hill, some four hundred yards in advance of his army's main position.

After an hour-long artillery duel, during which little damage was done to either side, Breckinridge prepared to advance. The Confederate line was reordered for the assault. The 23d Virginia Cavalry anchored the line on the turnpike and, with Colonel George S. Patton's 22d Virginia Infantry, Colonel Derrick's 23d Virginia Infantry advanced along and to the east of the roadway. At 2:00 P.M. Breckinridge ordered his troops forward.

Short work was made of Sigel's "breakwater" line. The 123d Ohio fired one volley and ran. The 18th Connecticut held on only a little longer. Neither regiment could be fully rallied. After losing one of his six guns to Confederate counter-battery fire, Von Kleiser limbered up and sped down the Valley Pike. From the former Federal positions, Breckinridge could clearly see Sigel's main line on Bushong's Hill and decided to gamble everything on one charge.

Once more the Confederate line went forward through the wet clover fields toward Bushong's Hill, with the cadets following in reserve. Cresting the rise around the Bushong farm, Wharton's men ran into a galling fire from the two Federal batteries on the right of Sigel's line and from Von Kleiser's guns, which were now positioned on the slope of Bushong's Hill, slightly in advance of the main Yankee battle line. Doubled-loaded with grapeshot, Von Kleiser's guns inflicted appalling casualties on Wharton's regiments. The 51st and 62d Virginia were particularly hard-hit and wavered. One by one men began trickling to the rear, unable to withstand the storm of shot and shell. The advance stalled and a gap opened in its center. East of the pike Patton's and Derrick's men were halted by fire from Federal cavalry.

It was the crucial stage of the battle. With his line stalled and a dangerous gap in the center, Breckinridge realized that is was time to commit his reserves—the Corps of Cadets. He agonized over the decision. His assistant ordnance officer, Major Charles Semple, urged the general to use the cadets; he argued that they would fight as well as the veterans. Breckinridge, however, recoiled from the prospect of exposing the cadets to the fusillades that had already devastated two experienced regiments. In turn, Semple correctly pointed out that if the gap in the line was not closed the battle would be lost. Confronted with the major's undeniably accurate analysis, the general reluctantly decided he had no other choice. "Put the boys in," he told Semple, "and may God forgive me for the order."[31] There were tears in his eyes as he spoke.

Semple galloped over to Lieutenant Colonel Ship. The gap in the line lay almost directly in front of the cadets and little direction was needed to move them into it. They began taking casualties almost immediately. A canister round from Von Kleiser's battery slammed into D Company, killing Cadet Privates Henry Jones and Charles Crockett instantly. First Sergeant William Cabell was hit in the chest by the full force of the explosion and lay in agony, tearing up clumps of grass as he expired. Private William McDowell also soon went down with a bullet in his chest, and he tore open his jacket to expose the wound as he died. The corps soon reached the Bushong house. Companies A and B passed it on the east, and Companies C and D went around to the west as Federal bullets thudded into the building's clapboard sides. Reforming on the other side, they entered the center of the storm, the Bushong orchard.

"The fire was withering," wrote Colonel Ship. "It seemed impossible that any living creature could escape."[32] Private Jack Stanard went down with a shattered leg. He and John Wise had earlier disobeyed orders and left their posts of safety with the cadets' supply wagons. Wise was wounded on Shirley's Hill and Stanard slowly bled to death despite the efforts of Cadet Edmund Berkeley, Jr., who attempted to stem the flow of blood with an old towel. Private Thomas G. Jefferson was shot in the stomach. Corporal Sam Atwill and Private Joseph C. Wheelwright were both shot. Cadet Captain Sam Shriver of C Company had his sword arm broken by a minie ball. Colonel Ship was hit in the left shoulder by a shell fragment and was so severely stunned that the senior tactical officer, Captain Henry A. "Old Chinook" Wise, took command, and then double-quicked the boys to the fence north of the orchard. The fence rails offered some protection from the enemy fire, but the situation was still desperate:

> For the first time, the cadets appeared irresolute. Some one cried out, 'Lie down!' and all obeyed, firing from the knee,—all but Evans, the ensign, who was standing upright, shouting and waving the flag. Some one exclaimed, 'Fall back and rally on Edgar's [26th Virginia] battalion!' Several boys moved as if to obey. [Andrew A.] Pizzini, first sergeant of B Company, with his Corsican blood at the boiling point, cocked his rifle and proclaimed that he would shoot the first man who ran. [Captain Frank] Preston, brave and inspiring, in command of B Company, smilingly lay down upon his remaining arm with the remark that he would at least save that. [Benjamin A. "Duck"] Colonna, cadet captain of D, was speaking low to the men of his company with words of encouragement, and bidding them to shoot close. The corps was being decimated.[33]

Sigel, unable to see the predicament at the center of the Confederate line because of the smoke of battle, thought that a cavalry charge against Patton and Derrick might bring victory and at 2:40 P.M., he sent his troopers galloping across the fields. But Breckinridge was ready, as the Federal troopers came charging toward the Confederate right through a rolling thunderstorm, they were torn apart by Confederate artillery. Only now, with his cavalry routed, did Sigel see the inviting opportunity offered by the confusion in the Rebel center. With the Confederates beginning to regain their momentum, he soon would lose the initiative he had stolen. Sigel, by this time so excited that he was giving commands in German, decided only an infantry counterattack could save him.

At approximately three o'clock the 34th Massachusetts, 1st West Virginia and 54th Pennsylvania moved forward under the command of Colonel Joseph Thoburn. Seventeen hundred Federals attacked twenty-seven hundred Rebels. It was too little too late. The 1st West Virginia advanced one hundred yards and ran into a hail of bullets from the cadets and from the 62d Virginia Infantry. Confederate artillery finished the job, and the West Virginians retreated. The 54th Pennsylvania on the left was turned back by Patton's and Derrick's men. The 34th Massachusetts advanced into this meatgrinder and suffered almost 50 percent casualties in a few minutes. The regiment's commander, unable to make himself heard above the din, grabbed the unit's color bearer and turned him about in order to get the men to withdraw to the old line. But there was no longer an "old line." The 1st West Virginia had not stopped, creating a huge hole between the 34th Massachusetts and the 54th Pennsylvania.

Now the Confederates charged. Another thunderstorm hit—"The most terrible storm I ever witnessed," said one participant.[34] As the Confederates surged forward, more cadets fell. Private Charles Randolph, whom Stonewall Jackson sent to VMI after his service as a fourteen year-old courier, was wounded in the head. Cadet Private Frank Gibson was shot in the leg, thigh, cheek, and hand. John Upshur dropped with a mangled leg. Old Chinook Wise, leading the charge, had his coattails shot away by a canister round fired from such close range that the bands had not yet burst. The charging cadets crossed a muddy depression that sucked the shoes from their feet, and fifteen-year-old Sam Adams stopped under fire to pull one of his out of the muck. This "Field of Lost Shoes" would, over time, become part of the New Market legend. Federal Captain Franklin E. Town watched the cadets advance across the field. "[T]hey advanced steadily without any sign of faltering. I saw, here and there, a soldier drop from their line and lie where he fell, as his comrades closed up the gaps and passed on. As a military spectacle it was most beautiful, and as a deed of war it was most grand."[35]

Von Kleiser's fire slackened as he began to limber his guns. The cadets, after pushing through the scattered remnants of the 1st West Virginia, paused to fire a volley at the battery's horses, dropping several of them. Von Kleiser was finished. With enough horses remaining to pull only four of his five guns, he ordered the abandoned gun spiked and moved off toward the pike only seconds ahead of the cheering cadets, who swarmed over the gun. Evans, the color bearer, straddled its hot barrel and waved the white battle flag. Some of Von Kleiser's gunners were captured as they attempted to flee. Cadet Lieutenant John Hanna hit one of them over the head with his saber while Winder Garrett chased another and stabbed him with his bayonet. The cadets also captured Lieutenant Colonel William S. Lincoln of the 34th Massachusetts. Lincoln, seriously wounded and pinned beneath his dead horse, watched the cadets' charge and later said he had never really seen discipline until he watched them advance.

By now the entire Federal line was in retreat. The cadets joined in the pursuit and captured between sixty and one hundred prisoners, including one German who cursed, "Dem lettle tevils mit der vite vlag."[36] General Breckinridge rode among the cadets during the pursuit. "Young gentlemen," he said, giving the cadets their due and then some, "I have you to thank for the results of today's operations."[37] He also rode over to the cadet battery, halted on the Valley Pike. "Boys," he proclaimed, "the work you did today will make you famous."[38] Cadet Dave Pierce, sitting on a limber chest, replied, "General, Fame's all right, but for Gawd's sake where is your commissary wagon? We like Fame sandwiched with bacon and hard-tack."[39] Even though proven soldiers, they were, after all, still the same irrepressible but irreverent cadets. To Breckinridge, they would forever after be "my cadets."

The corps paid a terrible price for the accolades it would receive. Five cadets—Cabell, Crockett, Jones, McDowell, and Stanard—lay dead on the field. Jefferson lingered until May 18, and then died in the arms of his friend Cadet Moses Ezekiel. Joseph Wheelwright, seemingly recovered from his wound, unexpectedly dropped dead on a Harrisonburg, Virginia, street on June 2. Alva Hartsfield succumbed to his wounds on June 26. Sam Atwill was taken to Staunton and seemed to be on the road to recovery until lockjaw set in. Superintendent Smith somewhat tactlessly wrote Sam's parents and informed them that their son died on July 17 "after three days of agonizing suffering."[40] Private Luther C. Haynes ended up in Richmond's Powhatan Hotel hospital and died there on June 15; the institute did not know of his death until almost fifty years later. Forty-seven other cadets were wounded. Twenty-four percent of those engaged were casualties. The cadets had finally "seen the elephant"; he was a bloody beast, terrible to behold.

The bodies of the dead were laid across an artillery limber and buried the next day. On May 17 the cadets marched from New Market and headed for Staunton "crestfallen and dejected. The joy of victory . . . forgotten in distress for the friends and comrades dead and maimed. We were still young in the ghastly game," a recovered John Wise later remembered, "but we proved apt scholars."[41] In Staunton the cadets boarded railroad freight cars for Richmond in accordance with orders that Secretary of War Seddon had dispatched before he was informed of the cadets' part in the battle. Enroute to the capital city, the cadets stopped in Charlottesville, "emptied all the ice cream saloons of their 'goodies,'" and spent some time sidetracked at Ashland, Virginia.[42] Lying alongside the tracks were the men of the Stonewall Division. "We had heard of them," wrote John Wise, "and looked upon them as the greatest soldiers that ever went into battle. What flattered us most was that they had heard of us."[43] In Richmond the cadets were reviewed by President Davis and received the

thanks of the Confederate Congress, along with a new battalion flag and
Enfield rifled muskets.

As their compatriots in Virginia were burying their dead, the cadets of
GMI returned to school from Resaca after their baptism of fire. However,
their return did not necessarily mean a resumption of studies because
Marietta was clogged with reinforcements rushing north and wounded
and refugees straggling south. Protecting government and private property from these transients became the cadets' job for the next several days.
During this time the appearance of the corps changed as resplendent
coatees were traded for more plain and practical gray jean uniforms, and
Belgian muskets, canteens, cartridge boxes, and knapsacks were issued.
The muskets were huge .69 caliber smoothbores, and the sixteen- and
seventeen-year-old soldiers complained loudly about being equipped with
such obsolete and inefficient "pumpkin slingers."

In early June the Georgia cadets were again called to active service.
"Slender, erect, with springy step and easy carriage," the 177 cadets
marched to the railroad station to board trains for West Point on the
Alabama-Georgia state line.[44] They would never see the school again.
With both armies moving toward Kennesaw Mountain, Marietta would
soon be in the war zone. The remaining sick and disabled cadets, the
dependents of the institute's officers, and the remnants of the faculty
started for Oglethorpe College in Milledgeville, where Capers had
arranged for the use of temporary facilities. The institute's abandoned
buildings would soon become a Confederate hospital.

The cadets detrained at West Point and went into camp in the valley
east of the Chattahoochee River. Although their assignment of guarding
the vital Chattahoochee railroad bridge, which linked Montgomery,
Alabama and Atlanta, was important, the cadets resented being shunted
off to far away West Point while the enemy advanced upon Marietta. The
high point of their stay was the presentation of a battle flag to replace the
"Stars and Bars" given to them by the ladies of Marietta in 1861. The gift
of Mary E. Jones, the flag and her presentation speech were mailed to
Major Capers at West Point. The superintendent read Miss Jones's speech
to the assembled corps, and Cadet First Lieutenant James R. McCleskey
of Company A responded with an acceptance speech on behalf of his fellow cadets. One of the color guard who would protect the battalion's new
colors was Color Corporal Julius L. Brown, the governor's son. The

cadets stayed at West Point until early July when they were recalled to assist in Atlanta's defense.

Since the declining fortunes of the Confederacy required the service of every man and boy to stem the tide of disaster, there was little rest for the bloodied VMI Corps of Cadets after the Battle of New Market. After the initial round of parades, speeches, and praise, the cadets encamped at Camp Lee in Richmond. Seven of the boys who had trained troops there in 1861 still remained with the corps. On May 28, after three days at Camp Lee, the cadets went into Confederate service. They took up positions on Richmond's intermediate defense line and occupied the trenches midway between the Brooke and Meadow Bridge roads.

As the cadets helped to defend Richmond, a new enemy was stirring in the Shenandoah Valley. After his inadequate performance at New Market, Franz Sigel took his army to Cedar Creek in the lower Valley to recover. Confederate authorities were so sure that Sigel would remain cowering there that they called Breckinridge and his division to join the Army of Northern Virginia. But General Grant had not given up on his plans for the Shenandoah, although he had given up on Sigel. The German was sacked and replaced as commander of the Department of West Virginia by Major General David Hunter. Hunter, a Shenandoah Valley native, hated Rebels and was not above destroying the property of those who swore allegiance to the Confederacy—even his own relatives were not spared. Hunter arrived at department headquarters on May 21, with orders to occupy the upper Valley, deny the upcoming harvest to the Confederacy, destroy Lynchburg and Staunton, and generally make a nuisance of himself. Hunter proceeded to reorganize his forces, fire some of Sigel's cronies, and bolster the morale of those remaining. On May 26 he marched south with ten thousand men and twenty-two guns.

With Breckinridge gone, only Imboden and some weak cavalry and partisan rangers stood between Hunter and his objectives, and the Federals made rapid progress. Hunter reached New Market on May 30. There his men were sickened by the sight of their dead comrades, thrown by the Confederates into hastily dug graves, many of which had been uncovered by the spring rains. A grim resolve to avenge their dead and erase the shame of New Market took hold of Hunter's men. Imboden was burning up the telegraph wires asking General Lee for assistance, but hard-pressed himself, Lee had none to spare. Instead, he asked Brigadier General

William E. "Grumble" Jones, who was camped near the Virginia-Tennessee border with three regiments of infantry and a battery of artillery, to gather all available men and move to Staunton.

Racing north, Jones collided with Hunter near the village of Piedmont, thirteen miles from Staunton, around noon on June 5. The Federals attacked shouting "New Market!" and fought better than they had on that battlefield. Jones fought well, given the circumstances, and might have even gained a victory if his cavalry had not let him down. As it was, the Confederate line was broken, Grumble was killed, and Hunter had a clear road to Staunton.

Jones's defeat caused near panic in the Confederate high command. On June 6, the VMI cadets were returned to state authorities and boarded trains for Lynchburg the following day. Lee now decided he could spare the remnants of Breckinridge's division, and he sent the new savior of the Valley and his twenty-one hundred men marching west the same day the cadets left Richmond. Hunter occupied Staunton on Monday, June 6. By the time he left the following Friday, he had destroyed the railroad, government workshops, a steam mill, a woolen factory, two stables, a foundry, and an enormous tax-in-kind warehouse; he had also confiscated over half a million dollars worth of equipment and provisions. Reinforced by George Crook's and William Averell's ten thousand men, Hunter now formulated a plan on how best to reach Lynchburg: He would advance by way of Lexington.

The VMI cadets arrived in Lynchburg at 9:00 P.M. on June 7, and boarded canal boats for the trip to Lexington, which they reached at 3:00 in the afternoon on June 9. On June 10, Hunter divided his army into four columns and set out on four separate roads leading east and south from Staunton. The cadets received word of Hunter's advance with little worry. "Well," said the veterans of New Market, "we'll have to whip 'em again."[45] But Hunter was no Franz Sigel, and by the evening of June 10, the Federals were skirmishing with Brigadier General John McCausland's troops near Midway. McCausland, an 1857 graduate of VMI and former faculty member with a deep affection for the college, knew full well what was likely to happen if Hunter got his hands on the institute, but his force was too weak to prevent its capture. He reluctantly sent word to Lexington to prepare the North River bridge for destruction and the town for evacuation. One of the cadet howitzers and a company of cadets under Captain "Old Chinook" Wise went to the bridge to carry out McCausland's orders as the superintendent continued loading provisions, school records, and other institute property aboard canal boats and wagons for removal. Although concerned for his college, Smith had no intention of throwing away the lives of his students by futile resistance to Hunter. Also, there was a misplaced hope that if the institute was captured without a fight, the Yankees might be more inclined to spare it.

Before dawn on June 11, McCausland's troops crossed the North River Bridge and fanned out to cover the retreat of their rearguard. The Federal advance chased these men back to the bridge, but was turned back by fire from McCausland's main body and the cadets. As soon as the rearguard galloped across, cadet sappers fired the turpentine-soaked hay bales that they had piled on and around the bridge, and the cadet howitzer fired at the bridge's pilings to weaken them. Their mission accomplished, the detached cadets double-quicked back to the institute to rejoin their companies while the Confederate cavalry, weary and dejected, passed along the pike in front of the barracks.

As the bridge burned, Captain Henry DuPont, Hunter's chief of artillery, placed some batteries on the high hills north of the river and began to shell the school. Two of McCausland's guns hurried up the hill past the statue of Washington, unlimbered on the northwest corner of the parade ground, and returned fire. The cadets fell-in beside the barracks, out of sight of the Federal gunners, and as each shot hit the building the cadets were subjected to a dangerous rain of brick and mortar.[46] Their officers soon moved them to a supposedly safer position on the reverse slope of the parade ground away from the barracks. But here the cadets were behind McCausland's artillery position on the parade ground, and enemy shells and shots directed at it exploded and bounded over their heads. Smith finally decided to remove the cadets from the institute altogether, and the boys retreated along the sidewalk in front of Washington College toward town as the Federal artillery pounded their home. They left behind their books, personal possessions, and five of their cannon, which could not be moved because of a lack of horses. Just past the Washington College campus, the veterans of New Market paused to tear up their colors to prevent its capture, and distributed the fragments among themselves.

McCausland's little force did not delay Hunter long, and he soon forded the river and moved into Lexington. Returning to Lexington was a homecoming of sorts for at least three of Hunter's men. Riding into town with the 3d West Virginia Cavalry was Charles H. McLane, dismissed from VMI for excess demerits in 1859. In the ranks of the 14th West Virginia Infantry marched William H. Gillespie, an 1862 graduate of the institute, and Theodore W. Boydston, who had entered VMI on April 19, 1861, and left twenty-five days later.

Colonel J. M. Schoonmaker, commander of Averell's First Brigade, was ordered by Hunter to burn VMI because his soldiers had been fired at from the buildings and because the cadets fought at New Market—a defeat that still weighed heavily on the minds of Sigel's former troops. Schoonmaker was the first to enter the cadet barracks and found "school books open on [the] desks and diagrams partly finished on the blackboard."[47] Instead of destroying the institute, however, Schoonmaker placed it and adjacent Washington College under his protection, an action which prompted Hunter to relieve him of his command.

Until the next morning when it was burned, Hunter's men rummaged through the school's property. "Both the Institute and Washington College were ransacked by the boys," wrote Private J. O. Humphreys on the unused pages of the commandant's January 17, 1862–May 7, 1864 letter book. In this diary he began to keep, Humphreys added, "the clothing of the cadets and the libraries received much attention. Indeed, it is doubtful if ever any army was so devoted to literature as was our Corps."[48] "There are some of the most extensive libraries here that I ever saw. I have procured some very good works," wrote another soldier.[49] Even those who disagreed with Hunter's destruction shared in the spoils. "General Hunter burns the Virginia Military Institute. This does not suit many of us . . . I got a pretty little cadet musket here which I will try to send to the boys," wrote future president Colonel Rutherford B. Hayes in his diary.[50] The bell attached to the clock above the barracks entrance was taken down and the statue of Washington was crated for shipment to West Point. Attached to the statue was a label proclaiming that it had been seized to "'rescue' it from the degenerate sons of worthy sires."[51] The institute's wells were polluted and obscenities scrawled on its walls. The Federals carted away or destroyed Professor Jackson's philosophical apparatus and ransacked the hospital.

At 9:00 A.M. Hunter torched the Virginia Military Institute over the protests of some of his officers. He set fire to the barracks and faculty housing. Hunter's incendiaries also ransacked and burned Governor Letcher's home, located close to the post. General Smith's home was spared because his daughter was convalescing from a recent childbirth, and Mrs. Smith convinced Hunter that moving her would cause her death. Also, Hunter made his headquarters there. The only other buildings that escaped the torch were the small Porter's Lodge, near the gate to adjoining Washington College, and what has become known to generations of VMI cadets as the "Old Hospital." The destruction of VMI represented a loss of $156,220 to the State of Virginia. Hunter also ordered the burning of

Washington College, but his cousin and chief of staff, David Hunter Strother, convinced him to spare the college since it was a civilian institution that had been endowed by General Washington himself.

So complete was the pillaging of the institute that even the college's slaves were robbed. Anderson, the school's slave baker, was stripped of his possessions, and when asked if he told the invaders that he belonged to the state, Anderson replied, "No indeed—if I had told the Yankee's that, they would have burnt me up with the other State property."[52]

Although a violation of the Federal Army General Order 100 which prohibited the damage of educational institutions, the conduct of Hunter and his men was not unjustified given the value of the institute to the Confederacy and the cadets' involvement in military operations against Federal troops. The war had transformed all of the South's military colleges from educational institutions into military establishments, and their destruction was justified by military necessity. A saddened General Smith recognized this hard fact and noted, "In a time of war it was not to be expected that the Va. Mil. Institute should escape the effects of the devastations which has visited by fire and rapine the fairest portions of our beloved commonwealth."[53]

The retreating cadets were not spared the sight of the institute's destruction. Marching southwest toward the mountains, "At a high point . . . we came in full sight of our old home," recalled Cadet John Wise. "The day was bright and clear, and we saw the towers and turrets of barracks, mess-hall, and professors' houses in full blaze, sending up great masses of flame and smoke."[54] Saddened and angered, the cadets marched to Balcony Falls, one of the mountain passes leading to Lynchburg. Here Smith had them construct breastworks, for he fully intended to fight if Hunter came that way. Since the pass was filled with refugees from the Lexington area, the cadets also served as a guard for them and their possessions.

Hunter remained in Lexington until June 14, when, strengthened by Duffie's brigade, he marched south toward Buchanan and the pass at the Peaks of Otter. When Smith received word of Hunter's movement he decided to abandon Balcony Falls and move the cadets to Lynchburg to join whatever Confederate troops were there. The cadets boarded freight boats and traveled there on the James River Canal. On the way to the city, a courier from Breckinridge, whom Lee had ordered to Lynchburg after the occupation of Staunton, flagged down the boats. The orders he delivered confirmed Smith's decision to move the cadets to Lynchburg. They arrived at the city wharves at 8:00 on the morning of June 16, and

Smith immediately reported to Breckinridge, the governor, and the board of visitors. Little more than Breckinridge's two thousand men and the cadets were in the city, far too few to stop Hunter, but along the railroad from the east reinforcements from Lee's army were hurrying.

In accordance with Lee's orders, Lieutenant General Jubal A. Early, on June 12, moved his Second Corps out of its position near Gaines Mill and marched it over eight miles to Charlottesville. There the corps boarded trains on the Orange and Alexandria Railroad for Lynchburg. Early had no confidence in the railroad's management, but Lynchburg's safety depended on how efficiently and rapidly it moved his soldiers. The general, therefore, made it very clear that he would tolerate nothing less than total cooperation and, if he did not receive it, warned, "I will hold all railroad agents and employés responsible with their lives."[55] The rail-road must have taken the crotchety bachelor at his word, for Early and his lead division, under the command of Major General Stephen Dodson Ramseur, arrived in Lynchburg around noon on the seventeenth, just barely ahead of the enemy. Hunter, who could have easily beaten Early to the city, had not yet arrived; he had been slowed by Imboden's and McCausland's delaying tactics, rumors that twenty thousand Confederate reinforcements were on the way to Lynchburg, and his two-day stay in Lexington. In Lynchburg, Early found Major General Daniel Harvey Hill, a veteran of the Army of Northern Virginia who happened to be in town, supervising the defenses on behalf of Breckinridge, who had been nearly incapacitated when his horse was blasted out from under him at Cold Harbor. Hill established a fortified line close to the city, with Breck-inridge's men in the trenches and the cadets in reserve in the Old Methodist Cemetery.

That night, Early brought up Breckinridge's troops and Major General John B. Gordon's division, which had just arrived in the city. The cadets remained with the tombstones, invalids, and militia in Hill's original line. Early on the morning of June 18, Hunter began an uncoordinated, half-hearted attack, which the Confederates withstood handsomely. But the men on the line were exhausted when the fighting ceased around seven o'clock at night; so around ten o'clock Early ordered the cadets into the front lines to relieve some of Ramseur's tired veterans. Colonel Ship commanded complete silence during the march and, to prevent straggling in the pitch-black darkness, ordered each boy to place his left hand on the cartridge box of the cadet in front of him. The cadets reached the trenches soon and moved in as Ramseur's men glided out like "shadows of darkness."[56] The trenches were no less gloomy than the graveyard according to Cadet Corporal John Wise:

The place was horrible. The fort was new, and constructed of stiff red clay. The rain had wet the soil, and the feet of the men who had been there had kneaded the mud into dough. There was no place to lie down. All that a man could do was to sit plump down in the mud, upon the low banquette, with his gun across his lap. I could not resist peeping over the parapet, and there, but a short distance from us, in a little valley, were the smoldering camp-fires of the enemy. Wrapping my blanket about me, its ends tucked under me, so as to keep out the moisture from the red clay as much as possible, I fell asleep hugging my rifle, never doubting that there would be work for both of us at daybreak.[57]

But there was no enemy to fight the next morning and, had Wise remained awake, he would have heard what Early heard—the sounds of an enemy in retreat. Early promptly launched a pursuit that continued for over sixty miles. When Hunter chose to retreat west toward Lewisburg, he took his army out of the war for several weeks and opened the Shenandoah, the Confederate's favorite invasion route north. Early took advantage of the opening and by July was knocking on the gates of Washington. Early's threat to the capital drew some troops from Grant's army, but not nearly enough to give Lee any relief. But while he was in the north, Early did take revenge for Hunter's destruction in the Valley; he sent John McCausland to ransom or burn Chambersburg, Pennsylvania. On July 30, McCausland carried out his orders to burn the town when its citizens were unable to raise the ransom, and got his personal revenge for the destruction of his beloved institute.

On June 24, the board of visitors ordered the cadets to return to Lexington; they reached it the next day. Smith had ordered tents, which didn't arrive, so the cadets stayed in buildings at Washington College. Smith, ever the optimist when it came to his school, viewed the physical destruction of VMI as little more than an inconvenience as long as the corps and the faculty remained intact. "[T]he Virginia Military Institute still proudly and defiantly stands," he reported to Adjutant General Richardson. "The brick and mortar which gave temporary shelter . . . constituted not the Military school of Virginia. Thank God, that still lives."[58]

The search for more permanent accommodations had already begun. As soon as rumors of the institute's destruction reached him, Adjutant General Richardson suggested moving the college to the University of Virginia, which at that time had only twelve students. Lynchburg College, Harrisonburg, Virginia's Mossy Creek Academy, and Randolph-

Macon College were also considered. Smith, however, was in favor of building cabins next to the destroyed barracks.

On June 27, the fourteen members of the class of 1864 graduated. Those cadets who were able to reach their homes or the homes of friends were furloughed until September 1. Only three or four cadets remained in Lexington. As Smith pondered the school's future, he received a letter from a friend of the institute:

> Camp Petersburg, July 4th, 1864
>
> I have grieved over the destruction of the Military Institute. But the good that has been done to the country cannot be destroyed, nor can its name or fame perish. It will rise stronger than before, and continue to diffuse its benefits to a grateful people. Under your wise administration, there will be no suspension of its usefulness. The difficulties by which it is surrounded will call forth greater energies from its officers and increased diligence from its pupils. Its prosperity I consider certain.
>
> With great regard, yours very truly,
> R. E. Lee[59]

Lee's confidence was not misplaced, for fifty-three Virginians and twelve other Southerners had already been appointed as cadets for the fall 1864 session, and Smith had workmen combing through the ruins of the institute for tin to be made into buckets, plates, cups, and basins for the new cadets.

Meanwhile, GMI cadets, as part of the state Militia Reserves, were with Major General Gustavus W. Smith, the elected field commander of the Georgia Militia. The cadets were posted at Nickajack Ridge, three miles north of Turner's Ferry, on the Chattahoochee River west of Atlanta. Earlier, as they and other militia units moved to these positions, Federal gunners spotted the dust from their march and sent some shells in their direction. After crossing the river the cadets were again shelled as they made their way across an open field, but they came through unscathed.

The day before the cadets arrived at their new positions, the Federals occupied Marietta and Major General George H. Thomas seized the institute as headquarters for his Army of the Cumberland. A correspondent for *Leslie's Weekly* toured the grounds and told his readers that it was "situated about a quarter of a mile from the center of town and before

Sherman advanced to the neighborhood, contained 130 cadets who were training in treason and the art of war."[60] Another reporter visited the superintendent's quarters, adjacent to the institute, and, despite seeing the now trampled garden of prize roses that had been planted by Colonel Brumby, pronounced the modest home "a princely residence."[61]

While the newspapermen toured the abandoned institute, Sherman planned his next move. One of his immediate objectives was to force a crossing of the Chattahoochee at Turner's Ferry and fall upon Johnston's army if it crossed the river, as Sherman expected it would. His instructions to Major General McPherson revealed the importance he put on the operation. "If you ever worked in your life," he wrote the commander of the Army of the Tennessee, "work at daylight tomorrow on that flank, crossing the Nickajack somehow, and the moment you discover confusion pour in your fire."[62]

The Third Brigade, Fourth Division, of Major General Frank P. Blair, Seventeenth Corps, Army of the Tennessee, made contact with the Confederate militia's Nickajack Ridge positions on Independence Day. Smith, who had been skirmishing with the Federals since the previous day, "was determined to sacrifice the command, if necessary . . . to prevent the Federals from crossing the ridge" and reaching the fortifications at Turner's Ferry—yet unoccupied by Johnston's Confederates.[63] Smith held the Yankees in check throughout the day and, upon Johnston's orders, retired to the Turner's Ferry fortifications on the morning of July 5. When the militia reached the works, it found them already occupied by Johnston's men, who had earlier abandoned positions around Smyrna Station.

By July 11, with his Chattahoochee River positions flanked, Johnston settled into the fortifications around Atlanta. The Georgia "malish," including the cadets, joined the rest of the Army of Tennessee in the hot, dirty, and dangerous trenches the cadets had helped dig earlier that summer. One week later, Joe Johnston, out of favor with Jefferson Davis because of his continual retreats, was replaced with offense-minded Lieutenant General John Bell Hood, one of Lee's former division commanders. From their positions in the trenches, the cadets watched as Hood flung his army against the encircling Yankees: Peachtree Creek on July 20; Bald Hill on July 22; and Ezra Church six days later. But Sherman's siege continued to remain intact despite horrendous casualties on both sides.

It was not the battle, but the filth of the trenches that killed the first Georgia cadets; Cadets R. Commander, C. Baker, Edmund Jordan, J. Mabry, John McLeod, and G. Smith all died of disease in them. In

August, as the militia became more involved in the fighting, the cadets suffered their first battle casualties. Cadet Private Samuel W. Goode was wounded in the arm by a Minie ball on August 7, and Cadet Private A. H. Alexander was struck and killed by a twelve-pounder cannonball that same afternoon. On August 11, Cadet Corporal J. K. Anderson was shot in the knee and later died in the hospital. The following day, Cadet Third Lieutenant Frank E. Courvoisie took a bullet in the hip, and sometime during his stay in the trenches, Cadet Private A. T. Luckie was wounded in the eye. The corps had been bloodied and the luck that had been with it since Resaca had vanished.

In late July and early August, Major General George Stoneman launched his cavalry on a raid through Georgia in support of Sherman's efforts before Atlanta. Though the raid was not successful—Stoneman and five hundred of his men were taken prisoner—the raiders came in close proximity to the state capital at Milledgeville on several occasions, causing Georgians to clamor for better protection for their government seat. Consequently, Governor Brown requested Hood to relieve some of the Georgia militia for Milledgeville's defense. Hood chose the cadet battalion for this responsibility; it arrived at the capital around August 20.

In Milledgeville the cadets, now 190 strong, encamped on the grounds of the capitol building, "a picturesque edifice of stone—encircled by a ten acre square."[64] Capers was appointed commander of the post of Milledgeville, and the cadet battalion and local home guard constituted the garrison. Scout posts were established throughout the area and the garrison occupied the city's defenses daily, but for three months the young soldiers enjoyed relative peace and quiet. The classes abandoned in May were reinstituted, although "[the cadets'] studies were much interrupted by military demand[s] on their time."[65] Also, the precarious military situation was not conducive to academics, especially since the students longed for a chance to strike another blow at the enemy.

Nevertheless, the Georgia cadets had done well in their first campaign. In his report to Adjutant General Henry C. Wayne, Major Capers summed up their conduct in the field:

In no single instance, whatever may have been the duties assigned them or the position occupied by them, have our expectations been disappointed in either the bearing or efficiency of the command. There was fatigue and blood and death . . . but no white feather.[66]

Although Capers had no way of knowing, there would be more fatigue, blood, and death to come for his young soldiers.

The situation in Charleston that spring and summer, not much better than that around Atlanta, required every available soldier. Since the Confederate evacuation of Morris Island on September 2, 1863, the Federals had been inching their way across adjacent James Island ever closer to Charleston. As part of the Confederate effort to meet this threat, the Citadel cadets had been on guard duty in the Charleston military district and on James Island since early spring. On May 1, they were relieved as sufficient troops arrived to take their place. Brigadier General William B. Taliaferro, however, did not want to lose the cadets, especially when troops at Charleston were being siphoned off to Virginia to assist Lee in meeting Grant's new offensives. On May 24, Taliaferro replied to the order relieving the cadets: "The cadets will be sent back if the general wishes, as soon as they are relieved from picket. They do not wish to return."[67] The next day Taliaferro was granted permission to retain the cadets but was ordered to send one company of the 21st South Carolina Infantry to Virginia.

Beyond occasional Federal shelling of the picket line, the cadets' service on James Island was not dangerous. Even so, duty on the hot, humid island was unpleasant. But "not only was there no complaint, . . . there was no service they did not perform cheerfully and in the spirit of true soldiers."[68]

Occasionally that summer, the Citadel cadets escorted prisoners to the prison camp at Andersonville, Georgia. The prisoners were transported in railroad cattle cars, and one of the cadets' duties was to scrape the manure from the floors of the cars before the captured Federals were loaded.

The cadets spent most of the summer in the field and were then furloughed until October. At the expiration of their furlough, they returned to Charleston but were soon moved to a camp near the Magnolia Cemetery due to a yellow fever epidemic in the city. In November the camp was moved to Orangeburg, a town on the railroad between Charleston and Columbia. Whether the cadets would ever return to Charleston was doubtful. The Federals had taken the neighborhood around the Citadel under fire and twenty-seven shells had fallen on the post in one week. So far the only casualty was a cow killed by shrapnel while grazing on the Green, and the cadets remaining at the Citadel had great fun on nightly

excursions to the barracks' roof watching the shelling. However, General
James Jones pointed out to Governor Milledge L. Bonham that "the continued bombardment of the city of Charleston by the enemy, has rendered the Citadel in that city a dangerous habitation, and wholly unfit for
the academic duties of the Cadets. They must therefore be removed from
that vicinage."[69] If suitable quarters could not be rented, Jones recommended that $15,000 be provided for the erection of "temporary huts."
The cadets remained encamped outside the city until they were recalled
in December.

As the Citadel cadets returned from their furlough, the Arsenal battalion was at work guarding prisoners of war. For six days the cadets
served as guards at Camp Sorghum, across the Congaree River from
Columbia. The camp was new and lacked permanent quarters for the
guard, so the cadets built brush huts to protect themselves from the
elements. A cadet detail was also sent to the prison camp at Florence,
South Carolina. On October 3, prior to beginning their guard duties, the
cadets took part in a special muster to hear President Davis speak as he
was passing through Columbia.

As with GMI and VMI, the South Carolina Military Academy's academic program pretty much fell apart in 1864. Nevertheless, the board of
visitors expressed its pride in the cadets: "[A]lthough the frequent, and at
one time prolonged demand upon the Citadel Cadets for military service
in the field, and as Provost Guard by the Confederate military authorities,
had seriously interrupted their academic progress, yet the discipline of the
Academies had been preserved unimpaired."[70]

The Alabama Corps of Cadets was also on the verge of a busy summer.
Despite its relative lack of field experience, it was becoming a first-rate
military unit. On April 26, Major General Samuel G. French, a division
commander in Joe Johnston's Army of Tennessee, reviewed the corps. At
the close of the drill one of the brigadiers accompanying French remarked
that he had seen the "crack corps" of Europe and the cadets of West Point
at drill, but had never seen "anything to excel the wheel of the battalion
in double ranks, six companies front, at double quick, that closed the
exhibition drill of the Alabama cadets".[71]

Except for the excitement caused by Sherman's advance from Vicksburg to nearby Meridian, Mississippi, in mid-February, French's visit was
the year's biggest event until July's graduation ceremony. A fifteen-day
furlough was granted after the graduation exercises, and the cadets were

ordered to reassemble at Selma after their short vacation. As they made their way to their homes, however, Governor Watts issued a call for all cadets in or passing through Montgomery to assemble for the city's defense from Federal cavalry raiders under Major General Lovell H. Rousseau. Fifty-four cadets responded to the call and were placed under the command of Lieutenant George C. Redwood. They brigaded with Lockhart's Battalion (later designated the 62d Alabama Infantry Battalion) and a company of conscripts from Camp Watts. Although thousands of new British Enfields were in the warehouses at Selma, the cadets were issued old rebored and rifled smoothbore muskets because of the haste required to get them into the field.

The "brigade," totaling about five hundred men under the command of Colonel J. L. Davidson, quickly boarded a special train on the West Point and Montgomery Railroad and headed east toward Auburn. On July 18, they met the enemy at Beasley's farm, six miles east of Chehaw Station. Here the Yankees had prepared an ambush for the cadets and their comrades, but a premature shot by one of the Federal troopers gave it away. As the train screeched to a halt, Davidson and his men poured out of the cars and deployed for battle, with Redwood and the cadets sent forward as skirmishers.

The Union forces confronting the cadets consisted of detachments of the 5th Iowa Cavalry and the 4th Tennessee (Union) Cavalries under the command of Major Harlon Baird. Outnumbered, Baird called on Rousseau for support and the general sent Colonel Thomas J. Harrison's 8th Indiana forward. With Harrison's arrival the tide turned, and although the Confederates "stubbornly contested the ground" from behind a rail fence, when a detachment of the 8th Indiana turned the Rebel left and fell upon their rear, the butternuts "fell back in confusion."[72] Curiously, a later reminiscence of a former cadet, who was not even in the fight, recorded a different outcome. According to him the engagement ended with the cadets pursuing Baird and Harrison and driving them from the field.[73]

Among Baird's men three were killed and eight or ten were wounded; the Rebel amateurs, however, lost over eighty men, including two wounded cadets—the first casualties suffered by the Alabama Corps in the war. The fifty-four Katydids represented the corps well; the *Montgomery Daily Mail* reported that they "bore themselves most gallantly, fighting as if they were accustomed to such work, although it was the first time they were under fire. The State cadets deserve all the praise bestowed on them, doing credit to themselves and the training they have received."[74]

Soon after the fight at Chehaw the entire corps, approximately two hundred strong, reassembled at Selma. On July 29, they received orders to report to Blue Mountain Station (present day Anniston) at the northern terminus of the Alabama and Tennessee River Railroad. As the cadets departed, the *Selma Dispatch* assured them "the special prayers of many loving hearts" went with them.[75] After a week or more at Blue Mountain, the cadets were ordered south to guard the A. & T. R. R. bridge over the Coosa River. From here the cadets were directed to Pollard, Alabama, near the Florida state line.

The boys traveled by train to Selma and by steamboat to Montgomery, enroute to their new station. At the capital Governor Watts reviewed the cadets and they immediately boarded a train for Pollard afterward, where they arrived the next day. The cadets spent a few days in camp at Pollard, then transferred to a position near Blakely, Alabama, across the bay from Mobile. There, at their Saluda Hills campsite, the cadets ran afoul of the scourge of many Rebel soldiers—"coast" or "pernicious fever." Several cadets came down with the disease, but the tender, efficient treatment of the corps surgeon, Dr. John B. Read, pulled all of them through, "though many of them were walking skeletons when they were moved away."[76]

The cadets' most dangerous duty at Blakely was defending army supplies from pilferage by their own cavalry. One confrontation with the troopers was particularly tense. Shooting was avoided only when, faced with the cocked and loaded muskets of the cadet provost guards, the cavalrymen were convinced that the cadets would indeed shoot and thus retreated. After a month at Blakely the cadets, under the command of Captain Eugene A. Smith, were ordered to return to Montgomery where they were furloughed until September.[77] The Katydids' summer in the field was over.

As the Alabama cadets' summer campaign was winding down, the final campaign of the Georgia cadets was just beginning. On September 2, the city of Atlanta fell. With this victory achieved, the restless, energetic Sherman needed a new challenge, and on September 20, he proposed to his friend Lieutenant General Grant that he march his army across Georgia and into South Carolina. "I can make the march," wrote Sherman, "and make Georgia howl."[78] On November 2, Grant approved Sherman's plan.

In preparation for the march, Sherman issued orders on November 10 for the destruction of all public and private property in Atlanta, Rome, and Marietta that might be of value to the enemy. Three days later, the Georgia Military Institute, used as a hospital by both sides, a headquarters, and a barracks for Marietta's Yankee garrison, was torched. When the Federals marched out of Marietta on November 14, "gaunt chimneys were the only reminders of the proud school that had served Georgia and the south so well."[79] Only the superintendent's quarters escaped destruction.[80]

On November 15, Sherman moved his army, now reorganized into two wings, from Atlanta's smoking ruins. His ultimate objective was Savannah on Georgia's coast; his immediate objective was Georgia's capital at Milledgeville. To disguise this objective, and to keep the defenders off-balance, the southern wing of the army, Major General Oliver O. Howard's thirty-three-thousand-man Army of the Tennessee, feinted toward Macon. Meanwhile the northern wing, the thirty-thousand-man Army of Georgia, under the command of Major General Henry Slocum, followed the railroad toward Augusta. With nothing but the three thousand or so militia under G. W. Smith and Major General Joseph Wheeler's cavalry to oppose the march, the only sizable engagement between Atlanta and Milledgeville occurred at Griswoldville, when twenty-three hundred militia attacked one of Howard's brigades. The militia got the worst of it and "were badly cut up."[81]

As Slocum's Fourteenth Corps advanced on Milledgeville, the decision was made to evacuate the city. Governor Brown offered pardons to any prisoners in the state penitentiary who would join the rag-tag assembly of troops in the capital. He then followed the legislature out of the city. Accompanying Brown on the last train out of the capital, the night of November 19, was State Adjutant General Henry C. Wayne. The Milledgeville garrison, consisting of a battery of artillery, a company of cavalry, a company of militia, the factory and penitentiary guards, the convicts (dubbed the Roberts Guards), and the GMI Corps of Cadets soon followed. Wayne placed Superintendent Capers in immediate command of the five-hundred-man force. At the request of Major General Howell Cobb, Confederate commander of the District of Georgia, Brown posted the troops at Gordon, a rail junction south of Milledgeville, and then continued his flight. At 10:30 the next morning, Wayne's telegraphic communications were cut. Upon learning that the enemy was moving toward Milledgeville, he decided to abandon Gordon and take up new positions to the east, at the point where the railroad to Savannah crossed the Oconee River. The Federal advance entered Gordon around four o'clock that afternoon and fired after Wayne's trainload of troops as it chugged out of the station.

When Wayne arrived at the bridge an hour and a half later, he found 186 South Carolina cavalrymen and Georgia militia already in place, courtesy of Major General Lafayette McLaws in Savannah. For a position to be held "to the last extremity," the terrain around the bridge left a lot to be desired: It could be flanked on the right, and on the left at Balls' Ferry, and attacked frontally; swamps on the Confederate side prevented the use of artillery at either the bridge or Ball's Ferry; and no fieldworks existed to protect the inexperienced infantry.[82] To defend the bridge and other crossing points, Wayne's seven hundred men had to cover a line nearly five miles long.

Undaunted, Wayne got to work. Despite the cold and wind, the troops constructed trenches near the bridge and built a stockaded outpost two miles to the west of it. Pickets were sent to the crossing points on the right flank and to Ball's Ferry. Capers was placed in charge of the bridge's defenses while the cadets, under Commandant of Cadets Austin, and a detachment of the 4th Kentucky Mounted Infantry, on loan from Wheeler, occupied the perilously exposed outpost. Mounted on a flat car rolled one of Captain William H. Purden's guns to furnish mobile artillery support for both the stockade and the bridge positions.

At 10:45 on the morning of November 23, elements of Major General Giles A. Smith's division of the Seventeenth Corps and Major General Judson "Kill Cavalry" Kilpatrick's cavalry appeared in front of the outpost and attacked. The outnumbered cadets and Kentuckians, supported by Purden's railway gun, gave ground slowly. As they crossed the bridge, Wheeler's mounted infantry withdrew. The convicts and militia formed a line with the cadets on the east bank of the Oconee. Smith pressed the attack, but the cadets and others, minus the Roberts Guards, who ran for the rear when Federal artillery opened up, delivered such a punishing fire that he was repulsed. An attempt to cross the river at Ball's Ferry by units of the Federal Fifteenth Corps was also foiled before darkness brought an end to the fighting.

Early the next morning the Federals renewed their assaults on the bridge and on Ball's Ferry. Inconclusive fighting continued throughout the day. About eight o'clock that evening, a Federal detachment crept to the west end of the railroad trestle and set it ablaze. The trestle burned all night and into the next day, but as the fire reached the bridge, the Federals withdrew. This enabled Capers and a detachment of cadets to extinguish the flames before more than a few feet of the bridge were charred.

Despite this success, things were going badly for the Confederates. From Ball's Ferry the message came that the enemy was preparing to cross and probably could not be stopped. When informed by Wayne that further defense was futile, Lieutenant General William J. Hardee, in charge of the Confederate defenses of Savannah and central Georgia, ordered a withdrawal east along the railroad to Station No. 13. In defense of the Oconee Bridge, Cadet Sergeant J. Scott Todd lost an arm, Cadet Privates Thomas A. Hamilton and W. E. Myrick were wounded, and Cadet Private C. H. Marsh went down with an agonizing groin wound that would eventually kill him.

Wayne's force tarried at Station No. 13 only long enough to receive a new assignment: the defense of the Ogeechee River railroad bridge near the town of Sebastopol, Georgia. Wayne's orders were changed at the Ogeechee, however, in response to Kilpatrick's threat to Millen. Wayne reached Millen at 3:30 P.M. on the November 27, his command now numbering 426 effectives. At Millen, Wayne's fear that Kilpatrick's cavalry would strike the railroad in his rear and cut him off from Savannah began a game of railroad roulette along the Georgia Central that lasted for the next several days. Wayne abandoned his positions at Millen the following day, and retreated to the Little Ogeechee railroad bridge at Station No. 4 1/2. On December 1, he moved west to Station No. 6. The next day he was back at 4 1/2. He moved to Station No. 2 on December 3, whereupon Hardee sent him back to 4 1/2. But Wayne picked up troops along the way and by December 4 he commanded almost four thousand militia and Purden's three cannon.

Units of the Federal Seventeenth Corps began their advance on the Little Ogeechee River railroad bridge in the early afternoon of December 4. Cadet Private J. D. Coleman was on picket duty in advance of the bridge when a party of Yankees demanded his surrender. Coleman refused to surrender, shot the officer in charge of the Federal detachment, and ran for his life. Heavy skirmishing soon began on the left of the Confederate position and in front of the bridge. Around four o'clock that afternoon, Lafayette McLaws arrived from Savannah with orders from Hardee to assume command. McLaws judged the position indefensible and ordered a retreat to Savannah.

Wayne and his men arrived in Savannah on December 6, and were placed in position about three and a half miles west of the city, with the Central Railroad on the left and the Savannah River on the right. The cadets occupied the center of this thin gray line. Wayne then relinquished his command to G. W. Smith, who had recovered sufficiently from a recent illness to again take the field. In his official report to Governor Brown, Wayne singled out the cadets for special praise, commenting upon their "gallantry, discipline, and skill" and expressed his admiration for, "these youths, who go into a fight as cheerfully as they would enter a ballroom, and with the silence and steadiness of veterans."[83] Capers, with some justifiable pride, said of his young soldiers, "If I had a division of these boys I could repulse the whole Federal army."[84]

As the Georgia cadets filed into the Savannah fortifications, the cadets of the South Carolina Military Academy were trying to turn back a Federal advance in South Carolina in support of Sherman's effort to capture Savannah. Ordered from their Orangeburg campsite on November 30 by the governor, the cadets took a train to Charleston, where White reported to Major General Samuel Jones, commander of the District of South Carolina. Jones was facing a Federal advance from Union-held Port Royal, South Carolina. Its objective was to cut the Charleston and Savannah Railroad; so Jones was scraping together every military organization he could get his hands on for the defense of the railroad.

The Citadel cadets and their officers were ready and eager for this call to arms. In March, Superintendent White had offered the cadet battalion's services in the defense of Charleston. This gesture caused the *Charleston Courier* to praise them as "gallant scions of our noble nursery of soldiers," and it led General Beauregard to review the corps on the Citadel Green on March 14.[85] Two months later forty-five of them were called to James Island and returned to march through the streets of Charleston with their white underclothes poking through their worn uniforms—a condition referred to as "blossoming" by the tactful young women of the city.[86]

In early December, Captain Thomas and the boys from the Arsenal, who came in response to Jones's call, joined the Citadel cadets at Charleston. The reunited Battalion of State Cadets numbered 343 under White's overall command. Captain Hugh S. Thompson commanded Company A, and Thomas commanded his cadets in Company B.

On December 3, the cadet battalion boarded boxcars on the Charleston and Savannah Railroad and headed for the Pocotaglio River southeast of Charleston. The cadets' train stopped at the town of Pocotaglio, and White was directed to take his command to the defenses of the Tulifinny River railroad trestle. The Tulifinny, like the Coosawhatchie and Pocotaglio, is a tidal river that rises out of black, impassable swamps and winds through salt marshes on its way to Broad River, an extension of Port Royal Sound. Across each of these rivers the Charleston and

Savannah Railroad ran on its vulnerable bridges. Federal forces had tried to sever this lifeline between Savannah and Charleston near Grahamville, South Carolina, on November 30, but were repulsed with heavy casualties by the Georgia "malish" at Honey Hill. Some of these same troops were poised to try again.

The cadets marched from Pocotaglio throughout the afternoon and evening, and finally halted alongside the railroad near the Tulifinny. It was a hard, tiring march under trying conditions. "We had come without overcoats or blankets," remembered Arsenal Cadet Sergeant George M. Coffin, "and it was raining, and without breaking ranks we lay down company front on the cornbeds and tried to sleep. I remember putting my plate canteen over my face to keep the rain off."[87] The hungry cadets, whose midday meal was interrupted at Pocotaglio by the order to march, wolfed down some bacon and hardtack in the cold, wet camp.

The following morning, December 6, the 127th New York Infantry, veterans of Honey Hill, along with parts of the 157th and 56th New York, portions of the 25th Ohio, a unit that had suffered badly at Honey Hill, and a detachment of United States Marines, all under the command of Lieutenant Colonel Stewart L. Woodford, landed at Gregory's Plantation on the Tulifinny River, southeast of the railroad. Brigadier General Lucius J. Gartrell, commander of the Tulifinny defenses, sent 150 men of the 5th Georgia Infantry out to search for the enemy. Near the intersection of Gregory's Point Road and Beaufort Turnpike the Georgians found what they were looking for. Initially the men of the 5th Georgia drove in the enemy advance guards, but when Woodford realized how small the Rebel force was, he went on the offensive. Soon the Georgians were hard pressed. Belatedly, Gartrell sent the 1st and 3rd Georgia Reserves and a section of artillery to their aid.

General Jones, wanting to know what the Georgians were up against, sent Major John Jenkins of the 3d South Carolina Cavalry and the cadets forward on a reconnaissance to the scene of the fighting. The cadets moved at the "double-quick, manifesting an eagerness to encounter the enemy," to a position on the enemy's right flank.[88] Jenkins and White deployed the battalion, but before they could attack, the 5th Georgia and the reservists gave way, leaving the 5th's colors and its dead on the field. The Confederates retreated to the trestle while Woodford entrenched his men near the intersection. The Federal army had suffered five killed and twenty-two wounded.

Jones was not pleased that Gartrell had sent such a small force to oppose the Federal advance, thereby allowing them to gain a foothold between the Coosawatchie and Tulifinny that was within striking distance of the railroad bridges. On the evening of December 6, Jones collected all of his available men near the Tulifinny trestle. He managed to gather Colonel Aaron C. Edward's 47th Georgia Infantry, a battalion of the 32d Georgia, the 1st and 3d Georgia Reserves, one company of the 1st South Carolina Artillery, the 7th North Carolina Reserve Battalion, Captain Bachman's German Artillery, and the Battalion of State Cadets—an approximate total of fifteen hundred men. With this force, Jones established a line stretching from the village of Coosawhatchie northeast to the Tulifinny, covering the railroad and the two vital bridges.

Despite being outnumbered, Jones decided to take the offensive and hit Woodford's position at the intersection. He gave responsibility for the assault to Colonel Edwards, and commanded the out-of-favor Gartrell to mount a "spirited demonstration of attack" from the Coosawhatchie positions.[89] Edwards was to attack at dawn with a force of eight hundred regulars and militia, including the cadets. If Edwards succeeded, Gartrell was instructed to "press forward . . . with all vigor."[90]

At dawn on December 7, Edwards formed his troops for the assault, and placed three companies of the 5th Georgia and the Citadel's Company A of the cadet battalion forward as skirmishers. The Arsenal cadets of Company B were placed in the main battle line. Full of nervous energy, the cadets gripped their rifles, breathed a silent prayer, and moved forward. On the other side of the railroad tracks the skirmishers entered a woods and collided with Yankee pickets. At the point of contact Cadet Private Farish Furman saw "a stream of fire shoot out from the bushes in front of me, accompanied by the sharp crack of a rifle."[91] The bullet intended for Furman lodged in a tree beside his head. His companion Cadet Allen J. Green was not as lucky. He was shot in the face.

Heavy skirmishing continued for the next three hours, as the Confederates steadily pushed the Federal skirmish line back upon its entrenchments. The advance was not bloodless for the cadets. Second Lieutenant Amory Coffin, Jr., battalion adjutant and assistant professor of French and drawing, fell with a severe head wound, and was saved from death only by the visors of the two caps he was wearing. Cadet Private Joseph W. Barnwell was wounded in the left leg, but managed to talk a surgeon out of amputating it. Cadet Edward C. McCarty went down with a severe wound while Cadet Lieutenant Stephen F. Hollingsworth and Cadet Private Albert R. Heyward, and Corporal William A. Pringle were slightly wounded. Cadet Private James H. Boatwright was saved from death when the Bible in his breast pocket stopped a bullet. Somewhere in the woods and marshes during that three-hour fight Cadet Private William B. Patterson was mortally wounded.

At one point during the fight, the Citadel cadets fell in with the 47th Georgia behind the railroad embankment. Major White rode his horse back and forth behind his cadets, cautioning them to keep their heads down and to be patient and let the enemy "come well up."[92] The Federals soon waded through a swamp opposite the embankment and formed for an assault. White gave the order to fire and the cadets fired a perfect volley that, along with the Georgians' lead, broke the Federal assault. The Confederates then clambered over the tracks in pursuit and drove the disordered Yankees back.

While Company A traded blows with the enemy, the generally younger, less experienced cadets of Company B were held in reserve. "We lay down to avoid the bullets and shells, passing over us," recalled Coffin, "in a heavy rain on some swampy ground."[93] But they were not denied the opportunity to fight, and the order came to rise and move forward to relieve Company A, which had almost expended its ammunition. Under fire, the two companies exchanged places and the Arsenal cadets "stayed in a while firing at the Yanks," even though Cadet Coffin admitted, "I did not see any."[94]

Edwards had driven Woodford's men into their entrenchments, but Gartrell's supporting attack was "not made with any spirit" and he failed to push the enemy from his front.[95] Unable to assault the entrenched Federal positions with only eight hundred men, Edwards pulled back to the Tulifinny. In advance of the Confederate line, the Arsenal cadets occupied rifle pits in an open field until nightfall, when they were relieved and returned to camp. The rough camp with its warm fires and hot food was luxury to the boys. "And my!" proclaimed George Coffin, "it was good to get something warm to eat again."[96]

The performance of the cadets in the day's skirmish drew high praise from Colonel Edwards. In his report he singled out the Citadel cadets for "behaving with great gallantry" and commended the Arsenal cadets for acting with "conspicuous coolness and spirit."[97] One observer noted "the splendid bearing of the Cadets under fire."[98] But perhaps the greatest compliment of all came from an old veteran who said in awe, "Them fellers fights like Hood's Texicans."[99]

Jones decided his force was insufficient to renew the assault that had failed on December 7, and turned his energies to defending the railroad by occupying strong defensive positions instead of trying to drive away the numerically superior, well-entrenched Federals.

Both sides strengthened their positions, and on December 9, Woodford's self-styled "skirmish brigade," now commanded by a Colonel Silliman on detached duty from his 26th United States Colored Troops, launched its own assault. The Federal battle line, formed with the Marine Battalion on the right, the 157th New York in the center, and the 127th New York on the left, advanced toward the railroad a little after 9:00 A.M. Three hundred and fifty yards from the railroad the "skirmish brigade" struck the Rebel picket line and quickly drove it back to the main Confederate positions.

The 32d and 47th Georgia infantries, the 7th North Carolina Battalion, and the cadets, all under Colonel Edwards' command, held the left of the Confederate line. As soon as his pickets reached safety, Edwards blasted Silliman's center and right with "musketry, grape, and canister."[100] Silliman, felled by a serious leg wound almost as soon as the firing began, was carried from the field. Command once more passed to Woodford as senior officer.

The 5th Georgia, along with the 1st and 3d Georgia Reserves, occupied the right of the defensive line on the Coosawhatchie. A shell fragment wounded Gartrell before he reached the field, but the acting commander, Colonel Charles P. Daniel of the 5th Georgia, poured a enfilading fire into the Federal left. Companies G and K, the left flank companies of the 127th New York, suffered severely. The commander of G Company was grievously wounded, and K Company's Captain H. L. Long was shot through the right arm, but he hid the wound from Woodford and remained on the field. Between them, the two companies lost five killed and twenty-eight wounded. The three companies of the regiment's right and center fared little better, with three men killed and twenty-three wounded, including the E Company commander, who was shot in the face. Daniel's men did not escape unscathed, however, and lost six dead and thirty-five wounded.

Back at Tulifinny trestle, First Lieutenant Stoddard's Marines tried to flank the Confederate artillery positions. Under a galling fire, the leathernecks became entangled in a dense thicket and were forced to retreat after losing eleven men. Thereafter, the Federal pressure on Tulifinny lessened, and the cadets hurried to the right to aid in the repulse of the 127th New York.

The "skirmish brigade" held its positions within two hundred yards of the railroad until 2:30 that afternoon, when the men retired to their works after burying dead comrades. According to Woodford's report, Federal losses were nine killed, sixty-two wounded, and three missing.

However, the Confederates reported "quite a number of enemy dead were left on the field."[101] Confederate losses were eight dead and fifty-two wounded. Most of these were suffered by Daniel's command, with the 3rd Georgia Reserves alone accounting for thirty-one of the casualties. No cadets were among the fallen.

After the failed attack of December 9, the Federals gave up attempts to capture the railroad by assault and instead brought up artillery to close it by bombardment. During this "lull" the cadets settled into camp near the railroad, without tents, and had to cook on their own. Their culinary experiments were sometimes nearly fatal. "[T]he first biscuits I made without any 'rising' laid me out under the trees for several days," one of the young cooks recalled sixty-five years later.[102] An appeal appeared in the *Charleston Daily Courier* on December 10, asking for tea, coffee, sugar, spirits, and bandages for the cadets. A change of clothing would also have been welcomed, Cadet Farish Furman noted when he complained to his mother a week later that he had not pulled off his clothes for fourteen days.[103]

On December 14, the newly matriculated Arsenal class of 1865 marched into camp to begin its training. Though many of these fourteen- to eighteen-year-olds were unschooled as soldiers, some were veterans; one, A. F. O'Brien, had already lost an arm in Confederate service. Training began in the Tulifinny camp with the old cadets as drillmasters, and soon a nearby field was filled with marching cadets. This was too tempting a target for Federal gunners to pass up and they fired into the parade. The cadets scattered in less than military formation, but none were injured. However, a shell passing through the nearby campsite mangled Cadet William D. "Big Bill" Palmer's left hand. Palmer ran about the camp howling in agony until he fainted, whereupon his brother-in-law, an army surgeon, amputated the hand. The crippled Palmer soldiered on until the end of the war. He was the battalion's last combat casualty, although over the next four months Citadel Cadets R. F. Nichols, Robert E. Muldrow, George O. Buck, and John Culbreath, and Arsenal Cadets Thomas A. Johnson and Russell Noble, all died of disease contracted during field service. On May 9, 1865, Cadet William M. Parker was killed by Federal soldiers in Anderson, South Carolina, while visiting his home on furlough.

The Citadel cadets broke camp on Christmas Day and moved to new positions on James Island as infantry support for Battery No. 2 near Sec-cessionville. The Arsenal cadets returned to Columbia. Major General Jones praised the cadets "who for the first time felt the fire of the enemy, so bore themselves as to win the admiration of the veterans who observed and served with them."[104] Major White also had high praise for his cadets who, "upon the battlefield, in camp, on the march, on picket, or working upon defenses. . . were ready for every emergency; manifesting at all times, and under the most trying circumstances, a manly and soldierly aspect, not finding fault with those in authority, but doing their duty cheerfully and well."[105]

Down the coast from the Tulifinny, the Georgia cadets discovered that the fortifications at Savannah were very different from those around Atlanta. The opposing lines were well separated and the cadets found that they could venture above ground without much danger. The trenches themselves were well drained and fairly comfortable. But on December 10, portions of the Federal Twentieth Corps settled in on the other side of the abatis and swampland in front of the cadets' position. Skirmishing began all along the line, but no concerted effort was made to storm the Confederate defenses. Instead, Sherman worked his line to the left in an attempt to cut Hardee's line of retreat into South Carolina. Soon Twentieth Corps units were across the Savannah River in the Palmetto State. Hardee began constructing a bridge over the Savannah River on December 17, and during the night and early morning of December 20 and 21, abandoned the city. The cadets formed part of the army's rear guard and were unfortunately forced to abandon their cannon. Cadet Frank S. Loftin remembered that the guns "had served us well, had never failed us."[106] Colonel Orlando Poe, Sherman's chief engineer, found one of the little cannon and suggested it be sent to West Point as a trophy.[107]

Because they were state troops it was against Georgia law for the cadet battalion to be utilized outside of the state, so they marched to Bamberg, South Carolina, and boarded a train for Augusta, Georgia. When they arrived in Bamberg on Christmas Day, the cadets were greeted by an "abundant feast of such delicacies as they had not seen for a month, provided by the citizens of that hospitable neighborhood."[108]

The Virginia Military Institute did not reopen until December 12. When classes began it was not in cabins alongside the devastated barracks as Smith preferred, but in Richmond's City Almshouse, which was graciously made available by the city fathers at the request of the state and Confederate governments. However, in consequence of the controversial Special Order No. 102, the cadets were in Richmond long before the institute reopened.

Seddon's order was published on October 3, but even prior to this, Cadet Captain Andrew Pizzini gathered thirty-two cadets on furlough in Richmond, as well as "a few gentlemen from the basement offices in the State Capitol," and reported to Camp Lee.[109] After drawing some antiquated smoothbore muskets from the local arsenal, Pizzini received the order on October 1 to take his troops to the exterior line near the Osbourne Turnpike and act as skirmishers and sharpshooters. Pizzini and his cadets arrived at the works in time to witness Lieutenant Colonel John Atkinson's furious bombardment of a Federal reconnaissance led by Major General Alfred H. Terry. Lieutenant Colonel John C. Pemberton, the vilified and mistrusted Pennsylvanian who had lost Vicksburg, and accepted a commission as a lieutenant colonel of artillery to stay in the war after he was shelved as a lieutenant general, later chastised Atkinson severely for burning up vast quantities of precious ammunition and powder.

After the cannonade died away, Brigadier General Patrick T. Moore, commander of the Virginia Local Defense Brigade, sent the cadets out beyond the works to see if Terry was still lurking around. Pizzini was not enthusiastic about the mission and his first act was to swap his company's worthless smoothbore flintlocks for the rifled muskets of Major John Dooley's Richmond Ambulance Company. Re-armed, the company started forward. Pizzini was quite tense:

Slowly we moved ahead expecting every minute to receive the fusillade of concealed enemies, but after advancing out of sight of our works, I deemed it prudent to slowly retire. I had found nothing in front but burning houses and fields plowed up by the tremendous shells coming from our works behind.[110]

The cadets were soon replaced in the trenches by a regiment of local defense troops and were drafted by General Moore to serve as his headquarters guard. The cadets welcomed the change and Pizzini confessed, "we struck it rich. Nice tents to sleep in, plenty of grub, good music to sing by, nightly incursions into the city to see our girls, and plenty of visitors; and the stories of New Market filled the air."[111]

Within two weeks of Pizzini's adventure the institute's officers began to arrive: Ship on October 14 and Captains Wise and Preston four days later. In obedience to Special Order No. 102, cadets also began to trickle in. By November 11, 262 cadets were employed in defense of the city. Superintendent Smith remained in Lexington to attend to the details of reopening the college, so Ship reestablished the institute's high standards of discipline. The commandant halted the regular comings and goings of cadets between Camp Lee and Richmond. He wanted to move the cadets farther from the capital since he felt its close proximity was "prejudicial to good order and discipline."[112] In addition to "protecting" the cadets from the temptations of Richmond, Ship wanted to get the corps out from "under the command of officers of the Reserve Forces, Gen. Moore and men of that ilk, under whom I did not choose to serve if I could avoid it."[113]

An opportunity to make these changes presented itself on October 27, when Union Major General Benjamin F. Butler's Army of the James attacked Richmond's defenses near the Williamsburg, Yorktown, and Darbytown Roads. During the fighting Ship received orders to report with the cadets to Lieutenant Colonel Pemberton. Pemberton sent the boys to the intermediate line near Williamsburg Road and directed Ship to report to Colonel Atkinson. By the time they arrived at Atkinson's headquarters at 8:00 P.M., after a four-hour march in a cold, drenching rain, Butler had already been repulsed, and the cadets were ordered into camp on Poe's farm as infantry support for a nearby battery. The relocation suited Ship, and he asked Pemberton to take the corps into regular Confederate service. The request was granted and the Virginia cadets moved from the control of Major General James L. Kemper's reserve forces to the control of Lieutenant General Richard S. Ewell's Department of Richmond.

Life at the Poe farm camp was comfortable although the weather was not altogether agreeable. The cadets were quartered in tents and, since the camp was a "permanent" one, they built fireplaces and chimneys of sticks and mud, and later of scrounged bricks and ersatz mortar, to warm their canvas homes. Ship believed that most of the young men preferred the tents "to the Camp Lee Barracks. If we were ordered back to Camp Lee I think I should occupy tents in preference to the Barrack."[114] Unfortunately, one of the consequences of the liberal lifestyle at Camp Lee remained with the cadets, and caused the commandant to complain that "a large number of cadets are now unfit for duty in consequence of the Camp itch contracted in Camp Lee, some of the cases are of a very malignant nature and cause the unfortunate sufferer much pain."[115]

Despite being posted near the front line, the cadets lost none of their playfulness and the chimneys of the tents provided the vehicle for many practical jokes. "[O]ne night after taps," according to Cadet Francis H. Smith, Jr., "there was more than the usual volume of smoke in our tent. It was borne to the limit of endurance when a Rat was directed to investigate. . . . On going outside he discovered that some mischievous fellows had somehow found boards which they used in covering completely the chimneys."[116]

Throughout the cadets' service in Richmond's defense, Superintendent Smith labored for their release and their return to studies. Finally, on December 12, they left the field. Their last day in the camp at the Poe farm was not pleasant. Rain on the previous day turned to snow that night and the temperature dropped so suddenly that the next morning "the tents had to be cut to separate them from the frozen ground before we could strike them."[117]

The cadets moved to the new home of the Virginia Military Institute —a four-year-old stone structure on Second Street in north Richmond that had been used as a military hospital. The former Almshouse was not as comfortable as the old barracks. Cadet Porter Johnson reported to his sister, "We are poorly fixed here for study, twenty in a room, one small table, no chair or stools, but one gas burner attached to the side of the wall, instead of the center of the room, where it ought to be. There is but one little stove in the room and the meanest coal that you can imagine."[118] Smith, on the other hand, was grateful for the building and reminded the cadets, "The building has been secured by the liberal courtesy of the City Council of Richmond, and every care will be taken, on the part of officers and cadets, that no mutilation, defacement, or other injury, be committed."[119]

The boys found the Almshouse "a doleful place. Shockoe Hill Cemetery was just across the street in front of us. The Jewish Cemetery to our left, separated from us by an area used for a parade-ground; the Colored Cemetery to the rear, and just outside the enclosure, the 'Gallows,' with many gruesome associations."[120] In Shockoe Hill Cemetery, within sight of the Almshouse, was the grave of Claudius Crozet, the first president of VMI's board of visitors and the man instrumental in establishing the institute's military system. Crozet had died on January 29, 1864, at the age of seventy-five, but no notice of his death was ever sent to the institute—his body lay in an unmarked grave.

Given the destitute state of the school, the use of the Almshouse was indeed a godsend. VMI's condition was best illustrated by the requirements levied on the cadets for the spring 1865 session. Each cadet had to furnish his own underwear; a gray jacket; one pair of gray pants; an overcoat; two pairs of shoes; a mattress and bedding; four towels; a comb, hairbrush, and toothbrush; a knife and fork; and one hundred pounds of bacon. The cadets were also requested to furnish their own textbooks if practicable. Despite the clothing requirements imposed by Smith, the Corps of Cadets would never again be the nattily dressed "foreign mercenaries" of New Market. Wartime shortages and the destruction of the institute had given the cadets uniforms of the "Confederate soldier variety."[121] "[I]t was pathetic," wrote one observer, "to see some of these boys marching in ranks through Richmond to their quarters with pants torn or worn out at the bottom and variegated in outfit, some with cadet jackets and plain pants, others with cadet pants and plain jackets."[122]

By December 28, enough cadets had reported back from furlough to begin the session. Smith opened with a speech reminding the nearly three hundred cadets and their faculty that despite the changed circumstances, the mission of VMI was still the training of officers for the armed forces and the education of the country's youths. "We now have our work distinctly before us," he declared. "It is a serious work. There is no child's play in it. It is a work which will tax every energy of your Professors and Officers, and it is a work which will demand, on your part, every effort that assiduity, self-denial, and resolution can call into requisition."[123]

As the cadets and officers busied themselves converting the poorhouse into a college, the glorious, destructive, and deadly year of 1864 mercifully drew to a close. Of the Confederacy's four major military colleges, one was in temporary quarters, one had been driven from its home state, another was practically closed with most of its cadets assigned to the defense of Charleston, while the fourth remained relatively unscathed in the Deep South, where the enemy had not yet penetrated in force. An optimist might have hoped for improvement in the fortunes of the military colleges, but "the glory of the year 64" was bought at too high a price to hope for much more than mere survival.

CHAPTER SIX

1865: "Come Retribution"

THE NOMADIC GEORGIA MILITARY INSTITUTE CORPS OF CADETS arrived at Augusta in January of 1865, but found themselves on the road to Milledgeville a few weeks later. Settling in the capital city for an extended stay, the cadets were finally able to think about their fallen comrades, resume their studies, and contemplate their futures. While the cadets were not ready to give up, others were, and the condition of the Confederacy probably caused even these young lions to question whether victory would be possible.

Civilians were especially doubtful of a successful conclusion to the great struggle that had already destroyed so much of their nation and claimed so many lives. "My faith fails me," wrote the formerly ardent Confederate, Mary Chesnut, in February, "it is too late. No help for us now—in God or man."[1] The military situation was certainly cause for despair: Grant had trapped Lee in Petersburg, Virginia; Mobile Bay was a Yankee lake; Hood's Army of Tennessee had been shattered at Nashville, leaving the Deep South temporarily without its main field army; Sherman had taken Savannah, as his Christmas present to Lincoln, and was now poised for a march through the Carolinas to link up with Grant.

To further dishearten the citizenry, everyday life in the Confederacy had become an ordeal. The Federal army and navy had isolated or captured most of the nation's ports, severing the vital lifeline of blockade runners from Europe. Consequently, warehouses in Bermuda and the Bahamas bulged with military supplies and consumer goods that could no longer be delivered. Crippling inflation continued. In January,

$16,000 Confederate currency purchased only $300 in gold, while a wooden bucket that sold for 25 cents before the war now commanded $50. The average citizen lost all faith in the country's economy and its currency, which one South Carolinian declared to be "mere waste-paper."[2] Perhaps it was a subconscious recognition of the situation that led the government, in February, to change its secret Vigenere cipher key from the boastful "Complete Victory" to the more ominous "Come Retribution."

February also brought Sherman's anticipated, but dreaded, link with Grant's army. Sherman abandoned Savannah on February 1, and turned his army north. The war was on its way to South Carolina with a vengeance and there was little the ragged, tired Rebel forces could do to stop it. Out of despair the government was blamed for the situation. "Does Jeff Davis so hate South Carolina that he means to abandon her to her fate?" an angry Columbia physician telegraphed Richmond.[3]

It was too late for blame, however, as Sherman's army crossed the Savannah River into the Palmetto State in force. Charleston residents waited for the onslaught, and the Citadel cadets, who were attached to Brigadier General Stephen Elliott, Jr's. brigade of Taliaferro's Division, waited with them. The people of Charleston had every reason to be apprehensive: Here was where the first shots of the war had been fired and here the Federals had been embarrassed by a city that had withstood bombardments and pummeled Fort Sumter into a shapeless pile of rubble. There was no reason for the Yankees to go easy on the city. Proud and unbowed, Charleston's citizens fearfully watched the advance of Sherman's "bummers."

If Charleston fell, "Benny" White was determined to make sure that the enemy would capture nothing more than an empty building on Marion Square: He quickly sent the Citadel's furnishings, records, textbooks, astronomical and surveying instruments, chemical and philosophical apparatus, and eight-thousand-volume library to the Arsenal Academy for safekeeping. Even the Citadel's blue silk flag, an 1857 gift from Charleston's Washington Light Infantry militia regiment, was packed off to Columbia.[4] White's actions were not unjustified, for Charleston had indeed been slated for destruction. "Should you capture Charleston," wrote Federal Chief of Staff Henry W. Halleck to Sherman, "I hope that by some accident the place may be destroyed."[5] Sherman promised that he would keep Halleck's "hint as to Charleston" in mind.[6] Sherman was no fan of Columbia either and allegedly told a lady in Savannah that he would "lay it in ashes" when he captured it.[7]

Charleston was spared Sherman's wrath, however, when the general decided to bypass the city and, instead, head directly for the capital via Barnwell and Orangeburg, both of which were looted and burned. In Columbia the Arsenal cadets, part of the city's provost guard, commanded by Major General Evander McIvor Law, patrolled the city's anxious streets and guarded seven hundred Yankee prisoners of war, confined in the Insane Asylum. On February 10, as Sherman closed in on the city, the cadets were dispatched to man a two-gun battery at the Congaree River highway bridge at the foot of Gervais Street. The battery fired on a portion of the Federal army, provoking Sherman with what he termed an unnecessary act of war. On February 15, under the fire of Federal sharpshooters, the cadets abandoned the battery and, as Confederate engineers burned the highway bridge, returned to the school.

By the next morning, Federal shells were falling around the Arsenal Academy; one struck the third floor while another exploded over a mess hall chimney as the cadets ate inside. Civil order disappeared as the Federals approached. General Law himself led the cadets, with fixed bayonets, against a drunken band of looters, and the general put a swift end to the confrontation by pulling the ringleader from his horse and sending him to jail in the custody of a cadet detail.

That evening it was apparent that the end was near. Governor Magrath, whose nineteen-year-old son Andrew, Jr., was a cadet, ordered Captain Thomas to take the 153 cadets off provost marshall duty and join State Adjutant General Albert C. Garlington's brigade, which was preparing to evacuate. There was no time to save either the Arsenal's or the Citadel's property, but Thomas did manage to retrieve the Citadel's handsome flag. At 11:00 P.M. the cadets joined Garlington, and marched out of the city before dawn the following day.

As Columbia's defenders fled, Mayor Jeff Goodwyn rode out and surrendered the city to Colonel George Stone of Sherman's Fifteenth Corps. Stone entered a city whose people were on the verge of anarchy. Confederate supply depots and local businesses were being ransacked as law and order departed with the retreating Confederate troops. "On every side were evidences of disorder," observed a Federal officer, "bales of cotton scattered here and there, articles . . . of furniture cast pell mell in every direction."[8] The conquerors did little to restore order and many soldiers joined in the looting. The situation deteriorated throughout the day, and that night—whether by accident or design—most of center-city Columbia burned. By the time the inferno was extinguished the next morning, 265 residences and 193 businesses and public buildings lay in ruins. The

Arsenal Academy survived the conflagration only to be burned later by Federal troops, with just the school's officer's quarters surviving Sherman's stay in the city.[9]

Although bypassed, Charleston did not escape the disgrace and trauma of surrendering to Sherman's troops. Isolated by Sherman's advance across its rear, on February 17 the city's garrison evacuated the defenses that had so long held the might of the Union army at bay. Federal troops under Lieutenant Colonel A. G. Bennett's command marched in on February 18 and raised the Stars and Stripes over the customs house, the Arsenal, and the Citadel. Only aged Professor William Hume remained at the Citadel to greet the invaders, and Bennett, worried that Rebel diehards might try to blow-up the school, which he had seized as his headquarters, held the old gentleman there until two o'clock in the morning as insurance against any such attempt. A few days later Bennett moved his headquarters to a nearby private residence, but kept a detachment stationed at the Citadel.

The Citadel cadets marched north with Lieutenant General William Hardee's dejected men and eventually crossed into North Carolina. The march was difficult and Major White was often seen carrying a large stack of cadet muskets across the withers of his horse, or walking miles in the mud while two or three exhausted cadets rode. While the corps, as escorts for a group of Federal prisoners, was enroute to Raleigh, Governor Magrath ordered White to join him at Spartanburg, South Carolina. Once relieved of their charges, the boys turned south, reaching Spartanburg in early March.

The Arsenal cadets were also North Carolina bound as Garlington's Brigade marched north from Columbia, along the Charlotte and South Carolina Railroad, to Winnsboro and White Oak. From there they set out to the northeast for Lancaster in hopes of avoiding Sherman's advance. At Lancaster a surprised Garlington found himself face-to-face with the Federal vanguard, which had turned from its expected route toward Charlotte. Rather than allow his weak brigade to be captured, Garlington disbanded it and ordered Thomas to report to the governor as soon as possible.[10] This order began a hard, adventurous march for the cadets.

Thomas stripped the cadets to light marching order, and after a day's march east, they had put Lynch's Creek between themselves and the Federals at Lancaster. From Lynch's Creek, the boys pressed on to Mount Croghan near the North Carolina line, where Thomas halted the weary cadets, who had been marching almost continuously since leaving Columbia. He then sent a courier to Hardee for information, who returned word that part of Sherman's four-column advance was heading for Cherhaw, due east of the cadets' Mount Croghan positions, and suggested that the cadets move there to help him confront the enemy. Thomas started the cadets on the road to Cherhaw, but it soon became apparent that they were moving through a countryside crawling with Yankees and might be gobbled up before ever reaching Hardee. After consulting his officers, Lieutenants Amory Coffin, B. H. Knight, John B. Patrick, Alfred J. Norris, Robert O. Sams, and Surgeon Melvin M. Sams, Thomas decided to head north toward Wadesboro, North Carolina, and toward the Wilmington, Charlotte, and Rutherfordton Railroad.

Reaching Wadesboro, the ragged cadets marched cross-country to a point on the railroad near Charlotte, where they clambered aboard a train for a ride into the city, now General Beauregard's headquarters. Beauregard sent the cadets on to Chester, South Carolina, where they left the train for another cross-country march to Unionville. They then secured rail transportation to Spartanburg. They marched into the governor's militia training encampment on March 8, with their colors, arms, and baggage intact. The Citadel cadets greeted them warmly and reclaimed their flag while Governor Magrath welcomed them with a speech, praising their "soldierly conduct on their trying march."[11] The Arsenal cadets were billeted in the buildings of Wofford College until March 10, when they received a fifteen-day furlough. While the Arsenal cadets were away on leave, Citadel Cadet Thomas A. Johnson died of "brain fever" at the Wofford encampment.

Upon the return of the Arsenal cadets, the Battalion of State Cadets moved to Greenville where they lived in "very comfortable" log huts of their own construction.[12] While here, the Arsenal corps was strengthened by the addition of new appointees ordered to the camp by the governor, as part of his plan to make the South Carolina Military Academy cadets the nucleus of a state guard. Until this new organization was formed, however, the boys were out of harm's way.

As the Citadel cadets were making their way toward Spartanburg, a tiny band of Florida cadets "saw the elephant" in an engagement that became one of the final footnotes in the history of this wasteful war.

The West Florida Seminary was established by an act of the Florida legislature in 1851 and began operations in Tallahassee as a civilian institution. In 1859 it merged with the Tallahassee Female Academy and thereafter offered coeducational primary and secondary instruction to more than two hundred boys and girls. In 1859 the seminary's principal, Duncan Turner, decided to offer military instruction to the male students, and in 1860, James Lucius Cross, a VMI graduate of 1856, was hired as the military instructor.[13]

The start of the Civil War hit the seminary hard. Enrollment decreased from 250 students in 1860–61 to about 58 by the 1864–65 academic year, and for a time, in 1862, the male department of the school was even closed.[14] The faculty was also caught up in the war. Cross resigned in 1862 to enter active service, and was replaced in 1863 by Captain Valentine Mason Johnson, another VMI graduate and a war veteran. Johnson was promoted to superintendent in early 1864.

By late 1863, the military system was firmly in place and a request was made of the legislature that the seminary's name be changed to the Florida Collegiate and Military Institute. A bill to change the name passed both houses, but Governor John Milton, who had visions of establishing a military school at the state arsenal in Mount Vernon, vetoed it. Nevertheless, the seminary thereafter became almost universally known as the Florida Military Institute.

By 1865 the institute's tiny Corps of Cadets had seen some service. In February 1864 a Federal force from Jacksonville, bent on the capture of Florida's capital at Tallahassee, was turned back by determined Confederate resistance in the piney flatlands of Ocean Pond, or Olustee, near present day Lake City. A contingent of Florida cadets participated in the victory.[15] One year later, Union Brigadier General John Newton, the Virginian in command of the Federal Department of West Florida and a combat veteran of both the eastern and western theaters, planned a strike in Tallahassee's direction again.

Newton chose to come from the sea, up the St. Mark's River with an amphibious force made up of nine hundred to one thousand men of the Federal 2d Florida Cavalry and the 2d and 99th United States Colored Infantry. They were supported by the Navy steamers *Magnolia, Mahaska, Honduras, Stars and Stripes, Spirea,* and *Fort Henry;* the schooners *O.H. Lee, Matthew Vassar,* and *Two Sisters;* and the *Proteus, Iuka, Isnomia,* and *Hendrick Hudson.* Once in the town of St. Mark's, which was fifteen miles south of Tallahassee, Newton planned to destroy its fort and railroad along with the Rebel gunboat *Spray* berthed there, and burn the bridges over the Aucilla and Ochhlockonee Rivers. Then he and his men would move on to the capital city.

On March 3, the ships carrying Newton's force attempted to enter the St. Mark's; but a "heavy gale" sprang up, causing the vessels to drop anchor and ride it out.[16] The only troops landed were a joint army-navy force of sixty Florida cavalrymen under Major Weeks and thirty blue-jackets commanded by Acting Ensign Whitman. These men were put ashore near the lighthouse with orders to capture the bridge over the St. Mark's River and open the way for an assault upon the town.

The following morning the fleet, led by the *Spirea,* set sail for the lighthouse and Newton's plan began to fall apart. The *Spirea* ran aground in heavy fog and the troopship *Honduras* quickly followed suit. Weeks and Whitman soon appeared on shore, with Rebel cavalry in pursuit. Their mission of seizing the bridge went unfulfilled. The main body of troops finally landed about 4:00 P.M. They moved a few miles inland to await the landing of their ambulances, ammunition, and artillery.

On the morning of March 5, the Federal force marched to the St. Mark's River bridge at Newport, where it found "the planking of the bridge taken up and the enemy's cavalry, with one piece of artillery, upon the opposite bank prepared to dispute the passage."[17] Frustrated in his attempt to cross the river at Newport, Newton searched his maps for another way. He found a place upstream called Natural Bridge, where the river dived underground beneath a natural limestone bridge.

Meanwhile, the naval force assigned to bombard St. Mark's fortifications in support of the army's assault was having troubles of its own. The *Mahaska, Spirea, Stars and Stripes,* and *Hibiscus* all ran aground. The closest any of the naval vessels ever came to St. Mark's was downriver from the abandoned site of Port Leon, where the navy was to land a force of seamen to support Newton. Commander R. W. Shufeldt made every effort "to get the vessels up the river to attack the forts" but failed.[18] By March 6, it no longer mattered because the army was falling back.

The citizens of Florida were acutely aware of the significance of their capital at this point. "Every state capital in [the] South except Tallahassee has been captured," wrote diarist Susan Bradford, "and we cannot expect to escape much longer."[19] All of the hullabaloo on the rivers, along with the report of a refugee, had alerted the commander of the Confederate Department of Florida, Brigadier General William Miller, to this latest threat to Tallahassee.

On the evening of March 4, Miller sent out a call for troops. Those who answered his summons were described by one Federal as "a moiety . . . from the vicinity, old men and young boys included."[20] The "old men" included the Gadsen Greys from Quincy, Florida, with no member younger than fifty. Prominent among the "boys" was the "Baby Corps"—twenty-five cadets from the seminary, some as young as twelve.[21] Sue

Archer, a student at the seminary and sister of one of the cadets, went to the train station to see her brother off. While there she saw "one little boy barefooted and wearing the cadets' uniform [who] stood apart from the others, and was crying, because Captain Johnson refused to let him go, as he was the only son of a poor blind woman. Captain Johnson told him that good soldiers did not cry."[22]

The cadets took the train to the Newport vicinity where they joined up with Lieutenant Colonel George Washington Scott's 5th Florida Cavalry Battalion late in the afternoon of March 5. The cadets occupied entrenchments on the west bank of the river and commanded the approaches to the bridge. Getting into the trenches was exciting since the cadets had to run two-by-two across some open ground under enemy fire. Cadet Sergeant John DuBose tripped and fell while entering a trench and fifteen year-old Cadet Charles L. Beard thought his companion had been shot.[23]

The Baby Corps skirmished with the Federals until nightfall. By morning the Yankees had moved to cross the river at Natural Bridge, and the cadets were ordered to join the rest of Miller's forces there. A mile from the battlefield, Cadets Tod Archer and fourteen year-old John Milton, Jr., the governor's son, were detailed to assist the surgeons. As they got closer to the fight the boys noticed pine trees torn by Union artillery, and saw their first dead man.[24]

At the Natural Bridge position the cadets joined Scott's 5th Florida, the Kilcrease Artillery, Gamble's Battery, Dunham's Light Artillery, the 1st Florida Reserves, Barwick's and Hodge's Reserve companies, Love's Militia, and twenty Confederate Marines dragooned by Miller himself from the gunboat *Spray*. Arriving well in advance of Newton, Miller posted his "moiety" in a crescent, with converging fields of fire covering the bridge. The cadets were posted in the center, directly opposite the crossing, and were armed with a hodgepodge of weapons, including flintlocks older than they.[25] They spent their time improving the trenches and polishing their bayonets to a bright silvery glow by sticking them repeatedly into the soft sand.

Newton, who had arrived at dawn on March 6, was surprised to see Confederates also waiting for him here. He sent Major Benjamin C. Lincoln with Companies B and G of the 2nd U.S. Colored Infantry forward to drive them away. Lincoln chased the Confederate pickets over the bridge but was stopped "by a superior force of the enemy behind intrenchments, having sloughs, ponds, marshes, and thickets in front and flanks as auxiliary defenses."[26] The sound of battle was heard almost to Tallahassee.

"The battle is on," Susan Bradford noted in her diary entry for March 6. "Since daylight we have been listening to the booming of cannon. . . . I am so hot with anger I would like to take part in the fighting."[27]

Newton searched for another crossing and thought he had found one a mile below the Natural Bridge. Unfortunately for him, the crossing point proved to be impracticable and "indeed already guarded by the enemy."[28] He was forced to attack Miller's main position again. Major Lincoln led the direct assault against the Confederate works with three companies of the 2nd Colored Infantry. Lieutenant Colonel B. R. Townsend was ordered to take three other companies of the regiment and turn the enemy's right flank. Lieutenant Colonel Uri B. Pearsall's 99th U.S. Colored Infantry was held in reserve. Some of the attacking black soldiers wore hat bands vowing "To Tallahassee or Hell."[29]

Townsend's advance went well, causing some of the defenders to abandon their positions. At the foot of the Rebel works, however, Townsend faced a wide, deep, and impassable slough which forced him to retreat. Newton now recognized that while "the enemy's position was too strong in numbers and strength to be carried," his position "was in a low salient in the marshes, exposed to [the enemy's] cross fire."[30] The Federals withdrew to a previously prepared position in a pine barrens three hundred yards to the rear.

During the attacks the cadets were not heavily engaged. As Cadet Lieutenant Byrd Coles recalled, "[We] amused ourselves watching the bark fly from the pine trees and twigs fall from bushes around us" as Union artillery swept the area.[31] The cadets were so interested in the spectacle of battle and so oblivious to danger that Coles later realized that "many of the cadets would have been struck if our teachers had not watched us constantly and made us keep behind cover."[32]

Sensing a retreat, Miller ordered an attack on the pine barrens with infantry and artillery, but ran upon "a perfect line of infantry supported by artillery" instead.[33] Twice Miller attacked and twice he was repulsed "with heavy loss," leaving the Federals "masters of the field."[34] After waiting an hour to see if the battle was to be rejoined, Newton gathered his wounded and retired, dropping trees and other obstructions to cover his retreat. Miller pursued for twelve miles, but gave up when the obstructions became too difficult to overcome.

Newton made it back to the safety of his ships and proclaimed that the enemy was "driven off the field near the Natural Bridge." He blamed his failure to follow-up this "victory" on the navy's inability "to cooperate in any manner" and denied that the "expedition was . . . undertaken to

. . . capture Tallahassee."[35] He also claimed that with his "500 men . . . a force of four to five times its number was decisively repulsed."[36] In reality, "Miller's Moiety" never exceeded 450 during the worst of the fighting. Newton bitterly excused his setback at Natural Bridge: "These men, who would not have stood before my troops in any other position, were impregnable at the Natural Bridge, which could have been defended by 200 resolute men, with a few pieces of artillery, against five times their number."[37] Having proclaimed victory, Newton sailed away with 148 officers and men less than what he had come with; they had been killed or wounded, or were missing.

Confederate losses totaled three dead and twenty wounded, none of who were members of the Baby Corps. Not many cadets took part in the battle because "only those with a written permit from their parents" were allowed to accompany Miller, and Superintendent Johnson had culled out the youngest at the Tallahassee train station.[38] Those who went, noted Susan Bradford, were "so proud and those who did not go [were] so chagrined."[39]

Some Tallahasseans picnicked on the battlefield in the days following the battle, but Susan Bradford declined such invitations. "How awful!" she observed. "I do not understand such curiosity. General Miller says dead negroes were actually piled upon one another in places and the river was covered with their floating bodies."[40] The fate of the captured black soldiers was not much better. On April 5, Confederate authorities at Andersonville Prison reported that "about thirty negroes, Louisiana slaves, captured at the Battle of Natural Bridge in Florida, have been ordered here . . . as laborers."[41]

Tallahassee had been saved again and would remain the only Confederate state capital east of the Mississippi not to fall to Federal attacks. The victory "seems to have put new life and hope in all of us," Susan Bradford exclaimed.[42] General Samuel Jones, commander of the Department of South Georgia and Florida, issued an order announcing "the success of our arms in driving back, with heavy loss, the enemy from our shores."[43] He especially praised the militia. "The conduct of the militia in the recent affair," the general noted, "has shown that for actual service they are equally available with the regular Confederate troops. They exhibited as much coolness and courage as veterans."[44]

The cadets became the heroes of the hour. "The cadets from the Florida State Seminary were in the fight and behaved in a most gallant manner," a local newspaper reported. "Their praise is on the lips of all who took part in the fight."[45] Some of the cadets returned to Tallahassee immediately after the battle and were welcomed along the way with wreaths of wild olive branches and songs composed in their honor.[46] The remaining cadets escorted twenty-five Federal prisoners back to the capital and arrived several days after the battle. At a ceremony in the Florida House of Representatives chamber, the combined company was honored with the presentation of a new company flag. The boys relished the attention, but were a bit puzzled by it. "Many were the brave & even desperate deeds performed by the cadets according to stories current in Tallahassee upon our return," Cadet Charles Beard recalled with some embarrassment, "but no cadet was sufficiently damaged to need more than a good square meal to render him fit for duty."[47] Although he didn't know it at the time, young Beard was witnessing the birth of a legend.

Another "elaborate entertainment, a celebration of the victory," was planned for April 9, to honor the troops who fought, including the Florida cadets, and to raise money for local hospitals.[48] Consistent with this spirit of "new life and hope," Governor John Milton of Florida bragged, "The enemy has not invaded our State with impunity but have on almost every occasion met with a bloody chastisement."[49] Milton, however, did not attend the Natural Bridge victory celebration. On April 1, 1865, despondent over the impending death of the Confederacy, the governor committed suicide at his plantation, "Sylvania," near Marianna, Florida.

When compared to the ordeals of their Florida and South Carolina brethren, the lives of the Virginia cadets occupying Richmond's former almshouse were much less hectic, even though Confederate authorities now viewed VMI as an almost exclusive source of trained augmentees for the capital's defenses rather than as an institute of academic viability. General Smith did not share this sentiment, and while he was willing to have the institute to do its part in the city's defense, he vigorously reinstated the curriculum of one of the state's few remaining colleges. When recitations began on January 1, the first class pitched into rhetoric, engineering, moral philosophy, natural philosophy, ordnance, and gunnery; the second class labored at Latin, math, chemistry, and infantry tactics; thirdclassmen worked at mastering math, Latin, and French; and the rats were assigned lessons in math, French, and geography. To make up for lost time, Saturday classes were introduced.[50]

It didn't take long for the war to intrude upon classwork, however. On January 29, General Ewell requested the corps' assistance in repelling a cavalry raid, led by Federal Colonel Andrew W. Evans, into the Rich-mond area. Adjutant General Richardson forwarded Ewell's request to Governor William "Extra Billy" Smith with the recommendation that the boys "be held in readiness, but that the academic course ought not to be interrupted without extreme necessity."[51] The governor agreed. The dan-ger disappeared by January 31, however, when Evans could find no use-able ford over the Chickahominy River.

Although life at the Almshouse was more spartan than in the Lexing-ton barracks, the day-to-day life of the cadets was little changed. "Grow-ley" continued to top the bill of fare at the cadet mess, although it may have been a bit watered-down and served in smaller portions than before. Card playing, smoking, and fighting, which were still against the rules, remained favorite cadet pastimes. Dress parade was still held precisely at five o'clock every afternoon, and it still drew large crowds of local citizens. Bucking and other forms of hazing continued to be part of a rat's rite of passage. And the professors, as if they had never heard of the war, contin-ued to labor mightily to hammer knowledge into hard young heads.

Some changes did have to be made, however, to account for present conditions. For one thing, the institute's regulations were less rigidly enforced. One fourteen year-old cadet praised his "free and independent life . . . constantly filled with recurring incidents to surprise, interest, and exhilarate."[52] In the crowded Almshouse, classroom conditions which would have caused consternation at Lexington were now accepted as a matter of routine. "The classes were so large," according to one scholar, "that many would have to stand grouped together, usually near the door. Before the lecture was finished the groups would be quietly thinned out, for from time to time while the professor was absorbed in his work or inspecting the black-boards the door would softly open and out would slip some member of the group."[53] Because of the large classes, examinations could no longer be conducted one cadet at a time, so several students were brought to the blackboard together and given the same exam. The honesty of some cadets also adapted to the circumstances; under the system of examination those examinees who were unprepared, "with much waste of chalk and many changes and corrections and with a sharp eye on his neighbor's work, . . . managed to construct a passable performance."[54]

In addition to running a college, some of the institute's officers served with army units in the Richmond area and sought other ways to aid the Confederacy. In February the school's administration became involved in the controversy concerning the use of blacks as soldiers. The institute's opinion on the subject was offered by Acting Superintendent Preston since Smith was in Lexington recuperating from an illness. Writing to the new secretary of war, John C. Breckinridge, Preston declared that public opinion supported the concept of black soldiers. Preston also suggested that should the decision be made to raise such regiments, Breckinridge "might command the services of the Corps of Cadets with their officers to perform the work of organization and drilling in the shortest time, and with the greatest efficiency."[55] The Confederate Congress approved the raising of black regiments on March 13. A few companies of black soldiers began training in Richmond soon thereafter; however, the cadets do not seem to have been involved in their instruction.

As the year progressed, calls for the corps' assistance continued. In March levies were made for cadet artillerists and cavalrymen. The former could be supplied, but the latter were practically nonexistent. Preston informed Governor Smith that since the cadets "have never been drilled as cavalry . . . I could not promise any special efficiency from them on horseback."[56] As it turned out, the cadets were spared the experience of riding to war "mounted on gentlemen's horses" and were instead called into the trenches as infantry on March 11.

The tocsin was sounded this time because of Federal Major General Phil Sheridan. After scourging the Shenandoah and destroying the remnants of Jubal Early's little army at Waynesboro, Virginia, in February, Sheridan made for Grant's siege lines around the Old Dominion's rail center at Petersburg. As part of this movement, Sheridan sent a strong scouting party from Colonel Charles L. Fitzhugh's Brigade toward Richmond. Believing Fitzhugh's entire brigade to be approaching, the military authorities called out the reserves and the cadets. On the morning of March 11, the corps marched west to a point between the James River Canal, down whose towpath the enemy was advancing, and the Westham Plank Road. Breastworks of logs and fence rails were hastily erected and the cadets were posted on the left of this fortified line, closest to the towpath; their positions were on the farm of Adjutant General Richardson. Too weak to break through defended works, however, Fitzhugh's scouting party retreated up the towpath. The cadets returned to the Almshouse on March 13, their thirteenth wartime call to arms ended.

The cadets were called out for the last time on the night of April 1. The alarms preceding the call were different from those seen in Richmond before. "Rockets and other signals were seen and a general air of excitement seemed to prevail," remembered the superintendent's son Francis Smith, Jr. "At taps many of us kept our clothes on and watched from the windows, expecting orders of some sort calling out the corps."[57]

Soon a courier reined up in front of the poorhouse and requested to see
General Smith. The horseman had indeed brought orders, and the cadets
were quickly formed in front of the building. Permission was given for
those under seventeen to fall out, but "none availed himself of the privi-
lege."[58] Although the boys were not told, they had been called upon to
relieve elements of Longstreet's First Corps. Longstreet's troops had been
dispatched to Petersburg to help reconstruct Lee's lines after Major General George Pickett's loss of the crucial Five Forks position earlier that day.

Early on Sunday, April 2, the cadets marched through the streets of
Richmond to the suburb of Rocketts and then nine miles out, along the
Darbytown Road, to Richmond's outer line. Here the cadets occupied the
rifle pits vacated by Brigadier General John Gregg's Texas Brigade. At
dawn pickets went forward to find the enemy and discovered the positions
of a black division a quarter of a mile in front of the cadets. A thick grove
of pines separated the opposing lines and obscured the Confederate view
of the Yankee soldiers. The suspense was nerve racking to the cadets, for
they expected an attack at any moment. "[W]hen the tremendous cheering of the enemy was heard, from time to time, we were sure our time had
come," wrote Francis Smith, Jr. "If anything more uncomfortable than
this waiting could have been found, we didn't care to experience it."[59]

Late that afternoon a squadron of dismounted cavalry appeared to
relieve the cadets; the corps pulled out of the line and quickly marched
back to the city. At Rocketts the boys were met by the fathers of some
of the Richmond cadets who told the corps that Petersburg had fallen
and that the capital was in danger of capture. The cadets marched on to
Capitol Square, where the crowded streets made it obvious that the government was leaving the city. As they weaved around great burning piles
of official documents, some cadets took souvenirs. "From one pile I took
out a roll of Confederate bonds with all coupons attached and from
another pile a bundle of official papers of various sorts," one admitted.[60]
At the square the cadets paused briefly around the Washington monument, a scene of so many proud moments for VMI, and then marched to
the Almshouse.

From all of the reports it seemed doubtful that the two hundred or so
cadets could reach any organized Confederate forces, so Smith disbanded
the corps and directed each cadet to escape as best he could. Some accompanied the superintendent up the James River Canal to Columbia, Virginia, where they were again disbanded on April 4. Others struck out
toward Lynchburg, headed for General Joseph E. Johnston's army in
North Carolina, or joined the first Confederate unit they were able to

find. Cadet Color Sergeant Francis T. Lee wrapped the institute's battle-flag around his body under his shirt and carried it through the Union lines to his home in Lynchburg; a year later he mailed it to Smith. One last detail carried Cadet William D. Buster, ill with typhoid fever, to an army hospital where he later died. Cadet Joel M. Hannah, suffering from a fever contracted in the Richmond trenches, was also left behind in the hospital. As the final VMI victim of the war, he died on April 17.

The last Confederate troops marched out of Richmond on the night of April 2. Among them were some other "boy soldiers"—the midshipmen of the Confederate States Naval Academy. After scuttling their schoolship, the *Patrick Henry*, in the James River, the midshipmen guarded the archives and gold of the Treasury Department on their flight from Richmond.

With the soldiers gone and much of Richmond in flames, as fires set to destroy the tobacco warehouses spread to government property downtown, normal order disappeared. A Richmond cadet made his way back to the Almshouse early on the morning of April 3 and "found it in . . . the possession of a horde of men, women, and children from all the neighborhood around, who had broken open the building and were carrying away everything moveable—furniture, cadets' trunks, books, guns and swords—indeed their vandalism spared nothing."[61] On his way home, the cadet saw a lone Federal cavalryman near Tenth and Broad streets "surrounded and followed by a howling, frantic mob of about five hundred negro boys."[62] A new order was coming to Richmond.

As the VMI cadet on a Richmond street corner watched the Old South die, Federal cavalrymen commanded by Brigadier General John T. Croxton rode hard for Tuscaloosa, Alabama. Croxton's Brigade was part of Major General James Harrison Wilson's horseborne invasion of Alabama and west Georgia, the Confederacy's last untouched industrial area. On March 30, Wilson had detached Croxton's fifteen-hundred-man brigade with orders to "proceed rapidly by the most direct route to Tuscaloosa, to destroy the bridge, factories, mills, university (military school), and whatever else may be of benefit to the rebel cause."[63]

Colonel Garland was not unaware of the approaching threat since reports of Wilson's movements had reached him soon after the Federals left their encampment in northwest Alabama. For several nights after Wilson's advance was reported, the cadets guarded the bridge over the Black Warrior River at Northport, a suburb of Tuscaloosa. As Wilson moved south, pushing small detachments of Lieutenant General Nathan Bedford Forrest's cavalry before him, it became apparent that the raider's initial objective was Elyton, not Tuscaloosa. Consequently, Major Aaron Hardcastle, the military commander of Tuscaloosa, and the cadets, his most reliable troops, picketed the road from Elyton. The Northport bridge was left in the care of the old men and boys of the local militia. With no artillery at his disposal, Hardcastle asked Garland to loan the corps' two six-pounder cannons to some army artillerymen home on leave. Garland agreed, and the guns were moved to Baird and Hunt's Livery Stable in the city.

Croxton was, in accordance with his orders, attempting to reach Tuscaloosa by the "direct route" from Elyton. However, he didn't count on running into Brigadier General William H. "Red" Jackson's cavalry division. Realizing he could not butt his way through Jackson's superior numbers, Croxton decided "to effect by stratagem what I could not hope to accomplish directly"—he would circle around Jackson and enter Tuscaloosa over the Northport bridge.[64]

Once Croxton made up his mind, he moved rapidly. His scouts gathered all those who could spread the alarm, and arrived at the bridge at 9:00 P.M. on April 3. Croxton planned to launch an assault at dawn, but as he and a 150-man scouting party from the 2nd Michigan Cavalry moved toward the bridge, they could clearly hear the guards ripping up the structure's flooring. With his only pathway being torn to splinters, Croxton was forced to attack. From behind cotton bales the surprised militia opened a feeble fire, but by ten o'clock the bridge was in Federal hands. The fight cost the defenders one killed and one wounded in exchange for one dead Union cavalryman.

Croxton's advance quickly neutralized the city's defenses as it moved into Tuscaloosa. Federal "spies," aided by a black man named Columbus Harris, reported the location of the cadets' cannon, which were quickly seized along with artillery Captain John Perkins, who was hitching horses to one of the guns when the fifty-man Federal detail burst into the livery stable.

Awakened by the shooting at the bridge, the glare of the burning Leach Hat Factory on the Northport side of the river, and Croxton's advance scouts, who were "both bold and boisterous, roaming the streets quite freely," the citizens of Tuscaloosa began sounding the alarm.[65] A man on Market Street rushed to the Methodist Church near his home and rang the churchbell furiously. Patrick Keyhoe, supervisor of the Alabama Insane Hospital, mounted his horse and galloped down Broad Street to warn the cadets.

Cadet Corporal James G. Cowan was just coming on guard when the excited Keyhoe rode onto the campus. At 12:30 A.M. he saw Colonel Garland appear at the guardhouse, known to the cadets as the Roundhouse, and order the drummers to beat the long roll for assembly. The corps' musicians were heard cording down their drums and soon the long roll reverberated among the buildings of the university.

In less than five minutes, Company B, the color company, commanded by Cadet Captain Samuel Williamson John, formed-up in the center, while Company A, under Cadet Captain Ademar Brady, fell-in on the left, and Company C, commanded by Cadet Captain William H. Ross, assembled on the right. Commandant Murfee double-quicked the three hundred cadets to the corner of campus nearest the town. Then he directed Captains Digges Poyner; John H. Murfee, his brother; and Eugene Smith, all three graduates of VMI, to take charge of their respective companies. After these captains inspected the cadets and their .58 caliber Springfield-rifled muskets, Murfee ordered his brother to advance into the city with a platoon of Company C as skirmishers while the rest of the corps followed.

In the streets of Tuscaloosa confusion reigned. Slaves wearing gray army hats looted from Leach's Hat Factory strolled along the sidewalks. Federal troopers rounded up about sixty Tuscaloosa residents and held them prisoner in a warehouse by the river. Troopers from the 2nd Michigan, 8th Iowa, and 4th and 6th Kentucky cavalries began helping themselves to both public and private property, ransacking stores and warehouses, and opening them up to the city's poor and blacks, who were invited to take whatever they wanted. The Confederate States Depository was robbed of $100,000 in currency and $2,000,000 in vouchers. Cherokee Place, the townhouse of Confederate Senator Robert Jemison, was searched and threatened with the torch. One roving Federal detachment even interrupted the wedding of Miss Emily Leach and Captain James S. Carpenter by taking the groom prisoner. All the while, flames from the burning Confederate tax-in-kind warehouse on Drish's Row lit the pandemonium with a flickering glow.

Into this nightmare marched the Alabama Corps of Cadets. The skirmishers marched down Broad Street, through a misty rain, with Captain Murfee a few paces in front. At Greensboro Street, the avenue leading to the Northport bridge, Murfee commanded, "Right wheel-forward march!" Almost immediately the cadets were challenged.

"Who comes there?"

"Cadets," answered Murfee cryptically.

"What regiment do you belong to?" asked a suspicious voice.

"Alabama Corps of Cadets," replied Murfee.

"Let them have it boys!" commanded the voice. A stream of bullets hissed through the mist.[66]

Murfee quickly ordered the cadets to load and fire from the prone position, and they rapidly did so. Suddenly the captain stumbled and fell. From the sidewalk Cadet Orderly Sergeant John Willingham called out, "Lieutenant Labuzen, take charge of the platoon; [Captain] Murfee has been shot."[67] Also felled by the Yankee volleys were Cadets W. R. May, Aaron T. Kendrick, and William M. King. All subsequently recovered.

Colonel Murfee soon arrived on the scene and was quickly at his brother's side. The commandant directed Cadet Corporal Cowan to find a litter and remove Captain Murfee, who had been shot in the foot. Cowan borrowed a litter from the Confederate hospital on the corner of Broad and Greensboro, and with the help of three orderlies, carried the captain to the nearby home of Colonel Murfee's mother-in-law. Along the way several more volleys were heard from the Greensboro Street battle-ground causing the wounded Murfee to say, "I'm afraid my poor boys will be butchered."[68]

However, back on Greensboro Street the fighting was winding down, and the Federal detachment soon galloped back to the bridge. Meanwhile, the bulk of the corps advanced up the street one block east of Greensboro while a platoon of Company B, under Cadet Captain John, established a blocking position across a sidestreet to the west near the bridge.

The cadets were rapidly pulled into a situation uncomfortable for even veteran soldiers—a night battle among the city's buildings. In such an engagement, intelligence is safety, for without the knowledge of your enemy's position, each sidestreet harbors an enemy column and each building becomes a nest for snipers. Murfee decided to use tactics instructor Captain John Massey as the eyes of the corps and sent him forward to reconnoiter the avenue between Broad Street and the river to prevent a Federal flanking movement.

After satisfying himself that the street was free of Yankees, Massey and his two scouting companions, Professors W. J. Vaughn and P. F. Tricon, found the main body of the corps drawn up across the road leading to the bridge. No movement could be seen down the mist-shrouded street, so Massey volunteered again to scout ahead of the cadets. Massey, Vaughn, and Tricon advanced about seven yards before they were challenged. They unwisely responded to the demand "Who goes there?" with the reply "A Rebel" and were promptly fired upon.[69] Immediately the cadets behind them returned fire, causing the scouting party to find itself caught in a lively crossfire. Fortunately, the shooting quickly died out and Massey and his companions were able to return to the corps' position. As he reached the cadet line, Massey was shocked to see a Federal soldier standing near the head of the corps, while nearby the superintendent and Colonel Murfee were deep in conversation with a Confederate officer.

The officer was the hapless bridegroom Captain Carpenter, who had been permitted by his Kentucky hometown acquaintance General Croxton to return under Union guard to inform his new wife that he was safe. On his way back, Carpenter passed the cadets, took Garland and Murfee aside, and explained the military situation to them. Carpenter told the university officers that they faced fifteen hundred Federal veterans armed with Spencer repeating rifles and further resistance would be futile. He urged Garland to return the cadets to the university as quickly as possible. Confronted with Carpenter's estimate of the situation, Garland reluctantly ordered the retreat and by 1:00 A.M. the city was entirely in Federal hands. Its capture had cost Croxton twenty-three killed and wounded.

The "Battle of River Hill" was the cadets' first and only combat as a unit and, while brief, it was not pleasant. Seventy years after the event, former Cadet John F. Ponder recalled that night and admitted, "It was the first and only time I ever heard the 'hiss' of a rifle bullet and to tell the truth, I had rather listen to our modern radio, bad as it is at times."[70]

The Katydids paused at the campus only long enough to gather rations and appoint a detail to remain behind to destroy the powder magazine. Garland, not wanting to see his gallant students captured, force marched them along the Huntsville Road to Hurricane Creek bridge, eight miles east of Tuscaloosa.

In the meantime, after an absence of about forty-five minutes, Corporal Cowan returned from his litter detail for Captain Murfee. When Cowan reached Greensboro Street his comrades were gone and, imagining them all captured, he began to panic. Cowan ran up the street until he met a citizen who told him that the corps had returned to the university. Cowan then headed for the campus at a marching pace "that would have made a professional sprinter green with envy."[71] Near the observatory, the terrified boy fell into one of the defensive trenches Garland had begun in 1863. Immediately a gunshot rang out nearby. Frightened beyond description, Cowan checked himself, found he had not been shot, and took off across the campus at an "accelerated speed."[72]

Spotting a lantern near the powder magazine, the corporal investigated and found the cadet detail charged with its destruction. Believing
the gunshot to be the herald of the Federal advance, the scared young soldiers abandoned their mission and followed their comrades. They reached
Hurricane Creek bridge near sunrise. Thirty-six years later, a still embarrassed Cowan admitted that the shot he heard near the observatory came
from the discharge of his own weapon as he fell.

On the morning of April 4, Croxton began his mission of destruction
at the university. Federal incendiaries made short work of Washington,
Jefferson, Madison, and Franklin Halls. The Rotunda, containing a
library of nearly five thousand volumes, was torched over the protests of
the librarian.[73] Troopers smashed equipment in the observatory, and the
Lyceum was burned to the ground. The Federals discovered the powder
magazine and finished the cadet detail's job. When the magazine went up,
the resulting explosion, said one resident of Tuscaloosa, "was unquestion-
ably the loudest noise ever heard around Tuscaloosa either since or before.
For many miles away the sound was heard. Our house a third of a mile
away, was considerably shaken at the time."[74]

Of the fourteen or so buildings on campus when Croxton arrived,
only four remained standing when he left two days later: the observatory;
the president's mansion, which was saved by the heroic actions of Mrs.
Garland; the Steward's Hall; and, ironically, the Roundhouse, the only
building on campus erected for a purely military purpose.[75]

At Hurricane Creek Bridge the cadets heard the explosion of the
powder magazine and saw the columns of black smoke boiling up from
the campus. Fully expecting pursuit, they removed the bridge's flooring
and entrenched on the opposite bank of the creek. But pursuit never
came. So after resting until nightfall, the homeless cadets headed for Marion, Alabama, sixty-seven miles south, in search of Forrest's command.

The Corps of Cadets arrived in Marion on the evening of April 7 and
were given a "cordial welcome and entertained . . . with lavish hospi-
tality."[76] The boys withstood the long march well and Professor Warfield
Richardson, writing to his wife on April 8, reported that "none of the
corps have straggled or fallen behind & all have done remarkably well,
wading & even swimming streams, cooning logs &c."[77]

In the city, Garland discovered that Wilson had captured Selma and
defeated Forrest on April 2. He then moved off in the direction of Montgomery. Garland also confirmed what all suspected—the university had
been almost completely destroyed. Faced with a precarious military situation and with no school to return to, Garland furloughed the corps on

April 13, ordering them to reassemble at Auburn on May 12 if the situation permitted.

Far to the north of the disbanding Alabama cadets, in North Carolina, General Joseph E. Johnston surrendered the remnants of the Army of Tennessee to Sherman on April 26, and the last Confederate army east of the Mississippi ceased to exist. That same day Governor Magrath furloughed the officers and cadets of the Citadel for thirty days, because they had been in the field almost continuously since December.

On April 27, the South Carolina Military Academy board of visitors met with the governor in Greenville. During the meeting the board optimistically passed resolutions to increase the enrollment of both academies to the maximum number possible and to arrange both schools' camps of instruction so that academic exercises might be resumed.

Around the time of the board's meeting, elements of Federal Major General George Stoneman's cavalry were raiding the Greenville area. The Arsenal Corps of Cadets, two companies of 140 rifles and the sole remaining organized body of troops in the state, evacuated its camp on May 1 and moved out along the Greenville and Columbia Railroad line. A few miles from Greenville the corps was overtaken by Lieutenant John F. Lanneau of the Citadel who again entrusted the Charleston college's flag to Captain Thomas. The cadets marched nineteen miles to the outskirts of Williamston and halted on a farm near Shiloh Church. Stretching out on the farmhouse lawn near a curve in the road, many of the exhausted cadets promptly fell asleep.

Suddenly a body of horsemen, possibly one of Stoneman's scouting parties or perhaps a group of renegades, rushed upon them from around the curve and opened fire. The shock of the unexpected assault resulted in momentary confusion. But when the Citadel flag was unfurled, Captain Thomas remembered, "The command promptly rallied around it, and the fire was returned by the Cadets with effect."[78] Only a few shots were exchanged, but as the attackers passed down the road, one of them fell from his horse and was carried off across a comrade's saddle. Two other horsemen may have been killed and wounded. The cadets, however, were unscathed, except for Cadet John Spearman who was slightly injured when enemy bullets shattered the stock of his musket.

It was obvious to Superintendent Thomas from this little skirmish that small bands of Yankee cavalry were all over the area. Therefore, he pushed the cadets on to Belton, through Cokesbury and Greenwood, finally halting them at the town of Ninety-Six, where they spent a week in camp before pressing on to Newberry. Here Thomas contacted Magrath for orders. On May 9, the governor ordered the superintendent to furlough the cadets for sixty days. They would reassemble for academic purposes at a place to be determined. Each cadet was to take his musket, accoutrements, and ammunition to his home and keep them until called for.

The GMI cadets, the only cadet corps that was still intact, remained on duty in the state capital until May 1, performing guard duty and hauling corn to destitute north Georgians. Major General Lafayette McLaws then ordered the corps to return to Augusta to protect surrendered Confederate government property from the masses of refugees, deserters, and paroled soldiers passing through the city. The cadets were to "suppress all disturbance and . . . make such detail for the preservation of order and property as may be called for."[79] Augusta was occupied by a brigade of Wilson's cavalry, yet McLaws ignored this and placed the burden of enforcing order in the city upon the cadets. "Upon the zeal and honor of this battalion," McLaws' order declared, "rests the good name of their State and the safety of Augusta."[80]

The cadets of GMI carried out their duties with "zeal and honor" until May 20, when the corps was surrendered and its members were paroled and sent home.

The young lions' war was finally over.

The Virginia Military Institute in 1857. *VMI Archives.*

The Virginia Military Institute in 1864. This photo taken in 1866 shows the Institute as it was left by Major General David Hunter. Washington's statue has been returned to its place in front of Washington Arch and some of the temporary cabins built to house the cadets are visible at right. *VMI Archives.*

Superintendent Francis H. "Old Spex" Smith in the uniform of a Confederate general. Smith was the Institute's superintendent for fifty years. *VMI Archives.*

Cadet Private John T. D. Gisinier strikes a suitably warlike pose for the photographer. He died of typhoid contracted during the McDowell campaign with Stonewall Jackson in May 1862. *VMI Archives.*

Cadet Lieutenant Andrew Pizzini. *VMI Archives.*

Cadet Private Sam Atwill, who was killed at the Battle of New Market. *VMI Archives.*

Cadet Private Jaqueline Beverly Stanard, also killed at New Market. *VMI Archives.*

The Citadel Academy in December 1860 with Charleston militia parading on the Green as depicted by an artist for *Frank Leslie's Illustrated Newspaper.* *The Citadel Archives & Museum*

The Arsenal Academy in 1856. The officers' quarters in the right foreground survived the war and were converted into the South Carolina Governor's Mansion. *The Citadel Archives & Museum*

Major James B. "Benny" White, who was superintendent of the Arsenal Academy 1859–61, and of Citadel Academy 1861–65. *The Citadel Archives & Museum*

Captain John Peyre Thomas, superintendent Arsenal Academy 1861–65, then of Citadel Academy 1882–85. *The Citadel Archives & Museum*

Citadel Cadet Moses Sanders Haynesworth, who was second corporal of the Citadel's Company B at the Battle of Tulifinny Trestle. *The Citadel Archives & Museum*

Cadet William Stewart Simkins, who alerted the crew of the sand battery to the presence of the *Star of the West.* *The Citadel Archives & Museum*

Citadel Cadet Corporal Edward Thomas. He served as a cadet first lieutenant at Tulifinny Trestle. | *The Citadel Archives & Museum*

A sketch by Captain D. R. Brown, 20th Connecticut, made during the Federal troops' occupation of the Georgia Military Institute.

Brigadier General Francis Withers Capers, superintendent of Citadel Academy 1852–59, and of Georgia Military Institute 1859–65. *Julia Yates Maloney Collection.*

Superintendent's Quarters, photo taken in 1988. This is the sole surviving Georgia Military Institute structure.

Unidentified cadet lieutenant in full dress uniform, c. 1850's. Epaulets are not in accordance with 1857 regulations. Note shako and shield incorporating the Georgia state seal. *Julia Yates Maloney Collection.*

Cadet Robert G. Stiles, c. 1856.
Julia Yates Maloney Collection.

Cadet Joseph Augustus
Mirabeau Beall Lamar Cotton,
c. 1860. Cotton's uniform
sports nonregulation
cheverons and epaulets and
may have been adapted for
his service as a drillmaster in
1861. *Julia Yates Maloney
Collection.*

GMI Cadet James A. Blackshear poses in full dress uniform in this 1861 photo. Blackshear survived the war, dying two years later of tuberculosis. *Julia Yates Maloney Collection.*

Unidentified cadet private. The forage cap indicates this photo was probably taken early in the war. *Julia Yates Maloney Collection.*

Cadet cannon on grounds of Marietta Country Club. Unveiled in 1928 by a descendant of the first superintendent, Colonel Arnoldus Brumby, it now awaits restoration in the basement of the Marietta Conference Center and Resort, which occupies the former GMI site.

Cadet cannon in Marietta Confederate Cemetery across the Powder Springs Road from the former campus of GMI.

A prewar view of the University of Alabama. The Rotunda is in the foreground, flanked by Washington, Jefferson, Madison, and Franklin Halls. The Lyceum can be seen in the middle background behind the Rotunda. *William Stanley Hoole Special Collections Library, University of Alabama.*

The Roundhouse. Used as the cadet guardhouse and the only building on campus built for a purely military purpose, it was one of only four structures to survive Croxton's Raid in 1865. *William Stanley Hoole Special Collections Library, University of Alabama.*

Colonel Landon Cabell Garland, president and superintendent of the University of Alabama, 1855–66. *William Stanley Hoole Special Collections Library, University of Alabama.*

Cadet George Washington Labuzen as a cadet private. He served as a cadet lieutenant at the Battle of River Hill. *William Stanley Hoole Special Collections Library, University of Alabama.*

Cadet First Lieutenant E. N. C. Snow, Company B, Alabama Cadet Corps 1864–65, in full dress uniform but with Army rank insignia rather than regulation chevrons. *William Stanley Hoole Special Collections Library, University of Alabama.*

CHAPTER SEVEN

"Entitled to All
the Honor of . . . Soldiers"

IN RESPONSE TO A POLITICIAN'S QUERY ABOUT WHY THE CONFEDERACY
could not be crushed, Abraham Lincoln supposedly replied, "It might be
done, were it not for a certain Military School they have which supplies
them with trained officers."[1]

Partisans of the Virginia Military Institute have always maintained
that Lincoln was referring to the Lexington school when he made this
remark. However, both VMI and the Citadel lay claim to the sobriquet
"West Point of the Confederacy," and similar claims have been made on
behalf of the other state military colleges. In truth, the Confederacy's
wartime "West Point" was not a single college but was formed instead by
the four major state military colleges in concert. The government viewed
the state military colleges in this manner and President Davis, when
given the opportunity in 1863 to recognize VMI as *the* Confederate West
Point, refused to do so. He told Adjutant General Richardson through
his aide de camp:

> The President takes a warm interest in the efficiency and suc-
> cess of the military schools of the several States of the Confederacy,
> but having had no opportunity to form any opinion by observation
> of the relative merits of the systems of education pursued at these
> institutions, he does not desire to be understood to express any
> especial preference for any.[2]

The record of the state military colleges' wartime and antebellum
alumni in the service of the Confederacy is impressive and amply

151

demonstrates their value in supplying the Confederacy's military leadership requirements. VMI furnished the South's armies with 20 general officers, almost 300 field grade officers, and over 500 company grade officers. The South Carolina Military Academy supplied 4 generals, 49 field grade officers, and 120 company grade officers. Detailed figures for GMI are unavailable, but graduate Pierce Manning Butler Young rose to the rank of major general and dozens of others also served; 465 Confederate officers, including 7 generals, were alumni of the University of Alabama.[3]

Lee's army attracted the majority of military college alumni and was particularly dependent upon VMI trained officers. During Pickett's famous charge on the third day of Gettysburg, thirteen of his fifteen regimental commanders were VMI men. The Battle of New Market was also a VMI affair; all of the brigade commanders except Imboden, and most of the regimental commanders, were alumni of the institute. Historiographer Douglas Southall Freeman was particularly aware of the Lexington school's relationship with Lee's army. "I am convinced," he wrote VMI's superintendent in 1938, "that the Army of Northern Virginia owed to the Institute such excellence of regimental command as it had. I do not believe the campaign of 1862 could have been fought successfully without VMI men."[4] Richard McMurry argues that the Army of Northern Virginia was more successful than the Army of Tennessee in part because of its large number of military college alumni.[5]

Support for the Confederacy's armies was not without cost, however. Of 193 South Carolina Military Academy graduates in Confederate service, 29 were killed in battle, 4 died of war-related causes, and another 29 were wounded. Of the 1,781 VMI alumni who served in the South's armed forces, 249 of them died. The University of Alabama was hardest hit by the war's destruction; 172, or almost 21 percent, of the 825 alumni who served were killed.

The Confederate leadership was not oblivious to the benefits of a military academy education or the need for a national military academy to produce future army officers. In April 1861, President Jefferson Davis proclaimed that "to secure a thorough military education it is . . . essential that officers should enter upon the study of their profession at an early period of life and have elementary instruction in a military school."[6] Despite this declaration, the Davis administration observed a laissez faire policy when it came to the state military colleges. This policy was particularly noticeable in several areas that adversely impacted the colleges.

Although the schools were undoubtedly aided by the central government on occasion, no concerted effort was made to assist the Confederacy's "West Points." Arming and equipping the cadet battalions, for example, which would have been a relatively simple matter for the government after the initial arms' shortage, was left to the individual states. Only after a great deal of begging and demanding by governors, adjutant generals, and superintendents did the Confederate authorities supply modern, serviceable weapons to the various corps of cadets. No orders were ever given to army commanders, quartermasters, or ordnance officers to routinely extend assistance to the colleges. Instead, these officers often ordered the seizure of school property for army use.

The government was also inconsistent in its policies toward the cadets themselves. The threat of conscription was ever present and although Davis, with the tacit approval of Congress, avoided drafting cadets as a matter of policy, no instructions were ever given to the Conscript Bureau to refrain from attempting to draft them. This failure led to several unnecessary confrontations between state and Confederate authorities.

Another area in which a cohesive administration policy would have helped not just the colleges, but the Confederate armed forces as well, was in the use of the cadet corps in the field. Davis refused to integrate the cadet battalions into the Confederate military establishment because he felt their services "in training officers for the army . . . were far more important to the Confederacy than service as a body in the field."[7] Yet he did nothing to discourage state authorities or his own officers from exposing the cadets to death by risking them in combat or from interrupting their studies by frequent field service.

Because of desertions and resignations, the number of wartime graduates of the military colleges was pitifully low. Of the 624 cadets who attended the University of Alabama and were eligible for graduation between 1861 and 1865, less than 200 graduated.[8] VMI's record was abysmal. Of the 529 cadets in the classes of 1861 through 1865, only 100 stayed the full term and graduated. President Davis was given an opportunity to help correct this situation by Adjutant General Richardson, who wrote the president and asked which he thought to be more valuable to the Confederacy: a premature soldier or a trained, graduated officer? Davis, in an overabundance of caution because of the Conscription Act, refused to take advantage of this opportunity and replied through his aide:

His Excellency is debarred from expressing any opinion as to whether the cadets . . . do better service to their country by pursuing their studies than by joining the Army, because his action in regard to the matter must necessarily conform to the law, which requires all citizens who are over eighteen years of age to enter the

service, and which leaves him no discretionary power to which the
case of cadets who have become liable to military duty can be properly referred.[9]

Richardson had no better luck when he attempted to get guidance
from the president on a less controversial subject: What character and
duration of instruction best served the nation? Davis's reply was limited
to his aide's curt response: "The pressure of public business will only
allow him to refer the Board [of Visitors] to a report made by him in
1860 on the subject of military education at West Point."[10]

Indifference was not the most beneficial policy for the Confederacy.
When the nearly identical regulations of the four major state military
colleges are compared and their almost symbiotic relationship is considered—VMI graduates aided and assisted Alabama while the South Carolina Military Academy supplied faculty and other officers for GMI—it
is apparent that their operation could have easily been supervised and
supported by the government, perhaps through a separate war department bureau. Such an arrangement would have had several advantageous
effects. First, it would have removed the Confederacy's most promising
source of trained and educated officers from the control of state authorities. Second, the wartime curricula could have been standardized and
perhaps compacted to allow for the graduation of more officers in less
time. Third, it would have allowed the cadets to enlist in the Confederate
Army, or Navy for that matter; this would have protected them from
conscription during their cadetship, prevented resignations at will, and
curtailed desertions by subjecting the cadets to the jurisdiction of the
Articles of War. Finally, the government would have been able to formulate a sensible assignment policy rather than allow graduates to choose
their regiments, resulting in an unequal distribution of talent. The failure
to take these steps cost the Confederacy the opportunity to integrate
its major military colleges into some sort of West Point complex with a
centralized administration, rather than a group of independent, state-
controlled institutions.

Of course, seizing control of the state military colleges would have
been an extremely unpopular move given the attitude of the governors
and some members of Congress toward states' rights. But even several
half-measures would have relieved the schools of many problems. Davis
could have pushed for a conscription exemption for cadets. He could
have ordered his officers to not call upon the cadets for field service, and
he could have encouraged state authorities to do the same. The colleges'

supply problems would have been greatly eased with a simple order to the army quartermaster and commissary generals to extend all practicable assistance to the schools and to keep their hands off of the colleges' supplies.

Any one of these courses of action would have helped the military academies immeasurably, but none was implemented. This is not to say that more interest and involvement in the affairs of the schools would have altered the outcome of the war. They would not have. But they would have helped the state military colleges establish a foundation for the Confederate officer corps of the future and produce more of the "West Point type" of officers that Davis, a West Pointer himself, felt necessary.

Instead of officially adopting and supporting the South's already existing and proven military colleges as its "West Point," the government created its own Confederate States cadets in the hope of later establishing a national military academy. On April 29, 1861, when the war was still young and expected to be short, Davis proposed to Congress that it authorize the grade of cadet and, until a Confederate States military academy could be established, attach the cadets to field companies for training. On May 16, Congress responded to the president's request and authorized him to appoint cadets from each state in relation to the number of representatives from that state plus ten from the Confederacy-at-large.

Several factors combined limited the effectiveness of the Confederacy's cadet program. For one thing the cadets were often exposed to death in combat—a good way to learn the art and science of war, but a merciless teacher when it came to failure, not to mention nonconducive to the academics required of each cadet. There was also a great deal of dissatisfaction among the cadets when on April 7, 1863, the army required them to be 21 years of age before they were eligible for examination for promotion to the grade of second lieutenant. Typical were the complaints of a father whose son had been in "sixteen battles—and yet the government refuses him a lieutenancy, because he is not quite twenty-one."[11] Another problem involved the convening of the requisite examining boards. The April 7 order of the war department laid the responsibility of convening these boards on the "Commanders of armies in the field," some of the busiest men in the Confederacy.[12] With more pressing matters than the examination of cadets to deal with, it is not surprising that the commanders often long delayed the boards. The case of Cadet Thomas B. Yancey is a good example. Appointed a cadet in June 1863 at age 20, by March 1865 Cadet Yancey had still not been promoted, although he promised Adjutant General Samuel Cooper that he would "forward the report of Examining Board, for [Yancey's] promotion, as soon as the Army is Stationary a sufficient length of time."[13] Even when the boards were assembled, it appears that in the absence of war department guidance, a cursory examination was often administered. On March 18, 1865, the adjutant general felt it necessary to issue guidance to future examining boards. Therefore, cadets would be tested on reading, writing, spelling, mathematics, "including fractions, the extraction of square roots, and the use of logarithms," algebra, geometry, plane trigonometry, mensuration, surveying, mechanics, and tactics.[14] Cadets were to be given three months advance notice of their examination. This was, needless to say, quite a curriculum to master in the middle of war.

Although the Confederate government refused to officially adopt the state military colleges as its "West Point," their existence probably had something to do with why the Confederacy never established a military academy, even though it did establish a Confederate States Naval Academy.[15] With some of the former Union's best military academies already producing Confederate officers, Congress undoubtedly felt no pressure to organize a Confederate States Military Academy.

Despite the contributions of the state military colleges, it is tempting to argue that any sort of military academy would have been an unnecessary luxury in the manpower-starved Confederacy. Furthermore, the cadet corps of those that did continue to operate were not utilized effectively. It is indisputable that the Confederacy could have fought the war without any military colleges. The argument that they were a wasteful luxury, however, presupposes that they constituted a drain on the material and personnel resources of the nation. This supposition is not supported by facts since the Confederacy only sporadically contributed material resources to the state military colleges. And it can further be proved false by an examination of the manpower which would have been released had the colleges been closed. Between 1861 and 1865 approximately four thousand young men entered the four major state military colleges. Many were under the age of conscription and, therefore, unavailable for service. But even under the assumption that all four thousand were placed in active military units, only forty, 100-man companies or four regulation strength regiments, could have been created. During any one year, however, only about one thousand young men, or the equivalent of one 10-company regiment, were enrolled at the state military colleges. This was hardly a force that would have had any appreciable impact on the war effort, and the potential of gaining one thousand "West Point type" officers each year was arguably of more value to the Confederacy than gaining an equal number of gun-toting privates.

Regarding the use of the cadets in the field, it is true that third-rate militia and home guards could have taken the cadets' place, but such a substitution would have been quantitative, not qualitative. Can one imagine a similar outcome at New Market had Breckinridge been forced to use the ill-trained old men of the Rockingham-Augusta Home Guards to plug the hole in his line? Nevertheless, the use of the cadets in the field went against President Davis's desire to not mobilize the youths of the Confederacy in general. "In making soldiers of them," he declared, "we are grinding the seed corn."[16] More importantly, combat was a misuse of the cadet corps. Their service in the early days of the war gave the South the advantage of fielding well-trained recruits, especially in Virginia. This advantage could have been maintained if the cadets had been used as drillmasters throughout the war. Although exact numbers are unknown, somewhere between forty thousand and fifty thousand recruits were trained by cadets from the four main Southern military colleges.[17] Additionally, cadet drillmasters who went to war with the regiments they had trained, as well as other cadets who left the colleges before graduation, supplied the Confederacy with a portion of its initial allotment of home-grown, trained company and field grade officers.

Although the cadet corps' greatest service was the initial training of recruits early in the war, their greatest glory came from their field service. Federal Major General John E. Wool, commander of the Union Army's Middle Department, was a general who understood the potential of boys in combat. When Wool's provost marshall ordered the conscription of Maryland boys sixteen and seventeen years of age, Wool became incensed. He feared that the order would cause Baltimore's youth to cross into Virginia and join Lee's army, and "with an army of boys, Lee could whip the world. They are the best soldiers in the world, as they are incapable of fear because they do not know the meaning of the word danger."[18]

In the postwar years, however, the probably apocryphal story of General Wool's comments set the stage for similar exaggerations. Not unexpectedly, the role of the cadets in their battles grew. New Market was a particularly fertile field for sowing the seeds of legend. It did not take long before the capture of Von Kleiser's abandoned gun became the capture of an entire Federal battery after hand-to-hand combat. Major Semple never guided the cadets into the gap in Breckinridge's line; they spontaneously moved in because they were great soldiers. The same thing happened wherever any of the cadet corps were engaged. Soon the sacrifices of other Confederate soldiers at the Oconee River bridge, the Tulifinny trestle, Tuscaloosa, or Natural Bridge were forgotten as attention focused on the relatively small cadet battalions.

With that said, though, the record of the Confederacy's cadets lends some credence to Wool's supposed comment. There were no recorded incidents of cowardice in the face of the enemy in any of the cadet corps, and, without exception, their performance in the field drew the praise of friend and foe alike. Cadets fired the war's first shots at the *Star of the West* and some of the last at a band of Federal raiders in South Carolina. In between, their service indicated that they were among the best state troops fielded during the conflict.

The frequency of the cadets' use in the field was a good indicator of the military misfortunes of the Confederacy. As the military situation deteriorated, the cadets were placed in harm's way more often with less opposition or reservation. There was regret, but no guilt, on the part of those who used them, for a nation fighting for its survival uses any means at its disposal, and the Confederacy was no exception. The use of the cadets of Chapultepec in the Mexican War and Hitler's destruction of his officer cadets and Hitler Youth in the final days of the Third Reich are examples of similar desperation.

Despite their excellence in the field, cadets failed to alter the outcome of any battle in which they participated, with the possible exception of New Market, which historian William C. Davis concluded "could not have been won as it was without them."[19] This was not any fault of the cadets, for their combat experience came at a time when the Federals could command overwhelming numbers in almost every engagement. Unfortunately, the truth is, that from a purely operational view point, the cadet battalions contributed little to the war effort; this naturally raises the question of whether the sacrifice of young lives was worth the results gained. If one regards winning as the sole justification for a soldier's death, then over thirty cadets died and more than sixty were wounded for nothing. Regardless of battles won or lost, however, the cadets' performance on the battlefield won them something more valuable than a victor's laurels, as Federal Captain Frank Town realized after the smoke cleared from the rain-soaked field at New Market:

> When such young men fall in a cause which they believe in, whether it is intrinsically right or wrong, one may realize the sadness of cutting off a life so full of promise, yet all—those who

approved and those who opposed the cause they died for—will accord to them the tribute of sincere respect and admiration.[20]

It would be an injustice to the young lions to judge them solely by the length of their campaigns, the number of their engagements, their record in the won-lost columns, or the "superman" legends that swirl around them. Their real glory comes from the simple fact that as boys— as students not expected to fight and die—they did not hesitate to do a man's and soldier's job. While large numbers of their contemporaries served in the army's and the navy's ranks, the cadets bore the dangers and privation of common soldiers while still trying to master the classics and natural philosophy, as well as prepare themselves for leadership positions in the armed forces of their states and their country. This dual mission made the cadet battalions unique among Confederate forces; their élan ranked them with the most disciplined and spirited of Rebel formations. This dualistic existence was not without its cost to the cadets. As one admirer of the Citadel corps noted, "It was very hard on them—at one time ordered to take to the field as men and soldiers, and the next moment treated as mere boys in a military academy."[21]

Despite being used as pawns in their states' and the Confederate government's policy battles, deprived of supplies by the very army they were training to serve, and squandered on the battlefield by officers who were ambivalent about their presence, the cadets hold a justifiably special place in the history of the "Lost Cause." Lieutenant Colonel James T. Murfee best summed up the story of the young lions when he wrote of his corps of cadets:

[E]very member . . . was a Confederate soldier, displaying the highest virtue in camp and in field; and therefore everyone is entitled to all the honor of such soldiers, and their descendants to a share in their glory.[22]

CHAPTER EIGHT

Reconstruction

ONLY ONE OF THE STATE MILITARY SCHOOLS REOPENED IN 1865. On October 16, through the perseverance of Francis H. Smith and the sacrifices of his skeleton faculty, the Virginia Military Institute admitted eighteen cadets.

The war had changed VMI. The impressive buildings were now gutted ruins, and the cadets billeted in private homes until temporary quarters could be built on post. Eighteen of the pre-war faculty had been killed or wounded on the battlefields while others, such as former Commandant William Gilham, were forced by poverty to seek higher paying positions.

There was reason for hope, however. The reputation of the college attracted some new and distinguished faculty members. George Washington Custis Lee, son of Robert E. Lee, signed on as professor of civil and military engineering and applied mechanics. The new professor of practical astronomy, geology, physical geography, and meteorology was Captain John Mercer Brooke, one of the designers of the ironclad *Virginia* and developer of the Brooke rifled naval cannon. Matthew Fontaine Maury, the renowned as "Pathfinder of the Seas," also joined the faculty. In addition to the new faculty, some of the old stalwarts such as Commandant Ship returned.

Although some members of Virginia's Reconstruction government had no love for the institute, VMI grew during the post-war years, producing educated, disciplined men to lead Virginia into the twentieth century. VMI wore her battle honors proudly and her strongest link to that time became even stronger on May 15, 1866, when the bodies of

Cadets Atwill, Jefferson, Jones, McDowell, and Wheelwright were reburied on post.[1]

Colonel Garland boldly scheduled the reopening of the University of Alabama for October 1, 1865, with only one professor and no physical plant to speak of. When only one student, a son of former Governor Thomas Hill Watts, came to enroll, the superintendent reluctantly closed the school. Despite Garland's initial setback, the university was the next of the miliary academies to reopen. Garland, however, was not there to see it because he resigned in June 1866 to accept the position of professor of physics and astronomy at the University of Mississippi.

In October 1868 Alabama's Reconstruction government ordered the school to reopen with an administration and faculty of Northerners. The people of Alabama essentially boycotted their university in protest and the Ku Klux Klan intimidated those who did not. Garland's Yankee replacement was driven away by the Klan with threats of lynching, so in 1871, the first post-war "native" faculty was appointed. On April 4, President Nathaniel T. Lupton welcomed seventy-five cadets to the university. By this time, the ruins of the school were covered by mounds of dirt and loblolly pines, but a new barracks had been built behind the site of the Rotunda. Commandant of Cadets George D. Johnston was now in charge of military training and his cadets were proudly outfitted in uniforms of Confederate gray.

Throughout the remainder of the century the University of Alabama thrived, although its military system did not. On December 7, 1900, the corps rebelled against an unpopular commandant and demanded the resignation or removal of both the commandant and superintendent. Eight days later, after half-hearted efforts to break the mutineers, the board of trustees informed the cadets that both officers had tendered their resignations and that they would be accepted. The military discipline of the corps was destroyed by the success of the mutiny and, on March 3, 1903, the legislature gave the university's trustees authority to abolish the military system. But reversion to a civilian institution did nothing to stifle the university's growth. Today it is known nationwide as the home of the Crimson Tide and "Alabama's Capstone of Higher Education."

Like the rest of the South, Georgia's economy was destroyed by the war; what little capital remained did not go to reopening the state's colleges. Despite the somber financial situation, alumni of the Georgia Military Institute made strenuous efforts between 1870 and 1875 to reopen the school with former Confederate General Joseph E. Johnston as superintendent. In 1873, the aid of Congressman Pierce M. B. Young, alumnus of GMI and a former Confederate general, was sought. In a letter signed by three former cadets, Young was reminded:

[T]he 'Georgia Military Institute' exists only in the statute books and the memories of the past. The buildings destroyed, the libraries and apparatus all burned, and the appropriation denied, the grounds and academy building only remain. But there clusters around the spot memories dear to Georgians, and to every Southerner. . . . The name, the character, the reputation of the 'cadet' of the G M I is dear to us, and we would perpetuate the 'school of instruction' upon ground hallowed by memories of the past."[2]

Young was asked to secure muskets and accoutrements from President U. S. Grant for the training of a new Georgia Corps of Cadets.

While the merit of the proposal to rebuild the iInstitute was indisputable, there simply was no money to see it through and the school never reopened. All Marietta has to remind it of its military college are the superintendent's quarters, a cadet cannon in the city's Confederate cemetery, and another cadet cannon currently awaiting restoration in the basement of a hotel and convention center recently opened on the former site of the institute.

The future of the South Carolina Military Academy was also in doubt for many years after the war. The report of the board of visitors on December 7, 1865, detailing the extent of the war's depredation upon the academy explains much of this uncertainty. The Arsenal, except for the officers' quarters, had been burned to the ground. The libraries, textbooks, furniture, and scientific apparatus had been destroyed or carried away as spoils of war. The Citadel, although physically unscathed, was occupied by Federal troops. The property of the Citadel, "consisting of room, mess hall, officer and section room furniture, records, textbooks, astronomical and surveying instruments, chemical and philosophical apparatus, cabinet of minerals and library, containing (8,000) eight thousand volumes," sent to the Arsenal Academy for safe keeping was all destroyed or carried away in the Arsenal's destruction.[3] With its physical plant gone, the governor and the board realistically gave up on reopening the Arsenal, but agreed that the Citadel should be placed back in operation. With the building in the hands of the U.S. military, however, little could be done to carry out the plan.

Three years later the Citadel almost lost its military feature entirely when, in response to the state constitutional convention's adoption of a provision declaring equal access to state schools for both races, Governor James L. Orr proposed that the Citadel be converted to a college for blacks. Again, since the building remained occupied by the Federal army, no action could be taken on Orr's proposal.

The military occupation of South Carolina ended in April 1877.

Almost immediately, nine South Carolina Military Academy graduates met at the Charleston Hotel to begin the work of reopening the Citadel. The most daunting problem that faced them was obtaining the building itself. Several times since 1869 the legislature had asked the Federal government for the return of the Citadel. Each request was refused based upon the argument that the school belonged to an insurgent state and its students had been employed in hostilities against the United States. In August 1877 Governor Wade Hampton renewed the request and was again refused.

The following year, the state took a different approach to the problem; it notified the federal goverment in Washington that it could keep troops at the Citadel for a yearly rental payment of $10,000 retroactive to its occupation in 1865. Congress decided it did not want the building that much and, in June 1878, a bill was introduced in the Senate which proposed the return of the Citadel to South Carolina. The only stipulations were that the state had to drop any claims for rent, and any claims over the destruction of the building's west wing, which burned in 1869. This time the state refused. Then, in April 1879, the Citadel was unexpectedly abandoned by the government and its garrison quietly marched out.

With the building now available, South Carolina Military Academy alumni, led by former superintendents Peter F. Stevens and Francis W. Capers, worked to obtain the legislature's support for reopening the school. The sentiments of the lawmakers were evenly divided when the bill to appropriate money for the reopening came to the floor in January 1882. A tie vote to kill the bill was broken in favor of debate on the measure, and on January 31, the bill was passed.

In 1910 the name given the Citadel and Arsenal academies in January 1861 was officially changed; the remaining military college would be known as The Citadel: The Military College of South Carolina. Another major change occurred in 1922 when a new, larger institute was erected on the site of Charleston's Washington Race Track. The old Citadel compound is now a hotel, and still stands on Marion Square, resplendent in its coat of "Charleston pink." It remains a memorial to the resiliency of Charleston and its military college.

The men who led the state military colleges through the war continued their contributions to the South and the newly reunited United States.

Francis Henney Smith served as superintendent of VMI until 1889, and then as superintendent emeritus until his retirement on January 1,

1890. During his long tenure at the institute, Smith remained a practical scholar, and taught classes until the early 1860s. He also made time to serve on West Point's board of visitors, write several mathematics textbooks, and author notes, which were assembled after his death, into the *History of the Virginia Military Institute*. Smith died on March 21, 1890. "The Institute's past and present greatness," wrote VMI historian, Colonel William C. Couper, "is and will for all time be indissolubly associated with the name of General Francis H. Smith."[4]

Scott Shipp returned to the institute as commandant of cadets and served in that position until 1889, when he became VMI's second superintendent. Shipp, who added the final "p" to his name around 1883, taught mathematics, Latin, and other subjects until 1888. Like Smith, he served on the West Point board of visitors; he was also named president of the board of visitors of the United States Naval Academy. Shipp served as superintendent emeritus of VMI from July 1, 1907 until his death at age seventy-eight on December 4, 1917. The 1859 graduate of VMI and commander of the cadets at New Market was remembered as "a stern disciplinarian. . . . absolutely just and fearless [whose] actions were always based on the right, as he saw it, and never on what might be popular."[5]

Peter Fayssoux Stevens, who in 1859 succeeded his brother-in-law Francis W. Capers as superintendent of the Citadel, resigned his position in October 1861 to enter the ministry. In November 1861 he tendered his services to South Carolina Governor Pickens and offered to raise a combined arms legion of infantry, cavalry, and artillery, which he proposed to honor with the governor's wife's maiden name: Holcombe. Stevens led his Holcombe Legion through the battles of Second Manassas and Sharpsburg, where he was wounded in the left arm. After the Confederate retreat from Maryland, Stevens felt that he was no longer serving in the defense of South Carolina, as he had volunteered to do, and resigned from the army to return to his parish near Black Oak, South Carolina. Here he devoted himself to ministering to the parish's black population. After the war, Stevens was appointed a bishop in the reformed Episcopal Church. He died on October 3, 1894, and was buried in Charleston's Magnolia Cemetery.

James B. "Benny" White did not resume his position as superintendent when the Citadel reopened in 1882. He continued to remain involved in educational endeavors, but he also became an insurance broker in Marion, South Carolina. He died in 1906 at the age of seventy-eight.

John Peyre Thomas, the last superintendent of the Arsenal Academy, had an eventful life after the war. In 1873 he founded the Carolina Military Academy at Charlotte, North Carolina. Then in 1881 he closed the school to accept the appointment as the Citadel's superintendent. He served at the Citadel until 1885, when he resigned due to a difference of opinion with the college's board of visitors. He served in the South Carolina House of Representatives from 1886 to 1888, and for a brief time in 1887 he was editor of *The Columbia Register*. He unsuccessfully attempted to procure a position on the faculty of the University of South Carolina, and after his wife's death in 1890, he established an "Academy of Lectures" in Columbia, where he also engaged in the insurance business. In 1892 he was appointed to the Citadel's board of visitors and served on it until 1900. In 1893 he published his *History of the South Carolina Military Academy* and was appointed State Historian of Confederate Records in 1897. He died in Columbia in 1912 at age seventy-nine.

Landon Cabell Garland remained a prominent force in Southern education after his June 1866 resignation as the University of Alabama's superintendent. He served as the University of Mississippi's professor of physics and astronomy and was named president of Vanderbilt University in 1875. He remained in this position until 1893 and died in his home on the Vanderbilt campus in 1895.

Alabama Commandant James T. Murfee became an architect after the war and designed some of the university's new buildings. In 1871 Murfee was named president of Alabama's Howard College (now Samford University), and in 1887 he founded the Marion Military Institute in Marion, Alabama which is still in operation today. Murfee died on April 23, 1912.

Francis Withers Capers, superintendent of both the Citadel and GMI, continued his career in education after the war. He taught in a private school in Augusta, Georgia, and in 1867 he was elected to the chair of mathematics at Charleston College, where he taught until 1890. Capers also remained involved in the affairs of the Citadel and was one of the moving forces behind its reestablishment. He died on January 12, 1892, at age seventy-two and was buried in the churchyard of Charleston's Bethel Methodist Church. He was eulogized as a "distinguished soldier, scholar and teacher, and much beloved gentleman," who was a "master builder of . . . character."[6]

Cadet John Sergeant Wise left VMI in 1864 and joined the army as a second lieutenant. After the war he graduated from the University of

Virginia and became a lawyer. However, he continued his interest in military affairs as captain of the Richmond Light Infantry Blues and as a member of VMI's board of visitors. He also served in Congress, but he is probably best remembered for writing *The End of An Era,* a reminiscence of the war. He died on May 12, 1913, and was buried in Richmond's Hollywood Cemetery.

Andrew Cameron Lewis Gatewood left VMI after one year and served with the 11th Virginia Cavalry as a second lieutenant. After the war he served as a colonel in the Virginia Militia and was brigadier general of the 1st Brigade, West Virginia Division of the United Confederate Veterans. He died on July 31, 1919. James Henry Reid left VMI to join Otey's Battery. He survived the war and became a farmer near Forestburgh, Virginia, until his death on March 2, 1921.

Moses Jacob Ezekiel, one of the few Jewish cadets to attend VMI, graduated in 1866 and studied art thereafter. He became a world-renowned sculptor and was knighted by the King of Italy. He died in Rome on March 27, 1917, and was buried in Arlington National Cemetery. Andrew J. Pizzini survived his New Market wounds and graduated from VMI in 1865. He was a post-war railroad entrepreneur and a captain in the Richmond Light Infantry Blues. Pizzini passed away on January 31, 1913. Francis H. Smith, Jr., graduated in 1869 and served on the Institute's faculty until his death on November 7, 1917.

Benjamin Azariah "Duck" Colonna graduated in 1864. He was employed as a civil engineer and as chief assistant to the United States Coast and Geodesic Survey. He died on March 14, 1924. Oliver Perry "Big" Evans became a lawyer and, later, judge of the Superior Court in San Francisco. He died at his home in Berkeley, California, on May 15, 1911, the forty-seventh anniversary of the Battle of New Market. Cadet John Breathed Snodgrass enlisted as a private in the Confederate Army after two years at VMI. He became a physician after the war and settled in Martinsburg, West Virginia, where he died on March 28, 1908.

Citadel cadet George E. Haynsworth was commissioned a second lieutenant of artillery in October 1861. After the war he became a lawyer and trial justice in Sumter, South Carolina. On December 30, 1887, he was accidentally shot dead while breaking up a fight in his courtroom. William S. Simkins was commissioned a second lieutenant in the 1st Regiment, South Carolina Artillery in August 1861. He later became a lawyer in Florida. C. Irvine Walker enlisted in the Confederate Army the day after his graduation in 1861. He rose to the rank of lieutenant colonel in the 10th South Carolina Infantry and was wounded at Atlanta and at Kingston, North Carolina. After the war he was a partner in and general

manager of Walker, Evans & Cogswell, president of the Charleston Man-
ufacturing Company; a member of the South Carolina Military Academy
board of visitors from 1878 to 1886; and brigadier general of South
Carolina volunteer troops from 1881 to 1883. Walker died in 1927.
Joseph Walker Barnwell became a legislator and a Charleston attorney.
He died in 1930 at the age of eighty-six. Farish Carter Furman also
became a lawyer and served as county judge in Milledgeville, Georgia. He
died young at age thirty-seven in 1883. George Mathewes Coffin, Jr., was
a produce dealer and banker in Charleston until his death in 1934.

John Kershaw was furloughed from the Arsenal in January 1865 to
join the staff of his father, Major General Joseph B. Kershaw. The younger
Kershaw was captured at Saylor's Creek, Virginia in April and imprisoned
at Fort Warren, Massachusetts. After the war he practiced law until 1873
and then was ordained as an Episcopal priest. He died in 1921. William
DeHon "Big Bill" Palmer overcame the loss of his hand to become a
planter in Berkeley County, South Carolina. His death came in 1912.

Georgia Cadet Joseph Augustus Mirabeau Beall Lamar Cotton
attended GMI from 1858 to 1860. He then left the institute to continue
his studies at Emory University. He enlisted in the 7th Georgia Infantry
and fought at First Manassas (Bull Run) in a company commanded by his
GMI classmate Captain T. S. Moyer. Cotton was slightly wounded in the
battle and Moyer was killed. Later in the war Cotton served as a captain
in Bonaud's Battalion of Artillery, performing provost duty in Quincy,
Florida. Cotton became an attorney and practiced in Thomaston, Georgia after the war. He died on Independence Day in 1907 and was buried
in Thomaston.

Alabama Cadet E. N. C. Snow finished his studies at the university
after the war and became a successful merchant and highly esteemed citizen of Tuscaloosa.

Those who survived the war never forgot their comrades who were
killed and would remain forever young. Memorials to the fallen cadets
were raised on each of the campuses or former campuses. As a cadet
private, Moses Ezekiel sat with his dying friend Tom Jefferson after the
Battle of New Market. As Sir Moses, Ezekiel sculpted a monument to
place over the graves of the New Market cadets who were buried on post.
Ezekiel put his heart into the work, and the resulting piece is *Virginia
Mourning Her Dead*—a poignant expression of the sentiments of all states
who sent and lost cadets to the war.

NOTES

CHAPTER 1

1. John Thomas Lewis Preston, "Historical Sketch of the Establishment and Organization of the Virginia Military Institute," 4 July 1889, VMI Archives, 2–3, (hereafter Preston, "Historical Sketch.")
2. *Rockbridge County News*, 14 October 1926.
3. Preston, "Historical Sketch," 3–4. Washington College is now known as Washington and Lee University.
4. Ibid., 6.
5. Ibid., 8.
6. Ibid., 9–10. These words are familiar to every VMI man since, as a rat, he was required to memorize them.
7. *Buchanan Advocate*, 20 Jan. 1836.
8. Ibid.
9. Preston, "Historical Sketch," 12.
10. Ibid., 17–18. This would be a common principle of all of the South's state military colleges.
11. William Couper, *One Hundred Years at VMI* (Richmond: Garrett and Massie, 1939), vol. 1, 69.
12. In the nineteenth century the proper reference of the institute was "The V.M.I." Over the years, the "The," as well as the periods, were dropped. Today the college is known universally simply as VMI. The institute was the first American college to become known by its initials. Claudius Crozet is usually credited with the first use of "The V.M.I."
13. Philip St. George Cocke as quoted in Jennings C. Wise, *The Military History of the Virginia Military Institute from 1839* (Lynchburg: J. P. Bell Co., 1915), 57.
14. John Peyre Thomas, *The History of the South Carolina Military Academy* (Charleston: Walker, Evans & Cogswell, 1893), 29, (hereafter Thomas, *Academy History*).
15. *Regulations of The Military Academies of South Carolina* (Columbia: R. W. Gibbes, 1858), 5–6, (hereafter *South Carolina Regulations*).

16. Jones served without pay as president of the board of visitors for the next twenty-two years.

17. Thomas, *Academy History*, 32. For convenience, the title South Carolina Military Academy will be used throughout when referring to both schools collectively.

18. Ibid., 33.

19. Bowling C. Yates, *History of the Georgia Military Institute, Marietta, Georgia, Including the Confederate Military Service of the Cadet Battalion* (1968), 1, (hereafter Yates, *GMI History*).

20. Sarah B. G. Temple, *The First Hundred Years: A Short History of Cobb County, In Georgia* (Atlanta: Walter W. Brown Pub. Co., 1935), 189, (hereafter Temple, *Years*).

21. *Southern Recorder*, 17 November 1857.

22. Temple, *Years*, 159.

23. *Selma Free Press* 12 August 1837.

24. Caleb Huse, "Personal Reminiscences and Unpublished History" in James B. Sellers, *History of the University of Alabama* (University: University of Alabama Press, 1953), vol. 1, 262, (hereafter Sellers, *University History*). During the 1850s, the strained relations between North and South gave rise to the establishment of many military colleges and preparatory academies, as well as to the adoption of military systems at civilian institutions. Two examples of this phenomenon are the Bastrop Military Institute and the North Carolina Military Institute. The civilian academy at Bastrop, Texas, was completely reorganized in 1858 as a military academy under the auspices of the Methodist Episcopal Church. Colonel T. P. Allen, formerly of the Kentucky Military Institute, was superintendent. In 1859, the North Carolina Military Institute was opened in Charlotte by Daniel Harvey Hill, brother-in-law of "Stonewall" Jackson and a future Confederate lieutenant general. In a letter to the author, researcher Bruce S. Allardice identified more than eighty independent military schools and academies operating in the South on the eve of the Civil War. Allardice is currently working on an in-depth history of the Southern military school antebellum alumni's wartime contributions to the Confederacy's military leadership.

25. Couper, *One Hundred Years*, vol. 1, 301–302. Smith wrote a lengthy letter to Garland on May 14, 1860, with his advice concerning the military organization of the university. Garland must have had some trepidation about assuming the superintendency of a military school. On this matter, Smith advised Garland, "It is not absolutely necessary that the Supt. of the Univ'y should be a military man . . . considering the experience of the present incumbent of the Presidency & his intimate acquaintance with the State, I would unhesitating advise his taking the superintendency of the University in its military organization with the military rank of Colonel." (Smith to Garland, May 14, 1860, VMI Archives).

26. Report, Garland to trustees, Sellers, *University History* vol. 1, 260.

27. H. Austill, *The University in '60 and '61*, William Stanley Hoole Special Collections, 1, University of Alabama, (hereafter Austill, *'60 and '61*).

28. Ibid., 3.

29. Ibid. James A. Anderson, transcript of radio broadcast April 21, 1941, 4 William Stanley Hoole Special Collections, University of Alabama.

30. E. B. Thompson to uncle, 26 November 1860, Sellers, *University History*, vol. 1, 262.

31. Preston, "Historical Sketch," 7–8.

32. Thomas L. Law (ed.) *Citadel Cadets: The Journal of Cadet Tom Law*, (Clinton: P. C. Press, 1941), 233, (hereafter Law, *Journal*).

33. *Regulations for the University of Alabama at Tuscaloosa* (Southern Methodist Publishing House, 1861), 10, (hereafter *Alabama Regulations*).

34. VMI applicants were required to be between the ages of 16 and 25; the South Carolina Military Academy considered only young men between 15 and 19. GMI applicants were required to be between the ages of 14 and 25; applicants for the University of Alabama could be no younger than 15.

35. *Alabama Regulations*, 18.

36. Ibid.

37. "Superintendent's Annual Report," in the *Annual Report of the Board of Visitors, July 1, 1871*, VMI Archives, 14.

38. *Alabama Regulations*, 12.

39. Law, *Journal*, note 1, 18.

40. Francis H. Smith, *History of the Virginia Military Institute* (Lynchburg: J. P. Bell Co., 1912), 138, (hereafter Smith, *VMI History*).

41. John Esten Cooke as quoted in Wise, *Military History of VMI*, 78.

42. Ibid., 79. Thomas Jackson came to VMI in 1852 as Gilham's replacement as professor of natural and experimental philosophy. Soon after his arrival, Jackson acted as commandant in Gilham's absence. Superintendent Smith later said "he gave no evidence of ability to command young men." Also considered for the position Jackson filled were Second Lieutenant George B. McClellan and Jesse L. Reno; William S. Rosencrans; and future Confederate Major General Robert E. Rodes.

43. *Southern Recorder*, 9 November 1858.

44. Law, *Journal*, 303.

45. Thomas, *Academy History*, 242.

46. Preston, "Historical Sketch," 20.

47. *Constitutional Union*, 20 May 1852.

48. Garland to Gov. John G. Shorter, 24 November 1862, Sellers, *University History*, vol. 1, 263.

49. Smith, *VMI History*, 242–243.

50. Garland to B. E. Norris, 6 November 1862, Sellers, *University History*, vol. 1, 268.

51. This and other descriptions of cadet life are, except when otherwise indicated, composites drawn from the regulations of all of the schools. There were minor differences in the life of a cadet or in the military organization among the various schools.

52. *Regulations for the Virginia Military Institute at Lexington, Virginia* (Macfarlane and Fergusson, 1854), 74.

53. Law, *Journal*, 24.

54. *Alabama Regulations*, 56.

55. Ibid., 55.

56. Ibid., 50.

57. Martha Lynn Midkiff, "The First One Hundred Years: A General History of Student Affairs At The University of Alabama." (Masters thesis, University of Alabama, 1978).

58. John Kershaw, "Reminiscences of Citadel Life: 1864–65," *1911 Citadel Annual*, 147, (hereafter Kershaw, "*Citadel Life*"). Faculty wore standard issue U.S. Army blue frock coats with state buttons until well into the war. The South Carolina Military Academy faculty traded theirs for Confederate gray in early 1863.

59. *South Carolina Regulations*, 17.

60. During the war the cadets were often taught the latest tactics by combat veteran graduates who returned to school on the commandant's staff.

61. Law, *Journal*, 23.

62. Ibid., 301.

63. Wise, *Military History of VMI*, 57. Gilham was a graduate of West Point and a Mexican War veteran who came to VMI in 1846 as commandant of cadets and professor of natural and experimental philosophy. Smith credited Gilham with making the "drill of the Corps the equal, if not the superior, of that at West Point." While at VMI, Gilham also developed and taught the South's first course in scientific agriculture and industrial chemistry. In 1860 Gilham wrote the *Manual of Instruction for the Volunteers and Militia of the United States*. It was used by the Federal Army until 1861 and by the Confederates, after the necessary changes in the title, throughout the war.

64. Couper disputes this story which is related in Smith's *History of VMI*. Couper claims that the cannon were obtained through the efforts of Adjutant General Richardson in 1847 and that President Taylor's gift was limited to the bronze barreled percussion muskets.

65. John S. Wise, *The End of an Era* (Cambridge: The Riverside Press, 1900), 101, (hereafter Wise, *Era*).

66. *Southern Recorder*, 15 November 1853.

67. "Official Register of the Officers and Cadets of the Georgia Military Institute" (1858) as quoted in Temple, *Years*, 186.

68. *Southern Recorder*, 7 July 1857.

69. O. J. Bond, *The Story of the Citadel* (Richmond: Garrett and Massie, 1936), 43, (hereafter Bond, *Citadel*).

70. Ibid.

71. Diary of Basil Manley, 23 January 1861, William Stanley Hoole Special Collections, University of Alabama. Manley would later give the invocation at Jefferson Davis's inauguration as president of the Confederate States of America on February 18, 1861.

72. Samuel Will John, "Alabama Corps of Cadets, 1860–1865," *Century Magazine*, 12 Jan. 1917, (hereafter John, "Alabama Cadets").

73. Preston to wife, 2 December 1859, Smith, *VMI History*, 164.

74. Ibid., 167–168.

75. Ibid., 167.

CHAPTER 2

1. Robert O. Sams, "The First Shot," December 1926, Citadel Archives, 4.

2. Statement, Sergeant S. E. Welch, as quoted in Bond, *Citadel*, 49.

3. Ibid., 50.

4. *New York Evening Post*, 20 January 1861.

5. C. Irvine Walker, "Reminiscences of Days in the Citadel," Citadel Archives, 14.

6. Letter, Joel D. Charles, 10 February 1861, South Caroliniana Library, University of South Carolina.

7. Couper, *One Hundred Years*, vol. 2, 24–25.

8. *Southern Recorder*, 13 November 1860.

9. Smith to Scott, October 1860, Couper, *One Hundred Years*, vol. 2, 59.

10. Ibid., 60.

11. Ibid.

12. Couper, *One Hundred Years*, vol. 2, 74.

13. Ibid., 63.

14. Bond, *Citadel*, 51–52.

15. J. B. Doorman as quoted in Couper, *One Hundred Years*, vol. 2, 63.

16. Smith to General William H. Richardson, as quoted in Couper, *One Hundred Years*, vol. 2, 80.
17. Wise, *Military History of VMI*, 131. There are various accounts of this incident which vary in small details.
18. Smith to General William H. Richardson, 18 April 1861, Couper, *One Hundred Years*, vol. 2, 81.
19. Letter to "My Dear parents . . . ," 18 April 1861, Andrew C. L. Gatewood Papers, VMI Archives, (hereafter Gatewood Letters).
20. Macon Abernathy to sister, 24 February 1861, William Stanley Hoole Special Collections, University of Alabama. Abernathy later joined the Confederate army and died in the war.
21. Letter to "My Dear parents . . . ," 18 April 1861, Gatewood Letters.
22. Cadets' petition and superintendent's answer, William Stanley Hoole Special Collections, University of Alabama, (hereafter *Petition*).
23. Ibid.
24. Ibid.
25. Wise, *Military History of VMI*, 145.
26. Couper, *One Hundred Years*, vol. 2, 107.
27. *Southern Recorder*, 2 July 1861.
28. Yates, *GMI History*, 6.
29. Wise, *Military History of VMI*, 148.
30. Letter to "My Dear parents . . . ," 28 April 1861, Gatewood Letters.
31. Sallie Brock Putnam, *Richmond During the War: Four Years of Personal Observation* (New York: G. W. Carleton, 1867), 34.
32. *Richmond Daily Examiner*, 27 April 1861.
33. Lee to Smith, 10 May 1861, Couper, *One Hundred Years*, vol. 2, 106.
34. Letter to "My Dear parents . . . ," 24 May 1861, Gatewood Letters.
35. Couper, *One Hundred Years*, vol. 2, 120.
36. Not all of the cadet drillmasters enlisted in the Confederate Army. After being furloughed from Camp Lee, Cadet Augustus B. Williams returned home in western Virginia and enlisted in the 8th Virginia (Union) Infantry. In 1862, Williams was a member of the Federal force opposing his former professor, T. J. Jackson.
37. Austill, *'60 and '61*, 4.
38. "Drummers and Fifers University Need in War of '61, Letter Shows," *Birmingham Age-Herald*, 4 November 1934, William Stanley Hoole Special Collections, University of Alabama.
39. "A University Cadet's Letter," *Alabama Historical Quarterly*, vol. 23, 1969, 289.
40. J. T. L. Preston as quoted in Couper, *One Hundred Years*, vol. 2, 97.
41. Couper, *One Hundred Years*, vol. 2, 108.
42. In his *Military History of VMI*, Wise refers to McCulloch as a volunteer acting captain at First Manassas and, in volume 2 of *One Hundred Years at VMI*, Couper lists Wight as such. Neither, however, are listed as volunteer acting captains in the *1984 VMI Register of Former Cadets*, although both are listed in the *Register* as being wounded in that battle.
43. Susan R. Hull, *Boy Soldiers of the Confederacy* (New York: Neale Publishing Co., 1905), 180, (hereafter Hull, *Boy Soldiers*).
44. J. L. Hempstead to Preston Cocke, 26 May 1899, Couper, *One Hundred Years*, vol. 2, 109.
45. Letter, Thomas D. Ranson, Hull, *Boy Soldiers*, 150–151.
46. "Drummers and Fifers."
47. *Lexington Gazette*, 10 April 1862.

48. Smith, *VMI History*, 182.
49. Ibid.

CHAPTER 3

1. Letter to Gov. J. G. Shorter, 5 September 1863, Sellers, *University History*, vol. 1, 264.
2. Letter to Governor T. H. Watts, 14 May 1864, Sellers, *University History*, vol. 1, 264; "Drummers and Fifers." Both military and civilian schools, colleges, academies, and universities were affected by the war and the loss of students. The Bastrop Military Institute closed. Superintendent Hill took the faculty and cadets of the North Carolina Military Institute with him to the 1st North Carolina Infantry's camp of instruction. Most of the school joined the regiment. Bastrop reopened in September 1867, changed its name to the Texas Military Institute the following year, and moved to Austin, Texas, in 1870. The North Carolina Military Institute never reopened. For a general discussion of the war's effect on the South's educational system, see Steven A. Channing, *Confederate Ordeal: The Southern Home Front* (Alexandria: Time-Life Books, 1984), 54–55.
3. *Southern Confederacy*, 2 May 1862.
4. Letter to "My dear Sister . . . ," 29 March 1862, Snodgrass Collection, VMI Archives, (hereafter Snodgrass Letters).
5. *Alabama Regulations*, 19.
6. Letter to Governor T. H. Watts, 29 March 1864, Sellers *University History*, vol. 1, 270.
7. John B. Patrick, *A Journal, Mar. 1861–December 25, 1865*, 7 September 1863, South Caroliniana Library, University of South Carolina, (hereafter Patrick, *Journal*).
8. Letter to "My dear Sister . . . ," 29 March 1862, Snodgrass Letters.
9. Bond, *Citadel*, 64.
10. *VMI Order Book*, VMI Archives, 123.
11. Couper, *One Hundred Years*, vol. 2, 166.
12. *Official Records of the Union and Confederate Armies in the War of the Rebellion* (Washington, D.C.: Government Printing Office, 1880–1901), Series IV, vol. 1, 1084 (hereafter Official Records, Armies).
13. Ibid., 1106–1107.
14. Letter to "Dear Sister . . . ," 29 April 1862, Snodgrass Letters.
15. Letter to "Dear Kate . . . ," no date, Snodgrass Letters.
16. Benjamin A. Colonna as quoted in Wise, *Military History of VMI*, 204.
17. The Corps' cannon have a history all to themselves, and Couper dedicates a full chapter to the cannon of VMI. Early in the war the Institute turned the four six-pounders of the cadet battery over to William N. Pendleton's Rockbridge Artillery. Pendleton, an Episcopal priest, christened the guns, "Matthew," "Mark," "Luke," and "John." The "Four Gospels" were returned to VMI after the war and now occupy places of honor in front of the cadet barracks, flanking Sir Moses Ezekiel's statue of Stonewall Jackson. Each Founder's Day, the guns thunder forth a salute to VMI.
18. Couper, *One Hundred Years*, vol. 2, 150.
19. Ibid., 152.
20. Smith, *VMI History*, 189.
21. Ibid., 189–190.
22. Ibid., 190.

23. Wise, *Military History of VMI*, 206.

24. Ibid., 192–193.

25. Ibid., 207.

26. Letter to "Dear Kate . . . ," 18 May 1862, Snodgrass Letters.

27. Smith, *VMI History*, 192.

28. Wise, *Military History of VMI*, 209.

29. Letter to "Dear Kate . . . ," 18 May 1862, Snodgrass Letters.

30. Letter to "Dear Sister . . . ," 8 June 1862, Snodgrass Letters.

31. "Superintendent's Annual Report" in *Annual Report of the Board of Visitors, July 1862*, VMI Archives, 7.

32. Sellers, *University History*, vol. 1, 274.

33. Ibid.

34. Ibid., 275.

35. Patrick, *Journal*, 14 August 1862.

36. Letter to "Dear Pa . . . ," 3 November 1862, Reid Collection, VMI Archives (hereafter Reid Letters).

37. Early in the war, the Confederate Congress authorized the appointment of Confederate States' cadets in contemplation of the establishment of a Confederate States' military academy. One was never established. Most of the cadets were assigned to units of the Confederate Army with the rank of cadet and, after October 13, 1862, the pay of a second lieutenant in the unit to which they were attached. No concerted effort was made to turn VMI into the Confederacy's West Point. And although additional cadets were appointed to VMI in 1864, most were involved in a "work-study" program which involved fighting with their units and studying when not fighting.

CHAPTER 4

1. Letter to "Dear Aunt . . . ," 28 September 1862, J. Kent Langhorne Papers, VMI Archives, (hereafter Langhorne Letters).

2. Letter to "Dear Bro . . . ," 29 November 1862, Langhorne Letters.

3. Couper, *One Hundred Years*, vol. 2, 169.

4. Ibid., 251.

5. Joseph W. Barnwell MSS, South Carolina Historical Society, 160.

6. Letter to "Dear Pa . . . ," 30 September 1862, Reid Letters.

7. John G. Barrett and Robert K. Turner, Jr., eds., *Letters of a New Market Cadet, Beverly Stanard* (Chapel Hill: University of North Carolina Press, 1961), 54, (hereafter Barrett, *Stanard Letters*).

8. Letter to Governor J. G. Shorter, 16 October 1862, Sellers, *University History*, vol. 1, 266.

9. Letter to Superintendent Smith, 3 May 1864, Couper, *One Hundred Years*, vol. 2, 251.

10. Letter to Amos Jones, 19 September 1863, Sellers, *University History*, vol. 1, 267.

11. Letter to R. Weaver, 22 September 1863, Sellers, *University History*, vol. 1, 267.

12. Letter to "Dear Pa . . . ," 3 November 1862, Reid Letters.

13. Letter to "Dear Father . . . ," 28 September 1862, Atwill Collection, VMI Archives, (hereafter Atwill Letters).

14. *VMI Order Book*, 175.

15. Kershaw, "Citadel Life," 148.

16. Ibid.

17. Wise, *Era*, 251.
18. Ibid., 283.
19. Letter to Governor J. G. Shorter, 3 February 1863, Sellers, *University History*, vol. 1, 268.
20. Diary of Cadet Charles T. Haigh, 27 March 1863, VMI Archives, (hereafter *Haigh Diary*).
21. Wise, *Era*, 290.
22. *Haigh Diary*, undated entry.
23. Wise, *Era*, 290.
24. Ibid.
25. Ibid., 271.
26. Diary of Cadet Carey Thomas, 11 March 1863, South Caroliniana Library, University of South Carolina.
27. *Haigh Diary*, undated entry.
28. Letter to "My dear Father . . . ," 2 September 1862, Atwill Letters.
29. Patrick, *Journal*, 17 September 1861.
30. Barrett, *Stanard Letters*, 43.
31. *Haigh Diary*, 11 April 1863. Haigh left the institute and was commissioned a second lieutenant in the 37th North Carolina Infantry. He was killed at Spottsylvania, Virginia, on May 12, 1864.
32. Wise, *Era*, 281.
33. Ibid., 248.
34. Letter to "Dear Pa . . . ," 14 August 1862, Reid Letters.
35. Letter to "Dear Pa . . . ," 26 August 1862, Reid Letters.
36. Letter to "Dear Sister . . . ," 22 March 1863, VMI Archives.
37. *Virginia Annual Reports for 1863*, document no. 22, as quoted in Couper, *One Hundred Years*, vol. 2, 197.
38. Smith to Adjutant General Richardson, 17 June 1864, VMI Archives.
39. Letter to Governor J. G. Shorter, 7 May 1863, Sellers, *University History*, vol. 1. 276.
40. Ibid., 275.
41. Ibid., 278.
42. Wise, *Military History of VMI*, 222.
43. Couper, *One Hundred Years*, vol. 2, 184.
44. Ibid.
45. Wise, *Era*, 270.
46. Ibid.
47. Ibid.
48. Couper, *One Hundred Years*, vol. 2, 190.
49. Patrick, *Journal*, 11 July 1863.
50. *Official Records, Armies*, Series I, vol. 28, pt. 2, 383.
51. Patrick, *Journal*, 1 September 1863.
52. Couper, *One Hundred Years*, vol. 2, 209.
53. Ibid.
54. *Stanard Letters*, 9.
55. Couper, *One Hundred Years*, vol. 2, 211.
56. Ibid., 212.
57. Ibid., 217.
58. *Superintendent's Letter Book, July 1863–January 1864*, VMI Archives.
59. Barrett, *Stanard Letters*, 24–25.

60. Ibid.
61. Couper, *One Hundred Years*, vol. 2, 244.
62. Barrett, *Stanard Letters*, 24.

CHAPTER 5

1. Letter fragment, 1864, VMI Archives.
2. Barrett, *Stanard Letters*, 47.
3. Couper, *One Hundred Years*, vol. 2, 250.
4. Letter to L. K. Polk, March 1864, Sellers, *University History*, vol. 1, 273.
5. The horses were nevertheless seized in March 1865 by order of Brigadier General William H. "Red" Jackson of Lieutenant General Nathan Bedford Forrest's command.
6. Special Order No. 64, *VMI Order Book*, VMI Archives.
7. Richardson to Smith, 15 March 1864, Couper, *One Hundred Years*, vol. 2, 253.
8. Letter to Governor T. H. Watts, 25 January 1864, Sellers, *University History*, vol. 1, 272.
9. Couper, *One Hundred Years*, vol. 3, 61–62.
10. Letter to Governor T. H. Watts, 17 March 1864, Sellers, *University History*, vol. 1, 273.
11. Capers to Wayne, 27 October 1864, Richard B. Harwell, ed., *The Confederate Reader* (New York: Longmans, Green and Co., 1957), 291 (hereafter Harwell, *Confederate Reader*).
12. Sherman was a former military school superintendent. In 1859 Sherman was hired as the first superintendent of the Louisiana Seminary of Learning and Military Academy, near Alexandria. Sherman resigned his post in January 1861. The academy's buildings burned in 1868 and the students, library, and equipment were moved to Baton Rouge, where the academy was reopened as the Louisiana State University.
13. Robert L. Rogers, "An Historical Sketch of the Georgia Military Institute, Marietta, Georgia," in Robert L. Rogers, *History of the Confederate Veterans Association of Fulton County* (Atlanta: V. P. Sisson, 1890), 82, (hereafter Rodgers, *Sketch*).
14. Oliver O. Howard, "The Struggle of Atlanta," in *Battles and Leaders of the Civil War* (New York: Castle Books, 1956), vol. 4, 198.
15. Wise, *Era*, 288.
16. Ibid., 286 287.
17. William Couper, *Virginia Military Institute and the Battle of New Market, May 15, 1864,* 4–5, (hereafter Couper, *New Market*).
18. Wise, *Era*, 291.
19. Ibid., 296.
20. Ibid., 298.
21. William C. Davis, *The Battle of New Market* (Garden City: Doubleday, 1975), 91, (hereafter Davis, *New Market*).
22. Wise, *Era*, 307.
23. Davis, *New Market*, 92.
24. Ibid.
25. Letter of Eliza Clinedinst Crim, quoted in Henry A. Wise, *Drawing Out the Man: The VMI Story* (Charlottesville: University Press of Virginia, 1978, 41. Wise; *Military History of VMI*, 58.

26. Wise, *Era*, 299.
27. Read's twisted musket is on display at the New Market Battlefield Memorial Museum.
28. Wise, *Era*, 299.
29. Report, Lt. Col. Ship, 4 July 1864, VMI Archives.
30. Wise, *Era*, 301.
31. Davis, *New Market*, 119.
32. Report, Lt. Col. Ship, 4 July 1864, VMI Archives.
33. Wise, *Era*, 302. Preston was the son of Colonel J.T.L. Preston and had lost an arm in battle earlier in the war.
34. Davis, *New Market*, 132.
35. Hull, *Boy Soldiers*, 93–94.
36. Wise, *Era*, 304.
37. Wise, *Military History of VMI*, 334; John S. Wise quoted in Hull, *Boy Soldiers*, 95.
38. John S. Wise as quoted in Hull, *Boy Soldiers*, 95.
39. Ibid.
40. Letter, 28 July 1864, Atwill Letters.
41. Wise, *Era*, 307.
42. Couper, *One Hundred Years*, vol. 3, 11.
43. Wise, *Era*, 308.
44. Yates, *GMI History*, 8.
45. Wise, *Era*, 310.
46. Two of DuPont's solid shot are allegedly still embedded in the central tower of the "old barrack's" east wing; Couper, though, claims they are painted dumbbells placed in the shellholes to replace the cannonballs which fell out long ago. As a U.S. senator, DuPont introduced legislation in 1914 which resulted in the reimbursement of VMI for some of Hunter's destruction. Jackson Memorial Hall, the cadet chapel and home to Benjamin West Clinedinst's monumental painting of the cadets' charge at New Market, was built with the money received.
47. Affidavit, J. M. Schoonmaker to U.S. Senate Committee of Claims, 10 March 1914, Wise, *Military History of VMI*, 368.
48. Diary of Private J. O. Humphreys, Couper, *One Hundred Years*, vol. 3, 35.
49. Diary of F. S. Reeder, Couper, *One Hundred Years*, vol. 3, 33–34.
50. Charles R. Williams, *Diary and Letters of Rutherford B. Hayes* (1922), vol. 4, 473–474, Couper, *One Hundred Years*, vol. 2, 33.
51. George E. Pond, *The Shenandoah Valley in 1864* (New York: Scribners, 1883), 30. The statue was later returned to its place in front of Washington Arch by David Hunter Strother, Virginia's Reconstruction adjutant general and ex officio member of VMI's Board of Visitors.
52. Couper, *One Hundred Years*, vol. 3, 39.
53. Report, Smith to Adjutant General Richardson, 27 July 1864, VMI Archives.
54. Wise, *Era*, 312.
55. *Official Records, Armies*, Series I, vol. 37, pt. 1, 763.
56. Wise, *Era*, 314.
57. Ibid.
58. Report, Smith to Adjutant General Richardson, 27 July 1864, VMI Archives.
59. Couper, *One Hundred Years*, vol. 3, 53.
60. Temple, *Years*, 323.
61. *New York Tribune*, July 20, 1864.

62. *Official Records, Armies*, Series I, vol. 35, pt. 2, 505.

63. Gustavus W. Smith, "The Georgia Militia About Atlanta," *Battles and Leaders*, vol. 4, 333.

64. Yates, *GMI History*, 12.

65. Rodgers, *Sketch*, 92.

66. Capers to Wayne, 27 October 1864, Harwell, *Confederate Reader*, 291.

67. *Official Records, Armies*, Series I, vol. 35, pt. 2, 505.

68. Thomas, *Academy History*, 211.

69. 1864 Report of Board of Visitors as quoted in Thomas, *Academy History*, 176.

70. Ibid., 175.

71. John, "Alabama Cadets," 12.

72. *Official Records, Armies*, Series I, vol. 38, pt. 2, 908.

73. John, "Alabama Cadets," 13. Soon after the skirmish, Rousseau, with some Rebels following at a discreet distance, withdrew east along the railroad toward Auburn on his way to join Sherman in Georgia. However, the stand at Chehaw had saved the two railroad bridges there from destruction. Sherman, who ordered the raid, was not pleased with this result.

74. *Montgomery Daily Mail*, 24 July 1864.

75. *Selma Dispatch*, 27 July 1864.

76. John, "Alabama Cadets," 13.

77. There is some evidence that not all of the cadets returned to the university. In a 1903 letter to former Cadet E.N.C. Snow, Commandant Murfee wrote that "one company remained in the [Liddell's] brigade and did heroic service in the engagement at Blakely in 1865" (*Alabama Historical Quarterly*, Spring 1943). The *Official Records* also contain a report by Federal Captain S.M. Eaton dated January 23, 1865, in which he states that information given him by a deserter indicated there were two hundred "Tuscaloosa cadets" in Mobile, (*Official Records, Armies*, Series I, vol. 48, 617). While their numbers were almost certainly exaggerated, the report does tend to confirm Murfee's statement that part of the corps was in the Mobile area in early 1865. Unfortunately, there appears to be no further information on the strength or activities of this detachment.

78. David Nevin, *Sherman's March: Atlanta to the Sea* (Alexandria: Time-Life, 1986), 33.

79. Yates, *GMI History*, 11.

80. The superintendent's house still stands off of Powder Springs Road near the Marietta Conference Center and Resort, which now occupies the former site of the Georgia Military Institute. During a visit to Marietta in 1988, I asked the gracious owner of the house, Mrs. Frank Owenby, how it managed to escape destruction. She related a local legend that it was spared by Sherman since he and Brumby were friends at West Point. Mrs. Owenby confessed that she did not believe this and it was her opinion that the Federals either forgot, overlooked, or lacked the time to destroy the building. This legend, while romantic, is probably nothing more than that since Brumby and Sherman were not cadets at West Point at the same time. The house was recently purchased by the city of Marietta.

81. Gustavus W. Smith, "The Georgia Militia During Sherman's March to the Sea," *Battles and Leaders*, vol. 4, 667.

82. *Official Records, Armies*, Series I, vol. 53, 32.

83. Ibid., 36.

84. *Atlanta Journal*, 27 April 1928.

85. *Charleston Courier*, 3 March 1864.

86.   Barnwell MSS, 168.
87.   George M. Coffin, "My Recollection of Fight at Tulifinny Creek, South Carolina, in December, 1864," in Bond, *Citadel*, 76 (hereafter Coffin, "Recollection").
88.   *Official Records, Armies*, Series I, vol. 56, 444.
89.   Ibid.
90.   Ibid.
91.   Farish C. Furman MSS, 28 December 1864, South Caroliniana Library, University of South Carolina.
92.   John C. Sellers MSS, Citadel Archives, 3.
93.   Coffin, "Recollection," 77.
94.   Ibid.
95.   *Official Records, Armies*, Series I, vol. 56, 444.
96.   Coffin, "Recollection," 77.
97.   *Official Records, Armies*, Series I, vol. 56, 448.
98.   Benjamin S. Williams, "A Gallant Soldier's Story," *Sunday News*, 2 September 1897.
99.   Thomas, *Academy History*, 212.
100. *Official Records, Armies*, Series I, vol. 56, 441.
101. Ibid. Arsenal Lieutenant R. O. Sams put Federal casualties from the engagements of December 7 and 9 at three hundred.
102. Coffin, "Recollection," 77.
103. Furman MSS, 28 December 1864.
104. *Official Records, Armies*, Series I, vol. 56, 445.
105. Thomas, *Academy History*, 208.
106. Yates, *GMI History*, 16.
107. The cadets' cannon were held as trophies of war for years. Two were finally returned to the state of Georgia and were placed on the grounds of the state capitol. Another was obtained by the citizens of Marietta in 1910 and placed in the city's Confederate Cemetery, almost directly across the Powder Springs Road from College Hill. The fourth gun, mounted on a rock taken from Kennesaw Mountain, was unveiled on the grounds of the Marietta Country Club, the former site of GMI, on April 27, 1928, in a ceremony attended by Cordelia Brumby, one of the superintendent's descendants, and eight of the fifteen surviving cadets of the institute. This gun was removed from its original location and is now stored in the basement of the Marietta Conference Center and Resort. The owners of the conference center plan to display the cannon on a replica gun carriage in the hotel lobby.
108. Rodgers, *Sketch*, 97.
109. 1900 *VMI Bomb*, 16.
110. Ibid., 17.
111. Ibid.
112. Ship to Smith, 2 November 1864, VMI Archives.
113. Ibid.
114. Ship to Smith, 11 November 1864, VMI Archives.
115. Ibid.
116. Article in "The Cadet," 3 January 1914.
117. Ibid.
118. Couper, *One Hundred Years*, vol. 3, 78.
119. General Order No. 23, 10 December 1864, in Wise, *Military History of VMI*, 394.
120. Article in "The Cadet," 3 January 1914.
121. "A Boy's Experiences in the Civil War, 1860–1865," in Hull, *Boy Soldiers*, 105, (hereafter "Experiences").

122. "Experiences," 106.
123. Wise, *Military History of VMI*, 404.

CHAPTER 6

1. C. Vann Woodward, ed., *Mary Chesnut's Civil War* (New Haven: Yale University Press, 1981), 733.
2. Ibid., 731.
3. Ibid., 704.
4. The flag, presented to the corps of cadets by the Washington Light Infantry Regiment in 1857, was "of blue Lyon's silk, displaying on one side the arms of the State of South Carolina and the name of the Institution, and on the other side an elaborate wreath of oak leaves, enfolding the inscription—Fort Moultrie, Cowpens, King's Mountain, Eutaw Springs, and below, 'Out Heritage'—the inscription being the same as that on the face of the Cowpens Monument erected on that battlefield by the Washington Light Infantry in the year 1856" (Thomas, *Academy History*, 203). The banner survived the war and now occupies a place of honor at the Citadel.
5. Robert L. Crewdson, "Burning Columbia," *Civil War Times Illustrated*, 12 October 1981.
6. Ibid., 13.
7. Ibid., 12.
8. Ibid., 13.
9. The Arsenal officers' quarters were later converted into the executive mansion for the governor of South Carolina. The records and equipment of the Citadel were also destroyed when the Arsenal was torched.
10. On February 21, Beauregard related to General Wade Hampton: "[The] State Cadets moved with General Garlington across the Catawba. Governor Magrath stated they cannot cross State line" (*Official Records, Armies*, Series I, vol. 47, pt. 2, 1245). Four days later, Magrath asked Beauregard to detach the cadets to oppose a rumored raid by Federal Major General George Stoneman (*Official Records, Armies*, Series I, vol. 47, pt. 2, 1274).
11. Thomas, *Academy History*, 198.
12. Robert O. Sams, "The Last Shot," (1926), Citadel Archives, 5.
13. During the seminary's first decade a number of VMI alumni served on the faculty.
14. As already noted, a loss of students was typical in all Southern educational institutions. However, the seminary also had to fight the effect of conscription and requested from President Davis an exemption from the draft for its students and faculty. Although Davis's reply is not recorded, the seminary had no better luck than the other military academies.
15. After the battle the cadets were used to guard Federal prisoners confined in Tallahassee's Masonic Hall, as well as the railroad bridges and commissary stores on various occasions throughout 1864. Cadet William Rawls recalled, "When the prisoners began to come in they had to be guarded, and the Cadets were placed in the Masonic hall, and the Baptist church, to guard those who were wounded. Afterward they were called upon at any time they were needed to perform military duty." (David J. Coles, "Garnet and Gray: The History of the West Florida Seminary During the Civil War.")
16. *Official Records of the Union and Confederate Navies in the War of the Rebellion*, (Washington, D.C.: Government Printing Office, 1894–1927), Series I, vol. 17, no. 1, 816, (hereafter *Official Records, Navies*).
17. Ibid., 817.

18. Ibid., 814.
19. Susan Bradford Eppes, *Through Some Eventful Years* (Gainesville: University of Florida Press, 1968), 256 (hereafter Eppes, *Eventful Years*). This statement, in common with other entries in Mrs. Eppes' "diary," is not quite true. Several of the Southern capitals were still in Rebel hands in early March, although their days were numbered.
20. *Official Records, Navies*, Series I, vol. 17, 819.
21. Gloria Jahoda, *The Other Florida* (New York: Charles Scribner's Sons, 1967), 176.
22. Coles, "Garnet and Gray," 6.
23. The only surviving example of a wartime Florida Military Institute cadet uniform belonged to Beard. The uniform, on display in the Museum of the Confederacy in Richmond, Virginia, is a butternut-colored shell jacket with Louisiana buttons. It was possibly among the equipment obtained by Superintendent Johnson during a trip to Virginia in early 1864.
24. In 1918, an "Old Confederate" writing in the Tallahassee *Daily Democrat* charged that the cadets became scared and refused to advance after seeing the dead man. A vehement debate ensured in the paper with some calling the charges "vile and untruthful." Recent research indicates that the "Old Confederate" may have been Susan Bradford Eppes (Coles, "Garnet and Gray," 8).
25. Based on a conversation with one of the cadets, Susan Bradford Eppes claims in her postwar "diary" that the cadets were posted as a sort of headquarters' guard "behind General Miller," the safest place on the field (Eppes, *Eventful Years,* 262).
26. *Official Records, Armies*, Series I, vol. 49, 60.
27. Eppes, *Eventful Years*, 260.
28. *Official Records, Armies*, Series I, vol. 49, 60.
29. Marjory Stoneman Douglas, *Florida: The Long Frontier* (New York: Harper & Row, 1967), 194.
30. *Official Records, Armies*, Series I, vol. 49, 61.
31. Coles, "Garnet and Gray," 9.
32. Ibid.
33. *Official Records, Armies*, Series I, vol. 49. 61.
34. Ibid.
35. *Official Records, Navies*, Series I, vol. 17, 819–820.
36. Ibid., 820.
37. *Official Records, Armies*, Series I, vol. 49, 64.
38. Eppes, *Eventful Years*, 261.
39. Ibid., 262.
40. Ibid., 261.
41. *Official Records, Armies*, Series I, vol. 8, 471.
42. Eppes, *Eventful Years*, 262.
43. *Official Records, Armies*, Series I, vol. 49, 63.
44. Ibid.
45. Coles, "Garnet and Gray," 10.
46. One song sung by young girls in Bel Air, Florida, was to the tune of "Dixie":
    The Young Cadets were the first to go
    To meet and drive away the foe . . .
    [They] fought against the combined powers
    Of Yanks and Blacks and shrapnel showers . . .
    (Coles, "Garnet and Gray," 10.)
47. Coles, "Garnet and Gray," 10.
48. Eppes, *Eventful Years*, 262.

49. *Jacksonville Union*, 8 April 1865.
50. Saturday classes remained a feature of cadet life until 1995.
51. Couper, *One Hundred Years*, vol. 3, 79.
52. "*Experiences*," 109.
53. Ibid., 109.
54. Ibid., 110.
55. *Official Records, Armies*, Series IV, vol. 3, 1093.
56. Couper, *One Hundred Years*, vol. 3, 82.
57. Article in "The Cadet," 3 January 1914.
58. Ibid.
59. Ibid.
60. Ibid.
61. "*Experiences*," 114.
62. Ibid., 115.
63. *Official Records, Armies*, Series IV, vol. 49, pt. 1, 418.
64. Ibid., 421.
65. Sellers, *University History*, vol. 1, 283.
66. John, "Alabama Cadets," 13.
67. James G. Cowan, "The Destruction of the University of Alabama," *Alabama University Bulletin*, (January 1901) vol. 1, no. 1, in William S. Hoole and Elizabeth H. McArthur, *The Yankee Invasion of West Alabama, March–April 1865* (University: Confederate Publishing Co., 1985), 43, (hereafter Cowan, "Destruction").
68. Ibid., 44.
69. John Massey, *Reminiscences* (Nashville 1916) in William S. Hoole and Elizabeth H. McArthur, *The Yankee Invasion of West Alabama, March–April 1865* (University: Confederate Publishing Co., 1985), 49.
70. John Flournoy Ponder, "Reminiscences of a Student of 1865," *University of Alabama Alumni News* (December 1938) vol. 22, no. 3, in William S. Hoole and Elizabeth H. McArthur *The Yankee Invasion of West Alabama, March–April 1865* (University: Confederate Publishing Co., 1985), 37.
71. Cowan, "Destruction," 45.
72. Ibid., 46.
73. Legend has it that the only book saved from the conflagration was a copy of the *Koran* taken by the Federal officer charged with the Rotunda's destruction. In reality, many volumes were later salvaged and some of the charred books are still in the university's library.
74. Thomas P. Clinton, "The Military Operation of General John T. Croxton in West Alabama, 1865," *Publications of the Alabama Historical Society*, (1904), vol. 4, 457, in Malcom C. McMillian, *The Alabama Confederate Reader* (University: University of Alabama Press, 1963).
75. On April 23, 1884, 46,080 acres of public land were given to the university by the United States Congress as payment for the damage inflicted by Croxton. In 1898 the university asked the state for $300,000 payment for the destroyed Rotunda and other buildings. The General Assembly refused, saying that the state of Alabama was not responsible for the destruction of the university.
76. Ponder, "Reminiscences," 40.
77. Letter of Warfield C. L. Richardson, 8 April 1865, Chenault Collection, William S. Hoole Special Collections, University of Alabama.
78. Report, J. P. Thomas, Bond *Citadel*, 85.
79. *Official Records, Armies*, Series I, vol. 53, 420.
80. Ibid.

CHAPTER 7

1. Wise, *Military History of VMI*, 168. This comment is often quoted but has never been, as far as this author has been able to determine, traced to its original source.
2. *Official Records, Armies*, Series I, vol. 2, 593.
3. VMI and Alabama figures are for alumni while South Carolina Military Academy's numbers count graduates only. The latter's numbers are based on research by Mr. Jim Moody as reported in Gary Baker's *Cadets in Gray*, 187. None of these figures includes graduates or alumni who served as enlisted men. VMI's statistics do include two deserters. It should be remembered that most of the Alabama alumni did not experience the university's military system.
4. Couper, *One Hundred Years*, vol. 3, 106.
5. Richard McMurry, *Two Great Rebel Armies* (Chapel Hill: The University of North Carolina Press, 1989). Chapter 6 of this book contains a discussion regarding the value state military school alumni added to the Army of Northern Virginia.
6. *Official Records, Armies*, Series IV, vol. 1, 267.
7. "University Cadet Corps," *Alabama Historical Quarterly* (Spring 1943): 56, (hereafter "University Corps").
8. "University of Alabama War Graduates 1865," William Stanley Hoole Special Collections, University of Alabama.
9. *Official Records, Armies*, Series IV, vol. 2, 593.
10. Ibid.
11. J. B. Jones, *A Rebel War Clerk's Diary At The Confederate States Capital* (1866; reprint, Alexandria: Time-Life Books, 1982), vol. 2, 7.
12. *Official Records, Armies*, Series IV, vol. 2, 472.
13. Yancey to Cooper, March 1865, courtesy of Deveraux D. Cannon, Jr.
14. *Official Records, Armies*, Series IV, vol. 53, 1157.
15. The Confederate States Naval Academy opened in July 1863 aboard the schoolship CSS *Patrick Henry*, anchored in the James River between Richmond and the Drewry's Bluff fortifications. Its cadets manned the James River defenses while on the schoolship and served on Confederate warships as part of their education. The Naval Academy was the only Confederate States military academy.
16. *Natchez Daily Courier*, 27 September 1861.
17. This estimate is based on an extrapolation of available figures for particular training encampments applied to other encampments of similar size for which figures were unavailable.
18. Hull, *Boy Soldiers*, 13. The term boy, as used in the Civil War, applied to those under conscription age as well as to young men who were unmarried, had never lived away from home, and who were not employed in a profession or trade.
19. Davis, *New Market*, 175.
20. Hull, *Boy Soldiers*, 94.
21. John F. Marszalek, ed., *The Diary of Emma Holmes* (Baton Rouge: LSU Press, 1979), 175.
22. "University Corps," 58.

CHAPTER 8

1. Of the years VMI is still in session, a special dress parade is held on May 15. On that day the names of the ten cadets killed at New Market are added to the normal roll call. As each name is called, a cadet steps forward and reports, "died on the field of honor, sir." This tradition was adopted from the ceremony used by the French Forty-sixth Regiment to honor the memory of La Tour d'Auvergne. In

recognition of his bravery and modesty, d'Auvergne was proclaimed "First Grenadier of France" by First Counsel Napoleon Bonaparte on April 27, 1800. When he was killed in battle at Oberhausen on June 27, Napoleon decreed: "His name is to be kept on the pay list and roll of his company. It will be called at all parades and a non-commissioned officer will reply '*mort au champ d'honneur*.'" (Couper, *One Hundred Years*, vol. 2, 323–324).

2. F. G. Rood, W. M. Roch, and A. J. Simpson to P. M. B. Young, 16 September 1873, Lynwood M. Holland, "The Georgia Military Institute, The West Point of Georgia: 1851–1864," *Georgia Historical Quarterly*, (1959), vol. 43, 246–247.

3. Thomas, *Academy History*, 229.

4. *The 1989 Register of Former Cadets of the Virginia Military Institute, Sesquicentennial Edition* (Lexington: VMI Alumni Association, 1989), 27.

5. Ibid., 27.

6. "288 S. C. Hist. and Genealogical Magazine," courtesy of Mrs. Julia Yates Maloney.

BIBLIOGRAPHY

UNPUBLISHED SOURCES

Abernathy Folder. William Stanley Hoole Special Collections. University of Alabama.

Anderson, James A. Radio broadcast transcript. Typescript in William Stanley Hoole Special Collections. University of Alabama. 21 April 1941.

———. "Major Caleb Huse." William Stanley Hoole Special Collections. University of Alabama.

Atwill Collection. VMI Archives.

Austill, H. *The University in '60 and '61*. William Stanley Hoole Special Collections. University of Alabama.

Barnwell, Joseph W. MSS. South Carolina Historical Society.

Charles, Joel D. MSS. South Caroliniana Library. University of South Carolina.

Coffin, Amory. Letter to "My dear Francis," Citadel Archives. 11 April 1911.

Coles, David J. "Garnet and Gray: The History of the West Florida Seminary During the Civil War." 1995.

Cotton, J. A. M. B. L. Letter to "Dear Aunt . . . ," Julia Yates Maloney Collection. 24 May 1861.

"Destruction of the University." William Stanley Hoole Special Collections. University of Alabama.

Duncan, D. P. Folder. South Caroliniana Library. University of South Carolina.

Furman, Farish C. MSS South Caroliniana Library. University of South Carolina.

Gatewood Collection. VMI Archives.

Haigh, Charles T. Diary. VMI Archives.

Jefferies, Richard M. *Address By The Honorable Richard M. Jefferies*. 18 December 1942.

Langhorne Collection. VMI Archives.

Manley, Basil. Diary. William Stanley Hoole Special Collections. University of Alabama.

McQueen, J. "The 1900 Student Rebellion at the University of Alabama." University History Folder, William Stanley Hoole Special Collections. University of Alabama. 1941.

Midkiff, Martha Lynn. *The First Hundred Years: A General History of Student Affairs At The University of Alabama*. Master's thesis, University of Alabama, 1978.

Patrick, John B. *A Journal, March 23, 1861–December 25, 1865*. South Caroliniana Library. University of South Carolina.

Petition of Alabama Cadets and Superintendent's Answer. William Stanley Hoole Special Collections. University of Alabama. April 1861.

Preston, John Thomas Lewis. *Historical Sketch of the Establishment and Organization of the Virginia Military Institute.* VMI Archives.

Reid Collection. VMI Archives.

Report, Lt. Col. Scott Ship on Battle of New Market. 4 July 1864. VMI Archives.

Sams, R. O. *The First Shot.* Citadel Archives. December 1926.

Shield, John H. Letter. VMI Archives.

Simpkins, William Stewart. Statement. Citadel Archives. 24 May 1920.

Snodgrass Collection. VMI Archives.

Thomas, Carey. Diary. South Caroliniana Library. University of South Carolina.

"288 S. C. Hist. and Geneological Magazine." Julia Yates Maloney Collection.

University of Alabama Quartermaster Book. William Stanley Hoole Special Collection. University of Alabama.

"University of Alabama War Graduates 1865." William Stanley Hoole Special Collections. University of Alabama.

Van Adder, Charles. *Colonel Aaron B. Hardcastle, 45th Mississippi Infantry.*

Various Order and Letter Books. VMI Archives.

Various *Annual Report of the Board of Visitors.* VMI Archives.

Walker, C. Irvine. *Reminiscences of Days in the Citadel.* Citadel Archives.

ARTICLES

"A University Cadet's Letter." *Alabama Historical Quarterly*, vol. 23, 1969.

Agnew, James B. "Hellions From Marion Square." *Civil War Times Illustrated*, vol. 21, May 1982.

Armistead, William. "Alabama Corps of Cadets." *North South Trader*, March 1975.

Barrett, John G. and Richard M. McMurry. "VMI in the Civil War." *A Crowd of Honorable Youths*, Ed. Thomas W. Davis. Lexington: VMI Sesquicentennial Committee, 1989, 31–45.

Coles, David J. and Robert Bruce Graetz. "The Garnet and Gray: West Florida Seminary in the Civil War." *United Daughters of the Confederacy Magazine*, January 1989.

Conrad, James L. "The Katydid Cadets." *Civil War Times Illustrated*, vol. 21, May 1982.

———. "Final Test of Courage." *Military History*, vol. 4, December 1987.

———. "Training In Treason." *Civil War Times Illustrated*, vol. 30, October 1991.

Crewdson, Robert L. "Burning Columbia." *Civil War Times Illustrated*, October 1981.

Davis, William C. "The Day at New Market." *Civil War Times Illustrated*, vol. 10, July 1971.

———. "Tall Tales of the Civil War." *Civil War Times Illustrated*, vol. 35, August 1996.

Grimsley, Mark. "Burning Down the South." *Civil War Times Illustrated*, vol. 34, September–October 1995.

Halsey, Ashley Jr. "Cadet Muskets." *American Rifleman*, October 1986.

Hathaway, Thomas C. Jr. "VMI Insignia." *VMI Alumni Review*, Spring 1985.

———. "One Hundred and Fifty Years of Virginia Military Institute Uniforms." *A Crowd of Honorable Youths*, Ed. Thomas W. Davis. Lexington: VMI Sesquicentennial Committee, 1989, 89–103.

Holland, Lynwood M. "The Georgia Military Institute, The West Point of Georgia: 1851–1864." *Georgia Historical Quarterly*, vol. 43, 1959.

John, Samuel Williamson. "Alabama Corps of Cadets, 1860–1865." *Century Magazine*, January 1917.

————. "Katydids Who Were Not Captured." *Confederate Veteran*, vol. XI, July 1903.

Kershaw, John. "Reminiscences of Citadel Life: 1864–65." *1911 Citadel Annual*.

Mann, B. David. "They Were Heard From: VMI Alumni in the Civil War." *VMI Alumni Review*, Spring 1985.

Martin, Abbott C. "The Cotton Letters." *Virginia Historical Magazine*.

McCorvey, Thomas C. "Southern Cadets In Action." *Harper's Magazine*, November 1889.

McMurry, Richard. "Sherman's Savannah Campaign." *Civil War Times Illustrated*, vol. 21, January 1983.

————. "Riding Through Alabama." *Civil War Times Illustrated*, vol. 20, August and October 1981.

Miller, Edward A. Jr. "VMI Men Who Wore Yankee Blue, 1861–1865." *VMI Alumni Review*, Spring 1996.

Naiswald, L. Van Loan. "Little Devils with the White Flag." *Civil War Times*, vol. 3, February 1962.

Reed, Thomas J. "Valley in Flames." *America's Civil War*, July 1989.

Riggs, David F. "'Put The Boys In'." *Civil War Times Illustrated*, vol. 18, January 1980.

Rudolph, Jack. "The Children's Crusade." *Civil War Times Illustrated*, vol. 21, May 1982.

Schafer, Elizabeth D. "Jaded Mules, Twisted Rails, and Razed Depots." *Civil War*, vol. 9, January–February 1991.

Selcer, Richard F. "Youthful Innocence Shattered." *America's Civil War*, March 1989. *The Cadet*, 3 January 1914.

"The Campaign for Atlanta." *Civil War Times Illustrated*, vol. 3, July 1964.

"The Georgia Military Institute at Marietta." *United Service Journal*, December 1881.

"University Cadet Corps." *Alabama Historical Quarterly*, Spring 1943.

Williams, Benjamin S. "A Gallant Soldier's Story." *Sunday News*, 2 September 1897.

Williams, Robert W. and Ralph A. Wooster, eds. "A Cadet At Bastrop Military Institute: The Letters of Issac Dunbar Affleck." *Texas Military History*, vol. 6, Spring, 1967.

BOOKS

Allardice, Bruce S. *More Generals In Gray*. Baton Rouge: Louisiana State University Press, 1995.

Baker, Gary R. *Cadets In Gray: The Story of the Cadets of the South Carolina Military Academy and the Cadet Rangers in the Civil War*. Columbia: Palmetto Bookworks, 1989.

Barrett, John G. and Robert K. Turner, Jr., eds. *Letters of a New Market Cadet, Beverly Standard*. Chapel Hill: University of North Carolina Press, 1961.

Bond, O. J. *The Story of the Citadel*. Richmond: Garrett and Massie, 1936.

Brice, Marshall M. *Conquest of a Valley*. Charlottesville: University of Virginia Press, 1965.

Buel, C. and R. Johnson, eds. *Battles and Leaders of the Civil War*. New York: Castle Books.

Capers, Ellison, IV. *Capers Connections 1684–1984*. Spartanburg: The Reprint Co., 1992.

Citadel Alumni Directory 1842–1959. The Citadel, 1960.

Channing, Steven A. *Confederate Ordeal: The Southern Home Front*. Alexandria: Time-Life Books, 1984.

Couper, William. *One Hundred Years at VMI*. Richmond: Garrett and Massie, 1939.

————. *Virginia Military Institute and the Battle of New Market, May 15, 1864*.

Davis, Burke. *Sherman's March*. New York: Random House, 1980.

Davis, William C. *The Battle of New Market*. Garden City: Doubleday, 1975.

Douglas, Marjory Stoneman. *Florida: The Long Frontier*. New York: Harper & Row, 1967.

Eby, Cecil D., ed. *A Virginia Yankee in the Civil War-The Diaries of David Hunter*. Chapel Hill: University of North Carolina Press, 1961.

Eppes, Susan Bradford. *Through Some Eventful Years*. Gainesville: University of Florida Press, 1968.

Fleming, Walter L. *Civil War and Reconstruction in Alabama*. New York: Columbia University Press, 1905.

Furgurson, Ernest B. *Ashes of Glory: Richmond at War*. New York: Alfred A. Knopf, 1996.

Georgia Senate Journal 1863.

Grimsley, Mark. *The Hard Hand of War*. New York: Cambridge University Press, 1995.

Harwell, Richard B., ed. *The Confederate Reader*. New York: Longmans, Green and Co., 1957.

Hoole, William S. *The Yankee Invasion of West Alabama, March–April, 1865*. University: Confederate Publishing Co., 1985.

Hull, Susan R. *Boy Soldiers of the Confederacy*. New York: Neale Publishing Co., 1905.

Jahoda, Gloria. *The Other Florida*. New York: Charles Scribner's Sons, 1967.

Jones, J. B. *A Rebel War Clerk's Diary At the Confederate States Capital*. 1866. Reprint. Alexandria: Time-Life Books, 1982.

Jones, James Pickett. *Yankee Blitzkrieg: Wilson's Raid Through Alabama and Georgia*. Athens: The University of Georgia Press, 1976.

Law, Thomas L. *Citadel Cadets: The Journal of Cadet Tom Law*. ed. John A. Law. Clinton: PC Press, 1941.

Lewis, Thomas A. *The Shenandoah In Flames: The Valley Campaign of 1864*. Alexandria: Time-Life Books, 1987.

Lucas, Marion Brunson. *Sherman and the Burning of Columbia*. College Station: Texas A & M University Press, 1976.

Marszalek, John F., ed. *The Diary of Emma Holmes*. Baton Rouge: Louisiana State University Press, 1979.

McMillian, Malcom C. *The Alabama Confederate Reader*. University: The University of Alabama Press, 1963.

McMurry, Richard. *Two Great Rebel Armies*. Chapel Hill: The University of North Carolina Press, 1989.

Nevin, David. *Sherman's March: Atlanta to the Sea*. Alexandria: Time-Life Books, 1986.

Official Records of the Union and Confederate Armies in the War of the Rebellion. Washington, D.C.: Government Printing Office, 1880–1901.

Official Records of the Union and Confederate Navies in the War of the Rebellion. Washington, D.C.: Government Printing Office, 1894–1927.

Pond, George E. *The Shenandoah Valley in 1864*. New York: Scribners, 1883.

Putnam, Sallie Brock. *Richmond During the War: Four Years of Personal Observations*. 1867. Reprint. Alexandria: Time-Life Books, 1981.

Ratchford, James W. *Some Reminiscences of Persons and Incidents of the Civil War*. Austin: Shoal Creek Publishers, 1971.

Regulations of the Georgia Military Institute. Atlanta: C. R. Hanleiter, 1857.

Regulations of the Military Academies of South Carolina. Columbia: R. W. Gibbes, 1858.

Regulations for the University of Alabama at Tuscaloosa. Southern Methodist Publishing House, 1861.

Regulations for the Virginia Military Institute at Lexington, Virginia. Richmond: Macfarlane and Fergusson, 1854.

Robertson, James I., Jr. *The Stonewall Brigade*. Baton Rouge: Louisiana State University Press, 1963.

Rodgers, Robert L. *History of the Confederate Veterans Association of Fulton County*. Atlanta: V. P. Sisson, 1890.

Sherman, William T. *Memoirs of General William T. Sherman*. Bloomington: Indiana University Press, 1957.

Smith, Francis H. *History of the Virginia Military Institute*. Lynchburg: J. P. Bell Co., 1912.

Sommers, Richard J. *Richmond Redeemed: The Siege at Petersburg*. Garden City: Doubleday, 1981.

Tanner, Robert G. *Stonewall In the Valley: Thomas J. "Stonewall" Jackson's Shenandoah Valley Campaign Spring 1862*. Mechanicsburg: Stackpole, 1996.

Temple, Sara B. G. *The First Hundred Years: A Short History of Cobb County, In Georgia*. Atlanta: Walter W. Brown Pub Co., 1935.

The 1989 VMI Register of Former Cadets: Sesquicentennial Edition. Lexington: VMI Alumni Association, 1989.

Thomas, John Peyre. *The History of the South Carolina Military Academy*. Charleston: Walker, Evans & Cogswell, 1893.

Turner, Edward Raymond. *The New Market Campaign*. Richmond: Whittet & Shepperson, 1912.

Vandiver, Frank E. *Jubal's Raid: General Early's Famous Attack on Washington in 1864*. Westport: Greenwood Publishers, 1960.

Warner, Ezra J. *Generals In Gray*. Baton Rouge: Louisiana State University Press, 1959.

———. *Generals in Blue*. Baton Rouge: Louisiana State University Press, 1964.

Wiles, A.G.D. *The Boys Behind the Gun*. Charleston: The Citadel, 1972.

Wise, Jennings C. *The Military History of the Virginia Military Institute from 1839*. Lynchburg: J. P. Bell & Co., 1915.

Wise, Henry A. *Drawing Out the Man: The VMI Story*. Charlottesville: The University Press of Virginia, 1978.

Wise, John S. *The End of an Era*. Cambridge: The Riverside Press, 1900.

Woodward, C. Vann, ed. *Mary Chesnut's Civil War*. New Haven: Yale University Press, 1981.

Yates, Bowling C. *History of the Georgia Military Institute, Marietta, Georgia, Including the Confederate Military Service of the Cadet Battalion*. 1968.

———. *Historical Highlights of Cobb County*. Marietta: Cobb Exchange Bank, 1973.

NEWSPAPERS

Atlanta Journal, 27 April 1928.

Birmingham Age-Herald, Alabama. 4 November 1934.

Buchanan Advocate, Virginia. 20 January 1836.

Charleston Daily Courier, South Carolina. 3 March 1864; 10 December 1864.

Charleston Mercury, South Carolina. 5 January 1861.

Frank Leslie's Illustrated Newspaper, 10 September 1864.

Harper's Weekly, 13 August 1864.

Lexington Gazette, Virginia. 10 April 1862.

Marietta Constitutional Union, Georgia. 20 May 1852.

Milledgeville Southern Recorder, Georgia. 15 November 1853, 7 July 1857; 9 November 1858; 22 April 1859; 3 May 1859; 19 July 1859; 13 November 1860; 2 July 1864.

Montgomery Daily Mail, Alabama. 24 July 1864.

Natchez Daily Courier, Mississippi. 27 September 1861.

New York Tribune, 20 July 1864.

Richmond Daily Examiner, Virginia. 27 April 1861.

Rockbridge County News, Lexington, Virginia. 14 October 1926.

Selma Dispatch, Alabama. 27 July 1864.

Selma Free Press, Alabama. 12 August 1837.

Southern Confederacy, 2 May 1862.

INDEX

Abernathy, Macon
  advice on soldiering, 36–37;
    death of, 173n.20
Adams, Daniel W., 50
Adams, Samuel, 98
Alexander, A. H.
  death of, 109
Anderson, J. K.
  death of, 109
Anderson, Joseph Reid, 4
Anderson, Robert, 31
Andersonville Prison, 111, 138
Anniston, AL, 113. See also Blue
    Mountain Station
Alabama and Tennessee River Rail-
    road, 114
Alabama Troops
  artillery: Lumsen's Battery, 42
  cavalry: Shockley's Cavalry Com-
    pany, 50; Stoor's Cadet Troop,
    50
  infantry: 41st Infantry, 42; 62d
    Battalion, 113; Lockhart's Bat-
    talion, 113
Alabama, University of
  alumni: in Confederate service,
    152
  cadets: called Katydids, 31; first
    trip to Montgomery, 26; train-
    ing of troops by, 41, 53; peti-
    tion to close the university, 37;
    reviewed by the governor, 41,
    114; desertions and resigna-
    tions, 41, 50, 53; units formed
    by cadet deserters, 50; respond
    to abolitionist raid, 74; in
    defense of Rouseau's raid,
    112–13; in engagement at
    Beasley's farm, AL, 113; sent to
    Blue Mountain Station, 114;
    sent to defend Coosa River rail-
    road bridge, 114; sent to Pol-

lard, AL, 113; confront Confed-
    erate cavalry, 114; sent to Blake-
    ley, AL, 114; in defense of
    Tuscaloosa, 143–47; in "Battle"
    of River Hill, 145–47; retreat to
    Marion, AL, 148; furloughed
    by superintendent, 149; in
    1865 engagement at Blakely,
    179n.77
  facilities: evacuation of, 147;
    destruction of, 148; compensa-
    tion for destruction, 183n.75;
    Ku Klux Klan opposes reopen-
    ing, 162
  school:disciplinary problems, 11;
    founding of, 11; introduction of
    military system, 12–13; lack of
    legislative support, 12; curricu-
    lum, 14–15; enrollment, 45,
    53, 60–61; abolishment of,
    162; reopening of, 162; short-
    ages, 65–66; tuition, 67;
    weapons and ammunition,
    68–69
Archer, Sue, 135–36
Archer, Tod, 136
Armstrong, N. W., 31
Arsenal Academy. See also South
    Carolina Military Academy
  cadets: training of recruits by, 38;
    first field service of 45; service
    in Charleston, 77; as prison
    guards, 112; on provost duty,
    131; retreat from Columbia,
    132; final engagement at Shiloh
    Church, SC, 149; furloughed
    by superintendent, 150
  facilities: description of, 8; evacu-
    ation of, 131; destruction of,
    132; plans to reopen aban-
    doned, 163; postwar use of offi-
    cers' quarters, 181

school: founding of, 6–8; regula-
    tions, 8; curriculum, 14
Ashland, VA, 99
Atkinson, John, 125, 126
Atwill, Samuel, F. 67, 71
  wounding of at New Market, 96;
    death of, 99; reburied at VMI,
    162
Aucilla River, 134
Augusta, GA, 115, 124, 129, 150
Austin, James S., 90, 116
Averell, William W., 102
  raids into Virginia, 79–83

"Baby Corps," 135, 136, 138. See
    also West Florida Seminary
Bagby, George, 38
Baker, C.
  death of, 109
Balcony Falls, VA, 105
Ball's Ferry, GA, 116
Bamberg, SC, 124
Banks, Nathaniel P., 55
Barclay, Hugh
  revives plan to convert Lexington
    Arsenal to school, 1–2;
    appointed to VMI board of visi-
    tors, 4; appointed as VMI trea-
    surer, 4
Barnwell, Joseph, 66, 73, 168
  wounded at Gregory's Plantation,
    120
Bartow, Francis, 44
Bastrop Military Institute, 170n.24
Bath Alum Springs, VA, 79
Beard, Charles L., 136, 139
Beauregard, Henry, T., 70
Beauregard, Pierre G. T., 133,
    181n.10
  at Battle of Bull Run, 43; praises
    South Carolina Military

Academy cadets, 77; reviews Citadel cadets, 118
Bee, Bernard, 43
Berkeley, Edmund, Jr., 65, 96
Belton, SC, 149
Bennett, A. G., 132
Beverly, WV, 80, 81
Big Shangy, GA, 39, 53
Birmingham, AL. *See* Elyton
Black Oak, SC, 165
Black troops:
  Confederate: 140–41
  Federal: 2d U.S. Colored, 134, 136, 137; 26th U.S. Colored, 122; 99th U.S. Colored, 134, 137
Black Warrior River, 143
Blair, Frank P., Jr., 109
Blue Mountain Station, AL., 114
Boatwright, James H.
  wounded at Gregory's Plantation, 120
Boydston, Theodore W., 103
Bradford, Susan. *See* Eppes, Susan Bradford
Brady, Ademar, 145
Bragg, Braxton, 63
Breckinridge, John C., 141
  during New Market campaign, 91–99; decides to commit VMI cadets to battle, 96; praises cadets after battle, 98–99; ordered to join Lee, 101; at defense of Lynchburg, 105
Brooke, John Mercer, 161
Brooke Road, 101
Brown, John
  trial and execution, 26–27
Brown, Julius, 70, 100
Brown, Joseph E., 16, 34, 39, 42, 52,
  increase number of cadets at GMI, 33–34; requests troops for defense of capital, 110; flees capital, 115
Brumby, Arnoldus V., 38
  hired as GMI superintendent, 9; supports purchase of GMI by state, 10
Buchanan Advocate, 3
Buchanan, VA, 3, 81, 82
Buchanna, James, 31
Buck, George O.
  death of, 123
Bull Run, Battle of, 43–44
Burgwyn, Henry King, Jr., 40
Bushong's Hill, 95
Buster, William D.
  death of, 143
Butler, Benjamin F., 125, 126

Cabell, William, 94, 99
  death of at New Market, 96
Confederate States Cadets
  establishment of, 175n.37; sent to VMI, 61; limitations of program, 155–56
California Furnace, VA, 80
Camp Brown, GA, 38, 39
Camp Jackson, VA, 78, 79
Camp Lee, VA, 39, 40, 43, 101, 125
Camp McDonald, GA, 39, 53
Camp Sorghum, SC, 112
Camp Watts, AL, 113
Capers, Francis W.
  replaces Brumby as GMI superintendent, 38; supervises training of recruits, 38–39, 42; promoted, 42; comments on cadets' impatience to fight, 89; at Battle of Resaca, 89–90; report to adjutant general, 110; with cadets against Sherman, 110, 114–18; praise for cadets, 118; assists in efforts to reopen the Citadel Academy, 164; postwar career, 166
Carpenter, James S., 145, 147
Castle Pinckney, 29
Cedar Creek, VA, 101
Centerville, VA, 43
Chambersburg, PA, 107
Chancellorsville, Battle of, 75
Charles, Joel D., 33
Charleston, SC, 6, 45, 59, 111, 130
  secession convention, 29; capture of, 132
Charleston Daily Courier, 118, 123
Charleston Mercury, 32
Charleston and Savannah Railroad, 118
Charlotte and South Carolina Railroad, 132
Charlottesville, VA, 99
Chattahoochee River, 100, 108, 109
Chattanooga, TN, 89
Chehaw Station, AL, 113
Cherhaw, SC, 133
Chester, SC, 133
Chesnut, Mary, 129
Citadel Academy, 12. See also South Carolina Military Academy
  alumni: in Confederate service, 152
  cadets: parade in honor of secession, 29; fire upon the *Star of the West,* 32; graduation exercise cancelled, 35; training of

recruits by, 38; first field service, 45; Cadet Rangers formed by, 118, 123; service at New Bridge, SC, 74; as guards for prisoners of war, 111; retreat from Charleston, 132; furloughed by governor, 149
  facilities: description of, 8; bombardment of, 111–12; evacuation of, 130; occupation of, 132; reopening of, 163–64; founding of, 6–8; flag, 181n.4
  school: curriculum, 14; enrollment, 45, 60; regulations, 8; shortages, 65; tuition, 69; weapons, 68
"Cives." *See* Preston, John Thomas Lewis
Clifton Forge, VA, 81, 83
Cobb, Howell, 115
Coffin, Amory, 33, 12, 133
Coffin, George M., 119, 121, 168
Cokesbury, SC, 149
Cold Sulphur Springs, VA, 82
Coleman, J. D., 117
Coles, Byrd, 137
Colonna, Benjamin A. "Duck," 55, 56, 58, 97, 167
Colston, Raleigh E., 33, 36, 42
Columbia, SC, 6, 112, 130
  secession convention, 29; captured by Federals, 131; burning of, 131–32
Columbia, VA, 142
Commander, R.
  death of at Atlanta, 109
Confederacy
  armies: 129–30; Army of Northern Virginia, 75, 101, 152; Army of the Potomac, 43; Army of the Shenandoah, 43; Army of the Tennessee, 109, 129, 149, 152
  military districts and departments: Department of Florida, 135; District of Georgia, 115; District of South Carolina, 118; Department of South Georgia and Florida, 138; Department of Richmond, 126; Department of Western Virginia, 91
  units: Bachman's German Artillery, 119; Longstreet's Corps, 142; "Stonewall" Brigade, 55; "Stonewall" Division, 99; Taliaferro's Division, 130; Gregg's Brigade, 142
Congaree River, 112, 131
Connecticut troops
  18th Infantry, 94, 95

Conscription Act, 51
  exemption for cadets, 52, 53,
    87–89, 153
Cooper, Samuel, 155
Coosa River, 114
Cossawhatchie River, 118, 120
Cotton, J. A. M. B. L., 168
Couper, William C., 152, 165
Courvoisie, Frank E.
  wounded at Atlanta, 109
Covington, VA., 81, 82
Cowan, James G., 145, 145–48
Crockett, Charles, 99
  death of at New Market, 96
Crook, George, 91, 102
Cross, James Lucius, 134
Croxton, John T., 143–44, 147,
    148
Crozet, Claudius
  appointed as first president of
    VMI board of visitors, 3; death
    of, 127; responsible for
    acronym, VMI, 169n.2
Culbreath, John
  death of, 123
Cumming's Point, 31
Cutshaw, William E., 79

Dalton, GA, 89
Daniel, Charles P., 122
Darbytown Road, 126
Dare, 87
Davidson, J. L., 113
Davis, Jefferson, 52, 109, 112
  views on military colleges, 151,
    153; views on mobilizing the
    Confederacy's youth, 157
Davis, Thomas B., 73
Davis, William C., 158
Derrick, Clarence, 95, 97
DeSaussaure, Wilmot G., 77
Dooley, John, 125
Droop Mountain, Battle of, 80
Dublin, VA, 80, 81
DuBose, John, 136
Duffie, Alfred N., 80, 81
DuPont, Henry, 94, 103, 178n.46

Early, Jubal, A.
  ordered to defend Lynchburg,
    106; raid on Washington, 107;
    defeated at Waynesboro, 141
East Tennessee and Virginia Rail-
    road, 80, 81
Ecole Polytechnique, 3
Echols, John, 80, 92, 93
Edgar, George M., 97
Edwards, Aaron C., 120, 122
  praises cadets, 121
Elliott, Stephen, Jr., 130

Elyton, AL, 74, 144
Eppes, Susan Bradford, 135, 137,
    138, 182n.24
Evans, Andrew W., 140
Evans, Nathan G. "Shanks," 43
Evans, Oliver "Big," 93, 98, 167
Eve, Joseph E., 39
Ewell, Richard E., 39
Ewell, Richard S., 126, 139
Ezekiel, Moses, 99, 167, 168

Fairfax Court House, 43
Faulkner, Charles, 95
Federal
  armies: Army of the Cumberland,
    108; Army of Georgia, 115;
    Army of the James, 125; Army
    of North Eastern Virginia, 43;
    Army of the Potomac, 43, 75;
    Army of the Tennessee, 109,115
  corps: Fourteenth, 115; Fifteenth,
    116, Seventeenth, 109, 116
  military departments: Middle
    Department, 157, Department
    of West Florida, 134, Depart-
    ment of West Virginia, 101
Ficklin, Benjamin, F., 51
Fitzhugh, Charles L., 141
Florida troops
  artillery: Dunham's Light
    Artillery, 136; Gamble's Battery,
    136; Kilcrease Artillery, 136
  cavalry: 2d Cavalry, 134; 5th Cav-
    alry Battalion, 136
  infantry; 1st Reserve, 136; Bar-
    wick's Reserve, 136; Hodge's
    Reserve, 136; Gadsen Greys,
    136; Love's Militia, 136
Florida Collegiate and Military
    Institute, 134. See also West
    Florida Seminary
Floriday Military Institute, 133. See
    also West Florida Seminary
Forrest, Nathan Bedford, 144, 148
Fort Moultrie, 29, 31
Fort Sumter, 27, 31, 35
Fort Wagner, 77
Franklin, Battle of, 57
Franklin, WV, 79
Franklin Society, 2
Freeman, Douglas Southall, 152
Fremont, John C., 79
French, Samuel G., 112
Furman, Farish, 120, 123, 168

Galloway, Thomas S., 36
Garland, Landon C.
  military system at University of
    Alabama, 11–12; appointed as
    superintendent, 13; attitude

toward military duties, 17; takes
    cadets to capital, 26; efforts to
    deter resignations and deser-
    tions, 37; dedication to sourth-
    ern cause, 47; attitude toward
    desertions, 49–50; fear of slave
    revolt, 59–60; on supplies and
    food, 65, 66, 67, 68–69; on
    university as a military objec-
    tive, 74–75; on Confederate
    policy toward cadets, 52, 89;
    furloughs cadets, 148; resigna-
    tion, 162, postwar career, 166
Garlington, Albert C., 131, 132
Gerrett, Winder, 95, 98
Gartrell, Lucius, J., 119, 120, 121,
    122
Gatewood, Andrew C. L., 36, 40,
    167
General Order No. 100, 105
Georgia Central Railroad, 117
Georgia troops
  1st Reserve Infantry, 119, 122; 3d
    Reserve Infantry, 119, 122; 5th
    Infantry, 119, 120, 122; 47th
    Infantry, 120, 121, 122; Geor-
    gia Militia, 108, 115, 119;
    Phillip's Brigade, 38; Robert's
    Guards, 115, 116
Gibson, Frank
  wounded at New Market, 98
Gilham, William H., 24, 26, 42,
    55, 161, 172n.63
Gillespie, William H., 103
Gilmor, Henry, 92
Gisinier, John T. D.
  death of, 58
Georgia Military Institute
  cadets: daily life, 10; at state
    encampments, 25; training of
    recruits by, 38–39, 53; resigna-
    tions and desertions, 39; at Bat-
    tle of Resaca, 89–90; as bridge
    guards, 100–101; ordered to
    defend Atlanta, 101; during
    Atlanta campaign, 108–110;
    ordered to defend state capital,
    110; evacuation of capital, 115;
    opposing Sherman, 116; skir-
    mish at Little Ogeechee River,
    117; in defense of Savannah,
    124; transferred to Augusta and
    Milledgeville, 129; final service
    at August, 150; surrender at
    August, 150
  cannon: abandoned at Savannah,
    124, description, 163; return of,
    180n.107
  facilities; as Confederate hospital,
    100; occupation of, 108;

destruction of, 114; superinten-
dent's quarters, 179n.80
school: curriculum, 14; enroll-
ment, 45, 61; postwar efforts to
reopen, 162–63; founding of, 9;
hiring of officers, 9; purchased
by the state, 10; shortages, 68,
100
Goode, Samuel W.
wounded at Atlanta, 10
Goodwyn, Jeff, 131
Gordon, GA, 115
Goshen, VA, 82
Graham, William F., 25
Grahamville, SC, 119
Green, Allen J.
wounded at Gregory's Plantation,
120
Greenville, SC, 25, 133, 149
Greenville and Columbia Railroad,
149
Greenwood, SC, 150
Gregg, John, 142
Gregory's Plantation, 119–21
Griffin, Charles, 44
Griswoldville, GA, 115
Grant, Ulysses S., 78, 91, 101,
114, 163

Haigh, Charles T., 70, 71–72,
176n.31
Hall, James, 42
Halleck, Henry W., 130
Hamilton, Thomas
wounded at Oconee River, 117
Hammond, James H., 7
Hampden–Sydney College, 11
Hampton, Wade, 38, 164
Hanna, John, 98
Hanna, W. J., 7
Hannah, Joel M.
death of, 143
Hardcastle, Aaron, 144
Hardee, Wiliam J., 90, 117, 124,
132, 133
Harper's Ferry, 26, 42, 43
Harris, Columbus, 144
Hartsfield, Alva
death of, 99
Hayes, Rutherford B., 104
Haynes, Luther C.
death of, 99
Haynsworth, George E.
fires "first shot" of Civil War, 32,
167
Hazing, 72, 74
"bucking," 72
"greening," 73
Hermitage Fairgrounds, 40. See also
Camp Lee
Hempstead, Junius L., 43

Herbert Alfred
appointed Arsenal Academy
superintendent, 8
Heyward, Albert R.
wounded at Gregory's Plantation,
120
Hill, A. Govan, 94
Hill, Daniel Harvey, 106, 170n.24
Hill, Ambrose Powell, 76
Hollingsworth, Stephen F.
wounded at Gregory's Plantation,
120
Honey Hill, Battle of, 119
Hood, John Bell, 109, 110
Hooker, Joseph, 75
Howard College, 166
Howard, Oliver O., 115
Hume, William, 16, 132
Humphrey, Miles B., 50
Humphreys, J. O., 104
Hunter, David H.,
replaces Sigel, 101; orders
destruction of VMI, 104;
repulsed at Lynchburg, 107
Hurricane Creek, AL, 147, 148
Huse, Caleb
appointed Alabama commandant,
13, 41–42

Illinois troops
9th Mounted Infantry, 90
Imboden, John D., 80, 81, 82, 92,
101
Indiania troops
8th Cavalry, 113
Iowa troops
5th Cavalry, 113; 8th Cavalry,
145

Jackson, Thomas J. "Stonewall,"
26, 34, 90, 97
inadequacies as professor, 16; at
Harper's Ferry, 42–43, at Battle
of Bull Run, 44; during
McDowell campaign, 53–58; at
Battle of Chacellorsville, 75;
wounding of at Chancel-
lorsville, 76; death of, 76; burial
of at Lexington, 76; as acting
VMI commandant, 171n.4
Jackson, William H. "Red," 144,
177n.5
Jackson, William L. "Mudwall," 79,
80, 82, 83
James Island, SC, 111, 123
James River Canal, 105, 141, 142
Jamison, David F.
introduces bill creating South Carolina Military Academy, 7;
appointed to board of visitors, 7;
elected president of South Car-

olina secession convention, 29
Jefferson, Thomas G.
wounded at New Market, 96;
death of, 99; reburied at VMI,
162, 168
Jemison, Robert, 145
Jenkins, Albert, 91
John, Samuel Williamson, 26, 145
Johnson, Edward "Allegheny," 55
Johnson, Thomas A.
death of, 133
Johnson, Valentine Mason
named West Florida Seminary
superintendent, 134; during
Natural Bridge campaign, 136,
138
Johnston, George D., 162
Johnston, Joseph E., 43, 50, 57, 89,
142, 149
relieved of command, 109; proposed as postwar GMI superintendent, 162
Jones, Henry
death of at New Market, 96;
reburied at VMI, 99, 162
Jones, James
opposes plan to convert arsenals
to military academies, 7;
appointed to SCMA board of
visitors, 7; orders cadets recalled
from field service, 59
Jones, Samuel, 82, 118, 121, 138
Jones, William E. "Grumble,"
101–102
Jordan, Edmund
death of at Atlanta, 109

Kanawha Valley, 80
Kemper, James, L., 126
Kendrick, Aaron T.
wounded at "Battle" of River Hill,
146
Kentucky troops
cavalry: 4th Cavalry, 145; 6th
Cavalry, 145
infantry, 4th Mounted Infantry,
116
Kentucky Military Institute,
170n.24
Kershaw, John, 68, 168
Kershaw, Joseph B., 68
Keyhoe, Patrick, 144
Kilpatrick, Hugh Judson, 116, 117
King, William M.
wounded at "Battle" of River Hill,
146
Knight, B. H., 133

Labuzen, George Washington, 146
Lancaster, SC, 132
Langhorne, Jacob Kent, 65

Lanneau, John F., 149
Law, Evander, McIvor, 131
Leach, Emily, 145
Lebanon Springs, VA, 58
Lee, Fitzhugh, 82
Lee, Francis T., 143
Lee, George Washington Custis, 161
Lee, Robert E., 13, 66, 78, 91, 101, 105, 161
    capture of John Brown, 26; on value of cadet drillmasters, 40; on value of VMI, 45; on destruction of VMI, 108
Leslie's Weekly, 108
Letcher, John, 34, 45, 52, 104
Lewisburg, VA, 80
Lexington Arsenal, establishment of, 1; objections to 1; conversion to school, 1–3
Lexington Gazette, 2
Lexington, VA, 1, 36, 54, 58, 76, 80, 81, 91, 102
Lincoln, Abraham, 29, 35, 59, 151
Lincoln, Benjamin C., 136
Lincoln, William S., 98
Little Ogeechee River, 117
Loftin, Frank S., 124
Long, H. L., 122
Louisiana Seminary of Learning and Military Academy, 177n.12
Luckie, A. T.
    wounded at Atlanta, 109
Lumsden, Charles L., 13, 42
Lupton, Nathaniel T., 162
Lynchburg, VA, 101, 102, 105, 143
    defense of, 106–107
Lynch's Creek, SC, 132

McCarty, Edward C.
    wounded at Gregory's Plantation, 120
McCausland, John, 102, 107
McCleskey, James R., 100
McCulloch, Robert D., 43
    death of at Bull Run, 44
McClellan, George B., 57, 171n.42
McDonald, Marshall, 80
McDowell, Battle of, 56
McDowell, Irvin, 43
McDowell, William, 162
    death of at New Market, 96; reburied at VMI, 99
McKinley, A. C., 39
McLane, Charles H., 103
McLaws, Lafayette, 116, 117, 150
McLeod, John
    death of at Atlanta, 109
McMurry, Richard, 152
McNeill, John S. "Hanse," 92
McPherson, James B., 89, 109

Mabry, J.
    death of at Atlanta, 109
Madison, Robert L., 57
Magrath, Andrew G., 50, 131, 132, 133
    furloughs Citadel cadets, 149
Magrath, Andrew G., Jr., 131
Manget, Victor E., 90
Manley, Basil, 172n.71
Manor's Hill, 93, 95
Marianna, FL, 139
Marion, AL, 139
Marion Military Institute, 166
Marines, C. S., 136
Marines, U.S., 119, 122
Marietta, GA, 9, 89, 100, 114, 163
    Federal occupation of, 108
Marsh, C. H.
    death of at Oconee River, 117
Massachusetts troops
    34th Infantry, 97, 98
Massey, John, 146, 147
Matthews, Joseph
    appointed second professor of Arsenal Academy, 8
Maury, Matthew Fontaine, 161
May, W. R.
    wounded at "Battle" of River Hill, 146
Meadow Bridge Road, 101
Means, J. H.
    appointed to SCMA board of visitors, 7
Meridan, MS, 112
Merritt, James L., 94
Michigan troops
    2d Cavalry, 144, 145
Midway, VA, 92, 102
Milledgeville, GA, 25, 100, 110, 115, 129
Milledgeville Southern Recorder, 39
Military colleges
    academic philosophies of, 17; altered by war, 47; admission requirements, 15, 171n.34
    alumni: number killed in war 152; unequal distribution of in Confederate armies, 152
    cadets: average ages, 70; acting as assistant professors, 15; impressions of curriculum, 16; daily life of, 10, 18–19; resignations and desertions, 39–41, 45, 49; training of recruits by, 37–41; efforts to stem loss of cadets, 50; conscriptions of, 50, 51–53; units created by deserters from, 50; food, 65, 67, 68; sources of amusement, 71–73; interest in women, 70–71; as "young lions," 74; postwar legends,

157–58; service in the field, 158–59; conclusions concerning wartime use of, 159; contributions to the Confederacy, 158–59; Confederate policy toward, 152
    corps of cadets: organization of, 20; statewide tours of, 23–27, 41
    military system: role of, 17; training, 23; objectives, 104–105; officers, 152; tactical officers, 23; uniforms, 20–21; changes in, 65
    schools: curriculum, 14–15, 112; disciplinary systems, 19–20; enrollment, 45, 60–61, 134; faculty, 41–42; grade insignia, 20, 22; graduates, 69, 69; shortages, 51, 63–67, 68–69, 85; Confederate seizure of, 87
Milton, John, 134, 136, 139
Millen, GA, 117
Miller, William, 135, 136, 137, 138
Milroy, Robert H., 55
Minge, Collier H., 93
Moffett, John S., 43
    death of at Bull Run, 44
Montgomery, AL, 26, 41, 100, 113, 114, 148
Montgomery Daily Mail, 113
Moor, August, 92, 93, 95
Moore, Andrew G., 26, 41
Moore, Patrick T., 125
Morris Island, SC, 31, 77, 111
Morrison, James H., 13
Morrison, Joseph H., 76
Morton, Tignal Jones, 40
Mount Croghan, SC, 133
Muldrow, Robert E.
    death of, 123
Munford, Thomas T., 75
Murfree, James T., 13, 42, 145, 159
    postwar career, 166
Murfree, John H., 145, 146

Nadenbousch, J. Q. A., 80
Natural Bridge, FL, 135, 136
Natural Bridge, Battle of, 136–38
Naval Academy (CSA), 143, 156, 184n.15
Newberry, SC, 25, 150
New Market, VA, 57, 92, 93
New Market, Battle of, 93–99
New Market Campaign, 91–99
New River, 80
Newport, FL, 135, 136
Newton, John, 134, 136, 137–38
New York Evening Post, 32
New York troops
    artillery: 30th Artillery, 95

infantry: 56th Infantry, 119;
  127th Infantry, 119, 122; 157th
  Infantry, 119, 122
Nichols, R. F.
  death of, 123
Nickajack Ridge, 108, 109
Ninety–Six, SC, 150
Noble, Russell
  death of, 123
North Carolina Military Institute,
  170n.24
North Carolina troops
  7th Reserve Infantry Battalion,
  120, 122; 18th Infantry, 76,
  26th Infantry, 40
Norris, Alfred J., 133
Norris, Charles R., 42, 43
  death of, 44
North Fork of the Shenandoah
  River, 95
Northport, AL, 143, 144
North River, 102

O'Brien, A. F., 123
Oates, James, 90
Ocean Pond (Olustee), Battle of,
  134
Ochlockonee River, 134
Oconee River, 115, 116
Ogeechee River, 116, 117
Ogletohorpe College, 100
Ohio troops
  25th Infantry, 119; 28th Infantry,
  94; 116th Infantry, 94; 123d
  Infantry, 94, 95
"Old Spex," 36. See also Smith,
  Francis H.
Orangeburg, SC, 111, 131
Orange and Alexandria Railroad,
  106
Orr, James L., 163
Osbourne Turnpike, 125

Palmer, William D. "Big Bill," 168
  wounded at Tulifinny, 123
Panther Gap, VA, 82
Parker, William M.
  killing of, 123
Patrick, John B., 60, 71, 78, 133
Patton, George S., 95, 96, 97
Patterson, William B.
  death of at Gregory's Plantation,
  121
Pearsall, Uri B., 137
Pemberton, John C., 59, 78, 125,
  126
Pennsylvania troops
  54th Infantry, 95, 97, 98
Perkins, John, 144
Petersburg, VA, 142
Phillips, William, 38, 39

Pickett, George, 142, 152
Pickens, Francis W., 31, 35, 165
Piedmont, Battle of, 102
Pierce, David, 99
Pizzini, Andrew, 97, 125, 167
Pocotaglio River, 118
Poe, Orlando, 124
Polk, Leonidas K., 87
Pollard, AL, 114
Ponder, John F., 147
Port Leon, FL, 135
Poyner, Digges, 145
Preston, Frank, 97, 125
Preston, John T. L., 87, 140, 141
  as "Cives," 2; vision for Lexington
  Arsenal, 2; appointed to VMI
  board of visitors, 4; appointed
  assistant professor, 4; thoughts
  on curriculum, 13–14; on
  advantages of military disci-
  pline, 17; at execution of John
  Brown, 27
Pringle, Wiliam A.
  wounded at Gregory's Plantation,
  120
Purden, William H., 116, 117

Ramseur, Stephen D., 106
Randolph, Charles
  wounded at New Market, 98
Randolph-Macon College, 11, 107
Ravenel, William
  death of, 78
Rawls, William, 181n.15
Read, Charles E.
  wounded at New Market, 94
Redwood, George C, 113
Reid, J. Henry, 60, 73
Resaca, Battle of, 89–90
Ricketts, James B., 44
Richardson, John M. 42, 49
Richardson, John P., 7
Richardson, Warfield C. L., 148
Richardson, William H., 69, 87,
  107, 151
  efforts to keep VMI open, 45;
  objects to use of cadets in the
  field, 54, 140; on cadet com-
  plaints concerning food, 66;
  obtains arms and ammunition,
  69
Ripley, Roswell, S., 77
River Hill, "Battle" of, 145–47
Robertson, James W., 8
Rocketts, VA, 82
Rockbridge County
  Unionist sentiment in, 35–36
Rockbridge County News, 1
Rodes, Robert E, 75, 71n.42
Rome, GA, 114
Ross, John D., 42

Ross, William H., 145
Rousseau, Lovell, H.
  raid into Alabama, 112–13
Rude's Hill, VA, 92
Ruffin, Edmund
  at execution of John Brown, 27;
  at Fort Sumter, 35

Samford University, 166
Sams, Robert O., 133
Sams, Melvin M., 133
Salem, VA, 81
Saluda Hills, AL, 114
Saunders, John Caldwell Calhoun,
  41
Savannah, GA, 115, 116, 117
  capture of, 124
Schoonmaker, J. M., 104
Scott, Winfield, 31, 34
Scott, George Washington, 136
Sebastopol, GA, 117
Seddon, James A., 87, 88, 99
Selma, AL, 148
Selma Dispatch, 114
Semple, Charles, 96
Shields, John H., 85
Shipp, Scott, 42, 125, 126, 161
  named VMI commandant, 49;
  commands escort at Jackson's
  funeral, 76; wounded at New
  Market, 96; postwar career, 165
Sheridan, Phillip, 141
Sherman, William T., 89, 109, 112,
  114, 124, 130, 149
  advance into South Carolina,
  130–33; as military school
  superintendent, 177n.12
Shirley's Hill, 93
Shockley, Bascom T., 50
Shorter, John G., 53, 59, 68, 75
  authorizes use of force to prevent
  cadet conscription, 52
Shriver, Samuel
  wounded at New Market, 96
Shufeldt, R. W., 135
Sigel, Franz
  during New Market campaign,
  91, 92, 94, 95, 97; relieved of
  command, 101
Silliman, Colonel, 122
Simkins, William S., 32, 167
Slocum, Henry, 115
Smith, Eugene A., 114, 145
Smith, Francis H. "Old Spex," 50,
  51, 125, 127, 128, 161,
  170n.25, 171n.42
  appointed as VMI superintendent, 4; on admission
  requirments, 15; on VMI as a
  "reform school," 18; as superintendent of John Brown's execu-

tion, 27; communication with Winfield Scott, 34; as "Old Spex," 36; appointed to governor's Committee of Three, 40; advocates closing VMI, 45–46; efforts to get supplies, 51; officers assistance of cadets to Jackson, 53; difficulties with board of visitors, 54–55; report on McDowell campaign, 58; on hazing, 73–74; on cadet qualities, 74; on use of cadets in the field, 79–80; praises cadets for service, 81; on cadet conscription, 88–89; orders evacuation, 103; moves cadets to Lynchburg, 105; on the destruction of VMI, 107; searches for new location, 107; disbands VMI corps of cadets, 142; postwar career, 164–65

Smith, Francis H., Jr., 126, 141, 142, 167

Smith, G. death of at Atlanta, 109

Smith, George H., 94

Smith, Giles A., 116

Smith, Gustavus w., 108, 115, 117

Smith, William "Extra Billy," 140

Snodgrass, John B., 53, 54, 58, 167

Snow, E. N. C., 168

South Carolina Military Academy board of visitors, 9, 149

cadets: statewide tour, 25; first field service of, 45; 1863 duty in Charleston, 77; in defense of Charleston and Savannah Railroad, 118–24; in skirmish at Gregory's Plantation, 119–21; received praise for conduct at Gregory's Plantation, 121; in skirmish at Tulifinny railroad trestle, 121–23; received praise for service, 123–24; encampment at Spartanburg, 132; encampment at Greenville, 133.

school: change of name, 164; creation of, 8; expansion of proposed, 60; efforts to reopen, 163; incorporated into state military establishment, 34

South Carolina Troops artillery: 1st Artillery, 120, 167; Washington Light Artillery, 45

cavalry: 3d Cavalry, 119; 6th Cavalry, 50; Cadet Rangers, 50, 59

combined arms: Hampton's Legion, 38; Holcombe Legion, 42, 165

infantry:, 4th Infantry, 38; 10th Infantry, 167; 21st Infantry,

111; Battalion of State Cadets, 8, 118, 133; Palmetto Guards, 27; Washington Light Infantry, 29

Spartanburg, SC, 133

Spearman, John wounded at Shiloh Church, 149

St. Marks, FL, 134, 135

St. Mark's River, 134, 135

Stanard, Jaqueline B. "Jack," 82, 85, 99 death of at New Market, 96

Staunton, VA, 54, 55, 58, 81, 82, 92, 101, 102

Stevens, Peter F. at engagement with Star of the West, 31–32; resigns as Citadel superintendent, 42; efforts to reopen Citadel, 164; postwar career, 165

Stoneman, George, 110, 149

Stoor, Charles P., 50

Strange, John B., 4–5

Strother, David H., 105, 178n.51

Sullivan's Island, 31

Sullivan, Jeremiah, 94

Tallahassee, 134, 135, 137, 138

Taliaferro, William B., 111

Taylor, Zachary, 24

Tennessee troops 4th (Union) Cavalry, 113; 53d Infantry, 40

Terry, Alfred H., 125

Thayer, Sylvanius, 1, 24

Thomas, Carey, 71

Thomas, George H., 108

Thomas, John P., 77 named Arsenal Academy superintendent, 42; during defense of Charleston and Savannah Railroad, 118; evacuates Arsenal, 131; retreat from Columbia, 132–33; at last engagement of Arsenal cadets, 149; furloughs Arsenal cadets, 150; postwar career, 166

Thompson, E. B., 13

Thompson, Hugh S., 50, 59, 118

Thompson, John K. "Put," 36

Thoburn, Joseph, 97

Todd, J. Scott wounded at Oconee River, 117

Town, Franklin E. on VMI cadets, 98; on sacrifices of cadets, 158–59

Townsend, B. R., 137

Tricon, P. F., 146

Tulifinny River, 119

Tulifinny trestle skirmish at, 121–22

Turner, Duncan, 134

Turner's Ferry, GA, 108, 109

Tuscaloosa, AL, 74, 143

Unionville, SC, 133

Upshur, John wounded at New Market, 98

Vaughn, W. J., 146

Vessey, Denmark, 6

Vicksburg, MS, 51, 78, 112

Virginia Military Institute alumni: in Federal service, 24, 103, 173n.36; in Confederate service, 152

board of visitors: apppointment, 3; opposes use of cadets to support Jackson, 54; operational control, 54

cadets: classifications of, 5; enrollment, 6, 60; prewar trips to Richmond, 24–25; at execution of John Brown, 26–27; confrontation with Lexington Unionists, 35–36; training of recruits by, 39; desertions and resignations of, 40–41; in McDowell campaign, 53–58; at Jackson's funeral, 76; in defense against Averell, 79–83; at "Camp Starvation," 82; in New Market campaign, 98; casualties at Battle of New Market, 99; in defense of Richmond, 88, 101, 124–27, 139–40, 141–42; in defense of Lexington, 102; in defense of Lynchburg, 106–107; at the Richmond Almshouse, 140; services offered to train black troops, 140–41; during evacuation of Richmond, 141–42

cannon: history of, 174n.17

facilities: inadequacies, 4; description of, 5–6; destruction of, 105–106; Richmond Almshouse, 124, 127; looting of Almshouse, 143; reopening of, 161; compensation for destruction of, 178n.46; flag, 24

military training: role in curriculum, 4; weapons, 68, 69

school: curriculum, 13–14, 33, 139; faculty, 161; hazing, 72–74; "rats," 39; supplies, 51, 65, 127, 67

Virginia troops ambulance: Richmond Ambulance, 125

artillery: Rockbridge Artillery, 43

cavalry: 4th Cavalry, 80; 11th

Cavalry, 167; 23d Cavalry, 95
infantry: 2d Infantry, 43; 4th
  Infantry, 42, 43; 5th Infantry,
  43; 18th Infantry, 43; 21st
  Infantry, 55; 22d Infantry, 95;
  23d Infantry, 95; 26th Infantry,
  97; 27th Infantry, 43; 33d
  Infantry, 43, 44; 51st Infantry,
  95; 62d Infantry, 94, 95, 97;
  Augusta–Rockingham County
  Reserves, 92, 157; Lexington
  Home Guard, 79, 80, 81, 82;
  Rockbridge Greys, 42; Rock-
  bridge Rifles, 36; Virginia Local
  Defense Brigade, 125
Von Kleiser, Albert, 95, 96, 98

Walker, C. Irvine, 33, 167
Wappoo Cut, SC, 45, 59
Washington College, 11, 103, 107
  VMI to be a part of, 3; spared
  from destruction, 104
Washington, DC, 44, 107
Watts, Thomas H., 75, 112, 162
Wayne, Henry C., 110, 115
  praises GMI cadets, 117
Waynesboro, VA, 141
Weeks, Major, 135
West Florida Seminary
  cadets: in skirmish at Newport,
  FL, 136; in Battle of Natural
  Bridge, 136–38; praised for
  conduct at Natural Bridge, 138;
  conscription of, 181n.14; post-
  war charges of cowardice,
  182n.24

school: enrollment, 134; founding
  of, 133; uniforms, 182n.23
West Point (USMA), 12, 112
  as model for southern military
  colleges, 3, 6, 13
West Point, GA, 100, 101
West Point and Montgomery Railroad, 113
West Virginia troops
  cavalry: 3d Cavalry, 103
  infantry: 1st Infantry, 94, 97, 98;
  8th
Western Military Institute, 12
Westham Plank Road, 141
  Mounted Infantry, 81; 14th
  Infantry, 103
Wharton, Gabriel, 91–92, 93, 95
Wheelwright, Joseph C.
  wounded at New Market, 96;
  death of, 99; reburied at VMI,
  162
Whilden, John M., 32
White, James B. "Benny," 77
  as Arsenal superintendent, 38;
  replaces Stevens as Citadel
  superintendent, 42; efforts to
  halt desertions and resignations,
  50; ordered to remove cadets
  from the field, 59; offers cadets
  to defend Charleston, 118;
  commands Battalion of State
  Cadets in defense of Charleston
  and Savannah Railroad, 118; in
  skirmish at tulifinny trestle,
  119, 121; praises cadets, 124;
  sends Citadel property to the
  Arsenal, 130; on retreat from

Charleston, 132; postwar career,
  165
White Oak, SC, 132
White Sulphur Springs, VA 79
Whitwell, A. C., 87
Wight, Charles C., 43
  wounded at Bull Run, 44
Wilderness Tavern, VA, 76
Williamsburg Road, 126
Willingham, John, 146
Wilson, James H.
  raid into Alabama, 143–49
Winchester, Va, 43, 79
Winder, Charles S., 55
Winnsboro, SC, 132
Wise, Henry A., 24, 26
Wise, Henry A. "Old Chinook,"
  70, 78, 102, 125
  takes command of cadets at New
  Market, 96
Wise, John S., 24, 70, 90, 91, 94,
  96, 99, 105, 107, 166
Wofford College, 133
Woodbridge, Jonathan, 93
Woodford, Stewart L., 119, 120,
  121, 122
Woodlief, Pierre
  wounded at New Market, 94
Woodstock, VA, 92
Wool, John E., 157

Yancey, Thomas B., 155
Yorktown Road, 126
Yorkville, SC, 61
Young, Pierce M. B., 152, 162